JUDICIAL REVIEW OF IMMIGRATION DETENTION IN THE UK, US AND EU

Immigration detention is considered by many states to be a necessary tool in the execution of immigration policy. Despite the apparently key role it plays in immigration enforcement, the law on immigration detention is often vague, especially in relation to determining the circumstances under which prolonged detention remains lawful. As a result, the courts are frequently called upon to adjudicate these matters, with scant legal tools at their disposal. Though there have been some significant judgments on the legality of detention at the constitutional level, the extent to which these judgments have had an impact at the lower end of the judiciary is unclear. Indeed, it is the lower courts which are tasked with judging the legality of detention through habeas corpus or judicial review proceedings.

This book examines the way this has occurred in the lower courts of two jurisdictions, the UK and the US, and contrasts this practice not only in those jurisdictions, but with judgments rendered by the Court of Justice of the European Union, a constitutional court at the other end of the judicial spectrum whose judgments are applied by courts and tribunals in the EU Member States. Although these three jurisdictions use similar tests to evaluate the legality of detention, case outcomes significantly differ. Many factors contribute to this divergence, but key among them is the role that fundamental rights protection plays in each jurisdiction. Through a forensic evaluation of 191 judgments, this book compares the laws on detention in the UK, US and EU, and makes recommendations to these jurisdictions for improvement.

Judicial Review of Immigration Detention in the UK, US and EU

From Principles to Practice

Justine N Stefanelli

•HART•
OXFORD • LONDON • NEW YORK • NEW DELHI • SYDNEY

HART PUBLISHING

Bloomsbury Publishing Plc

Kemp House, Chawley Park, Cumnor Hill, Oxford, OX2 9PH, UK

HART PUBLISHING, the Hart/Stag logo, BLOOMSBURY and the Diana logo are trademarks of Bloomsbury Publishing Plc

First published in Great Britain 2020

A catalogue record for this book is available from the British Library.

Library of Congress Cataloging-in-Publication data

Names: Stefanelli, Justine N, author.

Title: Judicial review of immigration detention in the UK, US, and EU : from principles to practice / Justine N Stefanelli.

Description: Chicago : Hart Publishing, an imprint of Bloomsbury Publishing, 2020. | Includes bibliographical references and index.

Identifiers: LCCN 2019040266 (print) | LCCN 2019040267 (ebook) | ISBN 9781509930456 (hardback) | ISBN 9781509930463 (Epub)

Subjects: LCSH: Emigration and immigration law—Great Britain. | Emigration and immigration law—United States. | Emigration and immigration law—European Union countries. | Alien detention centers—Great Britain. | Alien detention centers—United States. | Alien detention centers—European Union countries. | Illegal aliens—Great Britain. | Illegal aliens—United States. | Illegal aliens—European Union countries. | Court of Justice of the European Union. | Judicial review.

Classification: LCC K3275 .S74 2020 (print) | LCC K3275 (ebook) | DDC 342.08/2—dc23

LC record available at https://lccn.loc.gov/2019040266

LC ebook record available at https://lccn.loc.gov/2019040267

ISBN: HB: 978-1-50993-045-6
ePDF: 978-1-50993-047-0
ePub: 978-1-50993-046-3

Typeset by Compuscript Ltd, Shannon

To find out more about our authors and books visit www.hartpublishing.co.uk. Here you will find extracts, author information, details of forthcoming events and the option to sign up for our newsletters.

To my husband, who spent many early mornings with me and gave me endless support while I turned my research into a book worth publishing, and to my parents – my heroes

Foreword

CHILDREN ARE FASCINATED by medieval dungeons from which there was no means of escape or hope of release. We reassure them that the *oubliette* – the place where people are forgotten – is a thing of the past. We tend to forget that many thousands of immigrants – over 27,000 in the United Kingdom alone – are in administrative detention today. How can they be assured that they are not forgotten? How can we avoid a situation in which the expression 'administrative detention' becomes no more than a disingenuous euphemism for arbitrary imprisonment without trial, contrary to our fundamental conceptions of the Rule of Law? The law, and elementary respect for human dignity requires that lawful detention is subject to due process according to known laws impartially administered. This book examines how this is done.

Dr Stefanelli restricts herself to the law and practice of three jurisdictions: the Administrative Court of England and Wales; the District Courts of the United States Second Circuit; and the Court of Justice of the European Union. And she limits herself to cases that are concerned with the lawfulness of *continuing* detention, as opposed to the lawfulness of the initial decision to detain. This confines the discussion within manageable limits, while ensuring exhaustive and penetrating analysis within those limits.

England and Wales and the United States are countries of the common law, sharing the heritage of *Habeas Corpus* and the Rule of Law. In both jurisdictions there is an abundance of case law on the practice of administrative detention. But a divergence of approach has developed over the years for two main reasons. First, the law-makers have reacted in different ways to the inflow of immigrants and to the public demand for greater control. Second, the courts have differed in the extent to which they defer to the exercise of administrative discretion.

In addition, the courts of England and Wales must now take account of 'European law': the European Convention on Human Rights, interpreted by the European Court of Human Rights, and the law of the European Union, interpreted by the Court of Justice – notably the so-called 'Return Directive' on the return of illegal immigrants to their home country.[1] Although the case law is less abundant, it illustrates the way in which courts with international jurisdiction set about forging a common approach for the national courts of States that have very different legal traditions and historical background.

[1] Directive 2008/115/EC of the European Parliament and of the Council of 16 December 2008 on common standards and procedures in Member States for returning illegally staying third-country nationals.

It is a merit of this book that it is not a crusading manifesto against administrative detention as such. Dr Stefanelli starts from the assumption that States have the right to control the flow of immigrants and asylum seekers and, where necessary, to detain and expel them. Her concern is with the way in which courts perform their essential function, not only in applying the law, but in forming a workable structure within which the administrator can operate. As Dicey said, it is the task of judges to maintain the logic or symmetry of the law.[2]

I highly commend this book to those who are interested in how the law works and what can be done to make it work better.

David Edward
Edinburgh
3 September 2019

[2] A.V. Dicey *Law and Public Opinion in England*, Lecture XI, "Judicial Legislation", (Macmillan 1905 and subsequently), page 364 in the 1926 reprint.

Acknowledgements

THIS BOOK, AND the PhD that served as its basis, were an absolute joy for me to write – so much so, that I've mourned completing the book and having to leave these cases behind. But I could not have done this alone. The reality is that many people academically and emotionally contributed to this labour of love. I am foremost deeply indebted to my PhD supervisors, Professor Valsamis Mitsilegas and Professor Elspeth Guild. I have been consistently impressed by their wealth of knowledge and blessed by their innovative and enthusiastic input into my research. They made my experience an absolute dream, and I will be eternally grateful to them for encouraging me not only to embark on a PhD, but to turn my thesis into a book. I could never have imagined that both processes could be so enjoyable.

I am grateful to the team at Hart, especially Sasha Jawed, who helped bring this book to life, and to Chris Myers, who meticulously edited its text. I would like to thank the judges and lawyers who took the time to speak to me about their work and help me refine my writing with a clearer and more accurate picture of practice, particularly César Cuauhtémoc García Hernández, Professor Kees Groenendijk and Nicholas Nason. A special thank you goes to Giuseppe A Ippolito, Esq, Deputy Clerk to the Hon Hugh B Scott at the Western District Court of New York, who was instrumental in helping me to understand NY federal law and practice, and who I can now call a friend. I would also like to thank a number of people at the British Institute of International and Comparative Law, where I was employed for most of the time while I was conducting my research – in particular, Professor Robert McCorquodale, Professor Sir Jeffrey Jowell KCMG QC and Sandra Homewood. Their encouragement, support and understanding made juggling a full-time job with a PhD far less daunting than I had imagined. I am also indebted to Dr Lawrence McNamara, who provided me with brilliant advice on a regular basis, when he did not need to at all. Finally, I would be remiss if I did not thank my friends in the USA and the UK, particularly Alexa, Bart, Eva, Hannah, Kristin, Lois, Martyna, Mary, Sally and Zak for their emotional support and cheerleading. My greatest thanks go to my parents for their love and support (and not discouraging my pursuit of yet more research!), and my husband, who never let me doubt myself.

Table of Contents

List of Abbreviations

AEDPA	Antiterrorism and Effective Death Penalty Act
BIA	Board of Immigration Appeals
CEAS	Common European Asylum System
CFR	Code of Federal Regulations
CJEU	Court of Justice of the European Union
DHS	Department of Homeland Security
DOJ	Department of Justice
EC	European Community
ECHR	European Convention on Human Rights
ECtHR	European Court of Human Rights
EDNY	Eastern District of New York
EIG	Enforcement Instructions and Guidance
EOIR	Executive Office for Immigration Review
EU	European Union
EWCA	Court of Appeal of England and Wales
EWHC	High Court of England and Wales
FRA	Fundamental Rights Agency
IA	Immigration Act
ICE	Immigration and Customs Enforcement
IIRIRA	Illegal Immigration Reform and Immigrant Responsibility Act
INA	Immigration and Nationality Act
INS	Immigration and Nationality Service
LPR	Lawful Permanent Resident
NIAA	Nationality, Immigration and Asylum Act
NY	New York

OAYSys	Offender Assessment System
SDNY	Southern District of New York
SSHD	Secretary of State for the Home Department
TFEU	Treaty on the Functioning of the European Union
UK	United Kingdom
UKHL	House of Lords of the United Kingdom
UKSC	United Kingdom Supreme Court
UKVI	United Kingdom Visas and Immigration
UN	United Nations
UNHCR	United Nations High Commissioner for Refugees
USA	United States of America
USC	United States Code
USSC	United States Supreme Court
WDNY	Western District of New York

Table of Pool Cases

Key		
A	=	court attributes prolonged detention to detainee's pursuit of legal remedies
−A	=	court specifically indicates that pursuit of remedies should not count against detainee
CC	=	cookie-cutter judgment (US only)
−DD	=	court specifically criticises state's lack of due diligence in effecting removal
E	=	effectiveness principles (EU only)
F	=	forbearance policy (US only)
−F	=	forbearance policy discussed favourably toward detainee
L	=	Right to liberty, due process or fundamental rights specifically discussed by court
LR	=	detainee had legal representation
LR*	=	no data given on legal representation
MD	=	mandatory detention case (US only)
S	=	successful outcome (UK and US only)
Z	=	*Zadvydas*-based analysis (US only)

	Case Name	Citation	Judgment Date (Euro format)	Detained Since	Detention Length (years, days)	Markers
United Kingdom – Administrative Court of England & Wales						
1	*R (I) v SSHD*	[2002] EWHC 750 (Admin)	22/02/2002	07/02/2002	0 Y, 15 D	LR
2	*Hwez v SSHD*	[2002] EWHC 1597 (Admin)	29/07/2002	No data	–	S, LR
3	*Chen v SSHD*	[2002] EWHC 2797 (Admin)	05/12/2002	02/10/2000	2 Y, 64 D	LR
4	*R (Boukhalfa) v SSHD*	[2003] EWHC 991 (Admin)	28/01/2003	15/02/2002	0 Y, 347 D	S, LR, L
5	*R (Lubana) v SSHD*	[2003] EWHC 410 (Admin)	25/02/2003	14/08/2002	0 Y, 195 D	LR
6	*R (Kumar) v The Governor of HMP Lindholme*	[2003] EWHC 846 (Admin)	25/03/2003	01/07/2002	0 Y, 267 D	LR, L
7	*R (Badjoko) v SSHD*	[2003] EWHC 3034 (Admin)	12/09/2003	30/06/2000	3 Y, 74 D	LR
8	*R (H) v SSHD*	[2005] EWHC 1702 (Admin)	07/07/2005	28/02/2003	2 Y, 130 D	S, LR, L
9	*R (A) v SSHD*	[2006] EWHC 3331 (Admin)	07/12/2006	03/09/2003	3 Y, 96 D	LR, L
10	*R (MMH) v SSHD*	[2007] EWHC 2134 (Admin)	07/09/2007	31/07/2006	1 Y, 38 D	LR
11	*R (Bashir) v SSHD*	[2007] EWHC 3017 (Admin)	30/11/2007	25/03/2005	2 Y, 250 D	S, LR, A
12	*R (A) v SSHD*	[2008] EWHC 142 (Admin)	21/01/2008	A: 30/05/2006 B: 10/01/2007 MA: 03/10/2006 ME: 09/23/2006	A: 1 Y, 236 D B: 1 Y, 11 D MA: 1 Y, 110 D ME: 1 Y, 120 D	S, LR
13	*R (SK) v SSHD*	[2008] EWHC 98 (Admin)	25/01/2008	08/03/2006	1 Y, 323 D	LR, L
14	*R (Qaderi) v SSHD*	[2008] EWHC 1033 (Admin)	13/05/2008	05/10/2006	1 Y, 221 D	LR
15	*R (Lumba) v SSHD*	[2008] EWHC 2090 (Admin)	04/07/2008	23/06/2006	2 Y, 12 D	LR, L, –A

16	*R (YG) v SSHD*	[2008] EWHC 1735 (Admin)	08/07/2008	23/02/2007	1 Y, 136 D	S, LR
17	*R (IO) v SSHD*	[2008] EWHC 2596 (Admin)	09/10/2008	31/12/2006	1 Y, 283 D	S, LR
18	*R (Adewale) v SSHD*	[2009] EWHC 1289 (Admin)	14/01/2009	22/08/2007	1 Y, 146 D	S, LR, −DD
19	*R (M) v SSHD*	[2009] EWHC 629 (Admin)	05/03/2009	25/11/2008	0 Y, 100 D	LR
20	*R (Polanco) v SSHD*	[2009] EWHC 826 (Admin)	23/04/2009	22/06/2006	2 Y, 306 D	S, LR, L
21	*R (Asekun) v SSHD*	[2009] EWHC 1707 (Admin)	20/05/2009	09/07/2007	1 Y, 316 D	LR, A
22	*R (Abdi) v SSHD*	[2009] EWHC 1324 (Admin)	22/05/2009	30/11/2006	2 Y, 174 D	S, LR, L
23	*R (Daq) v SSHD*	[2009] EWHC 1655 (Admin)	25/06/2009	20/06/2006	3 Y, 6 D	S, LR, L
24	*R (Chahboub) v SSHD*	[2009] EWHC 1989 (Admin)	01/07/2009	21/09/2007	1 Y, 284 D	LR
25	*R (MM (Somalia)) v SSHD*	[2009] EWHC 2353 (Admin)	22/07/2009	24/09/2007	1 Y, 302 D	S, LR
26	*R (Saleh) v SSHD*	[2009] EWHC 2395 (Admin)	05/10/2009	19/08/2008	1 Y, 47 D	LR, A
27	*Hussein v SSHD*	[2009] EWHC 2492 (Admin)	21/10/2009	18/02/2009	0 Y, 245 D	LR
28	*R (Egal) v SSHD*	[2009] EWHC 2939 (Admin)	17/11/2009	14/04/2009	0 Y, 217 D	LR, A
29	*R (Abdullah) v SSHD*	[2010] EWHC 259 (Admin)	29/01/2010	20/02/2007	2 Y, 344 D	S, LR, L
30	*R (Said) v SSHD*	[2010] EWHC 365 (Admin)	03/02/2010	09/10/2006	3 Y, 118 D	LR
31	*R (A) v SSHD*	[2010] EWHC 808 (Admin)	09/02/2010	07/08/2007	2 Y, 187 D	S, LR, A
32	*R (A (Iraq)) v SSHD*	[2010] EWHC 625 (Admin)	19/02/2010	18/05/2008	1 Y, 277 D	S, LR, L, A
33	*R (Hussein) v SSHD*	[2010] EWHC 2651 (Admin)	30/03/2010	25/09/2009	0 Y, 186 D	S, LR, −DD
34	*R (HY) v SSHD*	[2010] EWHC 1678 (Admin)	12/04/2010	20/07/2006	3 Y, 267 D	S, LR, L
35	*R (Mohamed) v SSHD*	[2010] EWHC 1244 (Admin)	20/04/2010	29/06/2007	2 Y, 296 D	LR
36	*R (C) v SSHD*	[2010] EWHC 1089 (Admin)	30/04/2010	27/08/2008	1 Y, 246 D	S, LR

	Case Name	Citation	Judgment Date (Euro format)	Detained Since	Detention Length (years, days)	Markers
37	*R (Mahfoud) v SSHD*	[2010] EWHC 2057 (Admin)	04/08/2010	08/06/2007	3 Y, 58 D	S, LR, L
38	*MA & TT v SSHD*	[2010] EWHC 2350 (Admin)	21/09/2010	18/06/2009	1 Y, 95 D	S, LR, L
39	*Mohammed v SSHD*	[2010] EWHC 3323 (Admin)	23/09/2010	11/03/2010	0 Y, 196 D	LR
40	*R (Davies) v SSHD*	[2010] EWHC 2656 (Admin)	01/10/2010	1612/2008	1 Y, 289 D	LR, L
41	*R (Smith) v SSHD*	[2010] EWHC 2774 (Admin)	22/10/2010	10/12/2006	3 Y, 317 D	LR
42	*R (AK) v SSHD*	[2010] EWHC 3083 (Admin)	17/11/2010	06/09/2009	1 Y, 72 D	LR, A
43	*R (AE (Libya)) v SSHD*	[2011] EWHC 154 (Admin)	02/02/2011	30/09/2009	1 Y, 125 D	LR
44	*R (Aziz) v SSHD*	[2011] EWHC 554 (Admin)	16/02/2011	23/04/2009	1 Y, 299 D	S, LR, –A
45	*R (SM) v SSHD*	[2011] EWHC 338 (Admin)	23/02/2011	16/04/2009	1 Y, 313 D	LR
46	*R (Mjemer) v SSHD*	[2011] EWHC 1514 (Admin)	12/05/2011	31/12/2007	3 Y, 133 D	S, LR, L
47	*R (Raki) v SSHD*	[2011] EWHC 2421 (Admin)	06/10/2011	08/01/2007	4 Y, 271 D	S, LR, L
48	*R (Rashid) v SSHD*	[2011] EWHC 3352 (Admin)	21/10/2011	12/04/2009	2 Y, 192 D	LR
49	*R (Lamrani) v SSHD*	[2011] EWHC 3059 (Admin)	24/11/2011	09/06/2008	3 Y, 168 D	LR, L
50	*R (Yegorov) v SSHD*	[2011] EWHC 3358 (Admin)	25/11/2011	09/04/2009	2 Y, 230 D	LR
51	*R (Akram) v SSHD*	[2012] EWHC 1432 (Admin)	09/05/2012	23/04/2010	2 Y, 17 D	S, LR, L
52	*R (Noureddine) v SSHD*	[2012] EWHC 1707 (Admin)	22/05/2012	25/02/2009	3 Y, 87 D	LR
53	*R (Mhlanga) v SSHD*	[2012] EWHC 1587 (Admin)	12/06/2012	15/10/2006	5 Y, 241 D	S, LR, L
54	*R (Momoh) v SSHD*	[2012] EWHC 3740 (Admin)	21/12/2012	01/11/2009	3 Y, 51 D	S, LR, –DD
55	*R (Singh) v SSHD*	[2013] EWHC 380 (Admin)	28/02/2013	20/05/2011	1 Y, 285 D	LR
56	*R (Azaroal) v SSHD*	[2013] EWHC 1248 (Admin)	17/05/2013	13/10/2011	1 Y, 217 D	S, LR, L, –DD

57	*R (Belfken) v SSHD*	[2013] EWHC 4658 (Admin)	18/09/2013	18/03/2013	0 Y, 184 D	S, LR, L
58	*R (Giwa) v SSHD*	[2013] EWHC 3189 (Admin)	22/10/2013	01/05/2009	4 Y, 174 D	LR, L, −A
59	*R (Ismail) v SSHD*	[2013] EWHC 3921 (Admin)	13/12/2013	21/05/2012	1 Y, 206 D	S, LR, L, −DD
60	*R (Badah) v SSHD*	[2014] EWHC 364 (Admin)	28/01/2014	28/03/2011	2 Y, 307 D	LR, L
61	*R (JM) v SSHD*	[2014] EWHC 151 (Admin)	04/02/2014	19/10/2011	1 Y, 108 D	LR, L
62	*R (N) v SSHD*	[2014] EWHC 1593 (Admin)	01/05/2014	14/04/2012	2 Y, 17 D	S, LR
63	*R (Babbage) v SSHD*	[2016] EWHC 148 (Admin)	01/02/2016	07/10/13	2 Y, 117 D	S, LR, L
United States – NY Federal District Courts						
Eastern District of NY						
1	*Powell v Ashcroft*	(2002 EDNY) 194 F Supp 2d 209	04/04/2002	No data	–	Z, A
2	*Fraser v Ashcroft*	2003 WL 21143031 (EDNY)	13/05/2003	No data	–	MD, A
3	*Lovell v INS*	2003 WL 22282176 (EDNY)	21/05/2003	02/10/2000	2 Y, 231 D	MD
4	*Rajigah v Conway*	(2003 EDNY) 268 F Supp 2d 159	12/06/2003	19/06/2000	2 Y, 358 D	S, LR, Z, −A
5	*Sanusi v INS*	2003 WL 21696945 (EDNY)	15/07/2003	01/10/1997	5 Y, 287 D	Z, A
6	*Guang v INS*	2005 WL 465436 (EDNY)	28/02/2005	18/11/1999	5 Y, 103 D	LR, Z, A
Southern District of NY						
7	*Ncube v INS*	1998 WL 842349 (SDNY)	02/12/1998	27/07/1997	1 Y, 128 D	Z, A
8	*Copes v McElroy*	2001 WL 830673 (SDNY)	23/07/2001	23/10/1996	4 Y, 273 D	LR, Z, F

	Case Name	Citation	Judgment Date (Euro format)	Detained Since	Detention Length (years, days)	Markers
9	*Iturralde-Manosalva v Reno*	2001 WL 1398689 (SDNY)	09/11/2001	No data	–	LR*, Z
10	*Perez v Ashcroft*	2003 WL 22004901 (SDNY)	25/08/2003	No data	–	Z, A
11	*Reyes-Cardenas v Gonzales*	2007 WL 1290141 (SDNY)	30/04/2007	20/04/2000	7 Y, 10 D	Z, A
12	*Farez-Espinoza v Chertoff*	(2009 SDNY) 600 F Supp 2d 488	29/01/2009	27/10/2008	0 Y, 94 D	S, LR, MD
13	*Juma v Mukasey*	2009 WL 2191247 (SDNY)	23/07/2009	25/06/2008	1 Y, 28 D	Z
14	*Azad v Interim District Director, NY ICE and Riley*	2009 WL 2569132 (SDNY)	19/08/2009	14/08/2008	1 Y, 5 D	S, LR*, Z,
15	*Adler v US Department of Homeland Security*	2009 WL 3029328 (SDNY)	22/09/2009	12/06/2008	1 Y, 102 D	MD, A
16	*Agoro v District Director for Immigration and Custom Enforcement*	2010 WL 9976 (SDNY)	04/01/2010	16/01/2009	0 Y, 353 D	LR, Z, A
17	*Abassi v Secretary, Department of Homeland Security*	2010 WL 199700 (SDNY)	11/01/2010	28/10/2008	1 Y, 75 D	LR*, Z, A
18	*Miller v Shanahan*	2010 WL 481002 (SDNY)	29/01/2010	13/08/2007	2 Y, 170 D	LR, MD, A
19	*Monestime v Reilly*	(2010 SDNY) 704 F Supp 2d 453	09/04/2010	06/08/2009	0 Y, 246 D	S, LR, MD
20	*Andreenko v Holder*	2010 WL 2900363 (SDNY)	25/06/2010	01/10/2008[i]	1 Y, 267 D	LR*, MD, A
21	*Garcia v Holder*	(2011 SDNY) 788 F Supp 2d 326	01/06/2011	24/05/2011	0 Y, 8 D	LR, Z
22	*Johnson v Orsino*	(2013 SDNY) 942 F Supp 2d 396	24/04/2013	18/01/2012	1 Y, 97 D	LR, MD
23	*Araujo-Cortes v Shanahan*	(2014 SDNY) 35 F Supp 3d 533	05/08/2014	30/01/2014	0 Y, 187 D	S, LR, MD

24	*Martinez-Done v McConnell*	(2014 SDNY) 56 F Supp 3d 535	08/10/2014	26/03/2014	0 Y, 196 D	S, LR, MD
25	*Rodriguez v Shanahan*	(2015 SDNY) 84 F Supp 3d 251	30/01/2015	26/09/2014	0 Y, 126 D	S, LR, MD, L
26	*Reynoso v Aviles*	(2015 SDNY) 87 F Supp 3d 549	05/02/2015	09/10/2014	0 Y, 119 D	LR, MD
27	*Gordon v Shanahan*	(2015 SDNY) 2015 WL 1176706	13/03/2015	26/06/2014	0 Y, 260 D	S, LR*, MD
28	*Young v Aviles*	(2015 SDNY) 99 F Supp 3d 443	26/03/2015	28/08/2014	0 Y, 210 D	LR, MD
29	*Minto v Decker*	(2015 SDNY) 108 F Supp 3d 189	05/06/2015	28/03/2014	1 Y, 69 D	S, LR, MD
30	*Bugianishvili v McConnell*	2015 WL 3903460 (SDNY)	24/06/2015	28/10/2014	0 Y, 239 D	S, LR*, MD
31	*Giron v Shanahan*	2015 WL 5334046 (SDNY)	11/09/2015	03/09/2014	1 Y, 8 D	S, LR*, MD
32	*Richardson v Shanahan*	2015 WL 5813330 (SDNY)	06/10/2015	17/10/2014	0 Y, 354 D	LR, MD
33	*Faure v Decker*	2015 WL 6143801 (SDNY)	19/10/2015	27/04/2015	0 Y, 175 D	S, LR*, MD, L
34	*Raju v Shanahan*	2015 WL 7567455 (SDNY)	23/11/2015	31/07/2015	0 Y, 115 D	LR, MD
Western District of NY						
35	*Worrell v Ashcroft*	(2002 WDNY) 207 F Supp 2d 61	29/03/2002	29/11/1999	2 Y, 121 D	Z, A
36	*Pemberton v Ashcroft*	2002 WL 31011879 (WDNY)	09/08/2002	No data	–	LR*, Z, A
37	*Ellis v Ashcroft*	2004 WL 2202590 (WDNY)	30/09/2004	13/02/2002	2 Y, 230 D	Z, A
38	*Singh v Holmes*	2004 WL 2280366 (WDNY)	08/10/2004	No data	–	Z
39	*Pan v Ashcroft*	2005 WL 1398601 (WDNY)	14/06/2005	No data	–	Z
40	*Tam v Department of Homeland Security*	2006 WL 839425 (WDNY)	28/03/2006	23/12/2004	1 Y, 95 D	Z

	Case Name	Citation	Judgment Date (Euro format)	Detained Since	Detention Length (years, days)	Markers
41	*Roberts v Bureau of Immigration and Customs Enforcement*	2007 WL 781925 (WDNY)	13/03/2007	15/06/2006	0 Y, 302 D	Z
42	*Blackman v US Deprt of Homeland Security Bureau of Immigration and Customs Enforcement*	2007 WL 4404930 (WDNY)	14/12/2007	09/09/2005	2 Y, 96 D	Z
43	*Haidara v Mule*	2008 WL 2483281 (WDNY)	17/06/2008	15/02/2007	1 Y, 123 D	Z, CC
44	*Khaleque v Department of Homeland Security*	2009 WL 81318 (WDNY)	09/01/2009	28/12/2006	2 Y, 13 D	Z, A, F
45	*Ricketts v Mule*	2009 WL 102953 (WDNY)	13/01/2009	05/09/2006	2 Y, 131 D	Z
46	*Gabriel v Immigration and Customs Enforcement*	2009 WL 1272291 (WDNY)	23/02/2009	25/11/2008	0 Y, 90 D	Z
47	*Greenland v INS/Ice Dep't of Homeland Sec*	(2009 WDNY) 599 F Supp 2d 365	24/02/2009	01/03/2008	0 Y, 360 D	Z
48	*Gordon v Herron*	2009 WL 909640 (WDNY)	31/03/2009	19/07/2007	1 Y, 256 D	Z
49	*Ramos v Chertoff*	2009 WL 1563894 (WDNY)	02/06/2009	01/06/2007	2 Y, 2 D	LR, Z
50	*D'Alessandro v Mukasey*	(2009 WDNY) 628 F Supp 2d 368	29/05/2009	19/11/2007	1 Y, 192 D	S, LR, Z, –A, L
51	*Scarlett v US Department of Homeland Security Bureau of ICE*	(2009 WDNY) 632 F Supp 2d 214	10/07/2009	25/11/2003	5 Y, 228 D	S, LR, MD
52	*Duarte-Ceri v Napolitano*	2009 WL 1806694 (WDNY)	23/06/2009	08/05/2006	3 Y, 47 D	Z

53	*Gabriel v Cleary*	2009 WL 2413674 (WDNY)	04/08/2009	25/11/2008	0 Y, 252 D	Z
54	*Dogra v Immigration Customs Enforcement*	2009 WL 2878459 (WDNY)	02/09/2009	05/06/2008	1 Y, 89 D	Z, A
55	*Gumbs v Heron*	2009 WL 2958002 (WDNY)	11/09/2009	07/10/2007	1 Y, 340 D	Z
56	*Garcia v Heron*	2009 WL 3231924 (WDNY)	01/10/2009	16/06/2008	1 Y, 107 D	Z
57	*Diallo v Immigration and Customs Enforcement*	2010 WL 3769506 (WDNY)	05/05/2010	13/10/2005	4 Y, 204 D	Z, A
58	*Luna-Aponte v Holder*	(2010 WDNY) 743 F Supp 2d 189	10/09/2010	13/05/2007	3 Y, 121 D	MD, A
59	*Leslie v Heron*	2010 WL 4226561 (WDNY)	26/10/2010	25/11/2009	0 Y, 335 D	Z, −F
60	*Johnson v Phillips*	2010 WL 6512350 (WDNY)	20/12/2010	08/01/2009	1 Y, 346 D	LR, MD, A
61	*St Louis v Heron*	2011 WL 2746787 (WDNY)	13/07/2011	21/05/2010	1 Y, 53 D	Z
62	*Dover v Holder*	2011 WL 4054952 (WDNY)	12/09/2011	04/05/2010	1 Y, 131 D	Z, A, F
63	*Khan v Herron*	2011 WL 4899994 (WDNY)	14/10/2011	03/08/2009	2 Y, 72 D	Z, A, F
64	*Persaud v Holder*	2011 WL 5326465 (WDNY)	03/11/2011	17/12/2009	1 Y, 321 D	Z, F
65	*Muhury v Tryon*	2011 WL 6016606 (WDNY)	02/12/2011	10/11/2010	1 Y, 22 D	Z
66	*Adams v Holder*	2012 WL 1999488 (WDNY)	04/06/2012	13/08/2009	2 Y, 296 D	Z, F
67	*Andreenko v Holder*	2012 WL 4210286 (WDNY)	25/06/2010	22/10/2008	1 Y, 246 D	Z, F
68	*Lucien v Tryon*	2012 WL 5373455 (WDNY)	30/10/2012	05/07/2011	1 Y, 118 D	MD
69	*Toure v Holder*	2013 WL 1352288 (WDNY)	03/04/2013	06/03/2012	1 Y, 28 D	Z, CC
70	*Williams v Holder*	2013 WL 1352306 (WDNY)	03/04/2013	02/04/2012	1 Y, 1 D	Z, CC
71	*Gonther v Napolitano*	2013 WL 1569311 (WDNY)	12/04/2013	30/01/2012	1 Y, 73 D	Z, CC
72	*Tejeda-Estrella v Holder*	2013 WL 1570141 (WDNY)	12/04/2013	22/07/2011	1 Y, 265 D	Z, CC, F

	Case Name	Citation	Judgment Date (Euro format)	Detained Since	Detention Length (years, days)	Markers
73	*Rahel v Tryon*	2013 WL 1878914 (WDNY)	03/05/2013	26/09/2011	1 Y, 220 D	Z, CC, A, F
74	*Wynter v Phillips*	2013 WL 1879667 (WDNY)	16/04/2014	26/07/2012	1 Y, 264 D	MD
75	*Fofana v Holder*	(2013 WDNY) 947 F Supp 2d 329	03/05/2013	30/03/2012	1 Y, 34 D	Z, CC, A
76	*Haley v Holder*	2013 WL 1945704 (WDNY)	09/05/2013	04/08/2010	2 Y, 279 D	Z, CC, F
77	*Adegbite v Holder*	2013 WL 1945734 (WDNY)	09/05/2013	09/05/2012	1 Y, 0 D	Z, CC
78	*Dookhan v Holder*	2013 WL 1945950 (WDNY)	09/05/2013	08/06/2012	0 Y, 335 D	Z, CC, A
79	*Ahmed v Holder*	2013 WL 2468732 (WDNY)	07/06/2013	27/04/2012	1 Y, 41 D	Z, CC
80	*Mohamed v Holder*	2013 WL 2468738 (WDNY)	07/06/2013	19/06/2012	0 Y, 353 D	Z, CC, A, F
81	*Flores v Holder*	(2013 WDNY) 977 F Supp 2d 243	07/06/2013	10/06/2011	1 Y, 363 D	Z, CC, A, F
82	*Jones v Holder*	2013 WL 2898069 (WDNY)	13/06/2013	24/07/2012	0 Y, 324 D	Z, CC
83	*Bennett v Napolitano*	2013 WL 3282871 (WDNY)	27/06/2013	23/03/2012	1 Y, 96 D	Z, CC, F
84	*Gobin v Holder*	2013 WL 3784144 (WDNY)	18/07/2013	27/07/2012	0 Y, 356 D	Z, CC, A
85	*Bartholomew v Holder*	2013 WL 4780117 (WDNY)	05/09/2013	26/01/2012	1 Y, 223 D	Z, CC, A, F
86	*McKoy v Holder*	2013 WL 5211500 (WDNY)	13/09/2013	18/09/2012	0 Y, 360 D	Z, CC
87	*Mathews v Philips*	2013 WL 5288166 (WDNY)	18/09/2013	28/12/2011	1 Y, 265 D	LR, Z, CC, F
88	*Almonte v Holder*	(2013 WDNY) 983 F Supp 2d 234	19/09/2013	02/09/2011	2 Y, 18 D	Z, CC, A, F
89	*Newell v Holder*	(2013 WDNY) 983 F Supp 2d 241	26/09/2013	17/11/2011	1 Y, 314 D	Z, CC, A, F
90	*Jama v Napolitano*	2013 WL 5503965 (WDNY)	02/10/2013	25/09/2012	1 Y, 7 D	Z, CC
91	*Miller v Tryon*	2013 WL 5592484 (WDNY)	10/10/2013	04/10/2012	1 Y, 314 D	Z, CC, A, F

92	*Lumanikio v Holder*	2013 WL 5592807 (WDNY)	10/10/2013	21/07/2011	2 Y, 82 D	Z, CC, F
93	*Ruiz-Ibanez v Holder*	2013 WL 5964486 (WDNY)	08/11/2013	14/02/2012	1 Y, 268 D	Z, CC, A
94	*Charran v Philips*	2014 WL 296429 (WDNY)	24/01/2014	24/02/2012	1 Y, 335 D	Z, CC, F
95	*Morales v Holder*	2014 WL 1117827 (WDNY)	19/03/2014	10/05/2013	0 Y, 313 D	MD, A
96	*Wynter v Tryon*	2014 WL 1572356 (WDNY)	16/04/2014	26/07/2012	1 Y, 264 D	Z, CC, F
97	*Flores v Tryon*	2014 WL 2002830 (WDNY)	14/05/2014	10/06/2011	2 Y, 339 D	Z, CC, F
98	*McGowan v Tryon*	2014 WL 2931413 (WDNY)	25/06/2014	07/10/2013	0 Y, 261 D	MD
99	*Campbell v Tryon*	2014 WL 3809747 (WDNY)	30/07/2014	04/12/2012	1 Y, 238 D	Z, CC, A, F
100	*Vaskovska v Holder*	2014 WL 4659316 (WDNY)	17/09/2014	11/06/2013	1 Y, 98 D	LR, MD, A
101	*Hunt v Holder*	2015 WL 860778 (WDNY)	25/02/2015	26/06/2014	0 Y, 244 D	Z, CC
102	*Alzubi v Tryon*	2015 WL 860792 (WDNY)	25/02/2015	30/01/2012	3 Y, 27 D	Z, CC, A
103	*Islam v Philips*	2015 WL 1915106 (WDNY)	23/04/2015	20/10/2013	1 Y, 185 D	LR, Z, CC
104	*Farray v Holder*	2015 WL 2194520 (WDNY)	06/05/2015	03/02/2012	3 Y, 93 D	Z, CC, A, F
105	*Jiang v Holder*	2015 WL 3649739 (WDNY)	09/06/2015	20/05/2014	1 Y, 20 D	Z, CC, A
106	*Neil v Holder*	2015 WL 3937280 (WDNY)	25/06/2015	18/10/2013	1 Y, 250 D	Z, CC, A, F
107	*Salim v Johnson*	2015 WL 4094696 (WDNY)	01/07/2015	14/11/2013	1 Y, 229 D	LR, Z, CC
108	*Urrutia v Lynch*	2015 WL 7288698 (WDNY)	13/11/2015	09/12/2012	2 Y, 339 D	Z, CC, A, F
109	*Irving v Lynch et al*	2016 WL 231381 (WDNY)	13/01/2016	17/02/2015	0 Y, 330 D	Z, CC
110	*Beckford v Lynch et al*	2016 WL 827389 (WDNY)	02/03/2016	19/02/2014	2 Y, 12 D	Z, CC

	Case Name	Citation	Judgment Date (Euro format)	Detained Since	Detention Length (years, days)	Markers
European Union – Court of Justice of the European Union						
Category A Cases						
1	*Kadzoev*	Case C-357/09 PPU *Kadzoev* [2009] ECR I-11189	30/11/2009	03/11/2006	3 Y, 28 D	LR, L
2	*Arslan*	Case C-534/11 *Arslan* [ECR TBC]	30/05/2013	01/02/2011	0 Y, 176 D	LR
3	*G and R*	Case C-383/13 PPU *G and R* [ECR TBC]	10/09/2013	G: 24/10/2012 R: 11/11/2012	G: 0 Y, 321 D R: 0 Y, 303 D	LR, L, E
4	*Bero and Bouzalmate*	Joined Cases C-473/13 and C-514/13 *Bero and Bouzalmate* [ECR TBC]	17/07/2014	No data	–	LR
5	*Pham*	Case C-474/13 *Pham* [ECR TBC]	17/07/2014	No data	–	LR, L
6	*Mahdi*	Case C-146/14 PPU *Mahdi* [ECR TBC]	05/06/2014	23/03/2013	0 Y, 300 D	LR, L
Category B Cases						
7	*El Dridi*	Case C-61/11 PPU *El Dridi* [2011] ECR I-3015	28/04/2011	N/A	N/A	LR, E
8	*Achughbabian*	Case C-329/11 *Achughbabian* [ECR TBC]	06/12/2011	N/A	N/A	LR, E

9	*Md Sagor*	Case C-430/11 *Md Sagor* [ECR TBC]	06/12/2012	N/A	N/A	LR, E
10	*Mbaye*	Case C-522/11 *Mbaye* [ECR TBC]	21/03/2013	N/A	N/A	LR, E
11	*Filev and Osmani*	Case C-297/12 *Filev and Osmani* [ECR TBC]	19/09/2013	N/A	N/A	LR, E
12	*Zaizoune*	Case C-38/14 *Zaizoune* [ECR TBC]	23/04/2015	N/A	N/A	LR, E
13	*Celaj*	Case C-290/14 *Celaj* [ECR TBC]	01/10/2015	N/A	N/A	LR, E
14	*Affum*	Case C-47/15 *Affum* [ECR TBC]	07/06/2016	N/A	N/A	LR, E
Category C Cases						
15	*Mukarubega*	Case C-166/13 *Mukarubega* [ECR TBC]	05/11/2014	N/A	N/A	LR, L, E
16	*Boudjilda*	Case C-249/13 *Boudjilda* [ECR TBC]	11/12/2014	N/A	N/A	LR, E
17	*Zh and O*	Case C-554/13 *Zh and O* [ECR TBC]	11/06/2015	N/A	N/A	LR

[i] Specific date not provided. Opinion reads 'detained by the Department of Homeland Security in October 2008'.

Additional Cases

European Court of Human Rights

A and Others v UK [2009] ECHR 301
Abdi v UK [2013] ECHR 299
Abdulaziz, Cabales and Balkandali v UK [1985] ECHR 7
Aden Ahmed v Malta [2013] ECHR 720
Amuur v France [1996] ECHR 25
Bozano v France [1986] ECHR 16
Bykov v Russia [2009] ECHR 441
Chahal v UK [1996] ECHR 54
Dougoz v Greece [2001] ECHR 213
Draga v UK, Communicated Case [2015] ECHR 73
Gillan and Quinton v UK [2010] ECHR 28
JN v UK [2016] ECHR 434
Kolompar v Belgium [1992] ECHR 59
Lamy v Belgium [1989] ECHR 5
Litwa v Poland [2000] ECHR 141
MA v Cyprus [2013] ECHR 717
Maaouia v France [2000] ECHR 455
McMichael v UK [1995] ECHR 8
Megyeri v Germany [1992] ECHR 49
Quinn v France [1995] ECHR 9
Raynor v SSHD [2007] EWHC 1028 (Admin)
Saadi v UK [2006] ECHR 732
Saadi v UK [2008] ECHR 80
Tabassum v UK [2012] ECHR 223
Toth v Austria [1991] ECHR 72
Uppal and Singh v UK App no 8244/78 (Commission decision, 2 May 1979)
VM v UK [2016] ECHR 729
X v UK [1981] ECHR 9
Yoh-Ekale Mwanje v Belgium [2011] ECHR 2421

European Union

Case C-617/10 *Åkerberg Fransson* [ECR TBC]
Joined Cases C-20/00 and C-64/00 *Booker Aquaculture* [2003] ECR I-7411
Case 203/80 *Casati* [1981] ECR 2595

Case 6/64 *Costa v ENEL* [1964] ECR 585
Case C-465/07 *Elgafaji* [2009] ECR I-921
Joined Cases C-6 & 9/90 *Francovich and Bonifaci v Italy* [1991] ECR I-5357
Case C-40/11 *Iida v Stadt Ulm* [ECR TBC]
Case C-601/15 PPU *JN v Staatssecretaris van Veiligheid en Justitie* [ECR TBC]
Case C-144/95 *Maurin* [1996] ECR I-2908
Case C-528/15 *Policie ČR, Krajské ředitelství policie Ústeckého kraje, odbor cizinecké policie v Salah Al Chodor and Others* [ECR TBC]
Case 36/75 *Rutili* [1975] ECR 1219
Case 206/13 *Siragusa v Regione Sicilia – Soprintendenza Beni Culturali e Ambientali di Palermo* [ECR TBC]
Case 41/74 *Van Duyn v Home Office* [1974] ECR 1337
Case 14/83 *Von Colson and Kamann v Land Nordrhein-Westfalen* [1984] ECR 1891
Case 69/85 *Wünsche Handelsgesellschaft GmbH & Co v Federal Republic of Germany* [1986] ECR 947 [1986] EUECJ R-69/85

United Kingdom

House of Lords

A v SSHD [2004] UKHL 56
R (Alconbury Developments Ltd) v Secretary of State for the Environment [2001] UKHL 23
Chief Constable of North Wales Police v Evans [1982] UKHL 10
Council of Civil Service Unions v Minister for the Civil Service [1985] AC 374, [1984] UKHL 9
R (Khadir) v SSHD [2005] UKHL 39
Khawaja v SSHD [1983] UKHL 8
Tweed v Parades Commission for Northern Ireland [2006] UKHL 53
Zamir v SSHD [1980] UKHL 14

Supreme Court

R (Nouazli) v SSHD [2016] UKSC 16
Kambadzi (SK (Zimbabwe) v SSHD [2011] UKSC 23
Lumba (WL) v SSHD [2011] UKSC 12

Court of Appeal of England and Wales

A, X and Y [2002] EWCA Civ 1502
R (A) v SSHD [2007] EWCA Civ 804
R (Anam) v SSHD [2010] EWCA Civ 1140

R (Cheblak) v SSHD [1991] 1 WLR 890
R (Francis) v SSHD [2014] EWCA Civ 718
R (I) v SSHD [2002] EWCA Civ 888
R (LE (Jamaica)) v SSHD [2012] EWCA Civ 597
R (MH) v SSHD [2010] EWCA Civ 1112
R (Saadi) v SSHD [2001] EWCA Civ 1512
R (Saleh (Sudan)) v SSHD [2013] EWCA Civ 1378
WL (Congo) v SSHD [2010] EWCA Civ 111

High Court of England and Wales

R (Ahsan) v Governor of Brixton Prison [1969] 2 QB 222
R (Akangbe) v SSHD [2008] EWHC 2295 (Admin)
R (Botan) v SSHD [2017] EWHC 550 (Admin)
R (CM (Somalia)) v SSHD [2010] EWHC 640 (Admin)
G v SSHD [2016] EWHC 3232 (Admin)
R (Faulkner) v SSHD [2005] EWHC 2567 (Admin)
R (Hardial Singh) v Governor of Durham Prison [1983] EWHC 1 (QB)
R (Hassan) v Governor of Risley [1976] 1 WLR 971
R (Konan) v SSHD [2004] EWHC 22 (Admin) 30
R (Mahajna (Salah)) v SSHD [2011] EWHC 2481 (Admin)
R (Muboyayi) v SSHD [1992] 1 QB 244
R (NAB) v SSHD [2010] EWHC 3137 (Admin)
R (Rahman) v SSHD [2014] EWHC 1640 (Admin)
R (Venicoff) v Inspector of Leman Street Police Station [1920] 3 KB 72
Saleh v SSHD [2013] EWHC 61 (Admin)

Privy Council of the United Kingdom

Lam v Superintendent of Tai A Chau Detention Centre [1996] UKPC 5

United States

Supreme Court

Carlson v Landon (1952) 342 US 524
Clark v Martinez (2005) 543 US 371
Demore v Kim (2003) 538 US 510
Fong Yue Ting v United States (1893) 149 US 698
Haines v Kerner (1972) 404 US 519
Knauff v Shaughnessy (1950) 338 US 537
Nishimura Ekiu v United States (1892) 142 US 651
Shaughnessy v United States ex rel Mezei (1953) 345 US 206
Wong Wing v US (1896) 163 US 228
Zadvydas v Davis (2001) 533 US 678

Court of Appeals

Fleming v US (2d Cir 1998) 146 F 3d 88
Galarza v Szalczyk (3d Cir 2013) 745 F3d 634
Kim v Ziglar (9th Cir 2002) 276 F 3d 523
Lora v Shanahan (2d Cir 2015) 804 F 3d 601
Rodriguez v Robbins (9th Cir 2013) 715 F 3d 1127, cert granted 20/06/2016 as *Jennings v Rodriguez*, USA Supreme Court Docket No 15-1204 *USA ex rel Cadogan v LaVallee*, (2d Cir 1974) 502 F 2d 824
Williams v Kuhlman (2d Cir 1983) 722 F 2d 1048

Federal District Courts

Coita v Leonardo 1998 WL 187416 (NDNY) 1
Cruz-Taveras v McElroy 1996 WL 455012 (SDNY)
De Los Rios v United States 1994 WL 502635 (SDNY)
Louisaire v Muller (SDNY 2010) 758 FSupp2d 229
Rajigah v Conway (EDNY 2003) 268 F Supp 2d 159
US v Arena (NDNY 1995) 894 F Supp 580

Board of Immigration Appeals

Matter of Joseph (BIA 1999) 22 I&N Dec 799
In re Rojas (BIA 2001) 23 I&N Dec 117

Table of Legislation

Council of Europe

European Convention on Human Rights, signed 4 November 1950; entry into force 3 September 1953

European Union

Treaties

Charter of Fundamental Rights of the European Union [2012] OJ C326/391
Treaty on European Union [2012] OJ C326/13
Treaty on the Functioning of the European Union [2012] OJ C326/47

Directives

Directive 2001/55/EC of the Council of the European Union on minimum standards for giving temporary protection in the event of a mass influx of displaced persons and on measures promoting a balance of efforts between Member States in receiving such persons and bearing the consequences thereof [2001] OJ L212/12
Directive 2003/9/EC of the Council of 27 January 2003 laying down minimum standards for the reception of asylum seekers [2003] OJ L31/18
Directive 2004/38/EC of the European Parliament and of the Council of 29 April 2004 on the right of citizens of the Union and their family members to move and reside freely within the territory of the Member States [2005] OJ L158/77
Directive 2005/85/EC of the Council of 1 December 2005 on minimum standards on procedures in Member States for granting and withdrawing refugee status [2005] OJ L326/13
Directive 2008/115/EC of the European Parliament and of the Council on 16 December 2008 on common standards and procedures in Member States for returning illegally staying third-country nationals [2008] OJ L348/98
Directive 2011/95/EU of the European Parliament and of the Council on minimum standards for the qualification and status of third country nationals or stateless persons as refugees or as persons who otherwise need international protection and the content of the protection granted (recast) [2011] OJ L337/9

Directive 2013/32/EU of the European Parliament and of the Council on common procedures for granting and withdrawing international protection (recast) [2013] OJ L180/60

Directive 2013/33/EU of the European Parliament and of the Council laying down standards for the reception of applicants for international protection (recast) [2013] OJ L180/96

Directive 2001/40/EC of the Council on the mutual recognition of decisions on the expulsion of third country nationals [2001] OJ L149/34

Regulations

Regulation 603/2013/EU of the European Parliament and of the Council on the establishment of 'Eurodac' for the comparison of fingerprints for the effective application of Regulation (EU) No 604/2013 establishing the criteria and mechanisms for determining the Member State responsible for examining an application for international protection lodged in one of the Member States by a third-country national or a stateless person and on requests for the comparison with Eurodac data by Member States' law enforcement authorities and Europol for law enforcement purposes, and amending Regulation (EU) No 1077/2011 establishing a European Agency for the operational management of large-scale IT systems in the area of freedom, security and justice (recast) [2013] OJ L180/1

Regulation 604/2013/EU of the European Parliament and of the Council of 26 June 2013 establishing the criteria and mechanisms for determining the Member State responsible for examining an application for international protection lodged in one of the Member States by a third-country national or a stateless person (recast), [2013] OJ L180/31

Framework Decisions

Framework Decision 2002/584/JHS of the Council of 13 June 2002 on the European arrest warrant and the surrender procedures between Member States – Statements made by certain Member States on the adoption of the Framework Decision [2002] OJ L190/1

Framework Decision 2008/909/JHA of the Council of 27 November 2008 on the application of the principle of mutual recognition to judgments in criminal matters imposing custodial sentences or measures involving deprivation of liberty for the purpose of their enforcement in the European Union [2008] OJ L327/27

Framework Decision 2009/829/JHA of the Council of 23 October 2009 on the application, between Member States of the European Union, of the principle of mutual recognition to decisions on supervision measures as an alternative to provisional detention [2009] OJ L294/20

Miscellaneous

Council Decision 2010/124/EU relating to the operating rules of the panel provided for in Article 255 of the Treaty on the Functioning of the European Union (25 February 2010)
Court of Justice of the European Union, 'Rules of Procedure of the Court of Justice' [2012] OJ L254/1
Protocol (No 3) on the Statute of the Court of Justice of the European Union [2010] OJ C83/210

United Kingdom

Statutes

Borders, Citizenship and Immigration Act 2009, c 11, Royal Assent 21 July 2009
Constitutional Reform Act 2005, c 4, Royal Assent 24 March 2005
Criminal Justice and Courts Act 2015, c 2, Royal Assent 12 February 2015
Human Rights Act 1998, c 42, Royal Assent 09 November 1998
Immigration Act 2016, c 19, Royal Assent 12 May 2016
Immigration and Asylum Act 1999, c 33, Royal Assent 11 November 1999
Legal Aid, Sentencing and Punishment of Offenders Act 2012, c 10, Royal Assent 01 May 2012
Nationality, Immigration and Asylum Act 2002, c 41, Royal Assent 7 November 2002
Senior Courts Act 1981, c 54, Royal Assent 28 July 1981
UK Borders Act 2007, c 30, Royal Assent 30 October 2007

Statutory Instruments

Civil Legal Aid (Merits Criteria) Regulations 2013 SI No 2013/104
First-tier Tribunal and Upper Tribunal (Chambers) (Amendment) Order SI No 2011/2342
The First-tier Tribunal and Upper Tribunal (Chambers) (Amendment No. 2) Order SI No 2013/2068
The Supreme Court Rules 2009 SI No 2009/1603 (L 17)

Procedural Rules

Civil Procedure Rules 52, 87

United States

Constitution

USA Constitution, art III, s 1; amendment V

Statutes

Administrative Procedures Act, Pub L 79–404, 60 Stat 237, enacted 11 June 1946
Alien and Sedition Acts 1798: (1) An Act to Establish an Uniform Rule of Naturalization (Naturalization Act); (2) An Act Concerning Aliens; (3) An Act Respecting Alien Enemies; and (4) An Act for the Punishment of Certain Crimes against the United States (Sedition Act)
Anti-Drug Abuse Act of 1988, Pub L 100–690, 102 Stat 4181, enacted 18 November 1988
Antiterrorism and Effective Death Penalty Act 1996, Pub L No 104–132, 110 Stat 1214
Bail Reform Act 1984, Pub L No 98–473, 98 Stat 1976–87
Chinese Exclusion Act 1882 (An act to inaugurate certain treaty stipulations relating to Chinese), Session I, Ch 126, 22 Stat 58, 47th Congress, approved 6 May 1882
Geary Act 1892, Session I, Ch 60, 52nd Congress, 5 May 1892
Homeland Security Act 2002, Pub L 107–296, 116 Stat 2135, enacted 25 November 2002
Illegal Immigration Reform and Immigrant Responsibility Act 1996, Pub L No 104–208, Div C, 110 Stat 2009–546
Immigration Act 1882 (An act to regulate immigration), Session I, Ch 376, 22 Stat 214, 47th Congress, 3 August 1882
Immigration Act 1891 (An act in amendment to the various acts relative to immigration and the importation of aliens under contract or agreement to perform labor), Session II, Ch 551; 26 Stat 1084, 51st Congress, 3 March 1891
Immigration Act 1893, 27 Statutes-at-Large 570
Immigration Act 1990, Pub L No 101–649, 104 Stat 4978, 5049
Immigration and Nationality Act 1952, Pub L 82–414, 66 Stat 163, enacted 27 June 1952
Judiciary Act 1789, ch 20, 1 Stat 77
Judiciary Act 1875, 18 Stat 470
US Code Title 28 s 2241 – Power to grant writ
US Code Title 28 s 2243 – Issuance of writ; return; hearing; decision

Regulations

Code of Federal Regulations, Title 8, 'Aliens and Nationality', Parts 236, 241, 287, 1236

1

Introduction

I. THE DETENTION MACHINE

IMMIGRATION HAS TOPPED the political and legislative agendas in the UK, USA and EU in recent years. Economic austerity, political upheaval, terrorism and increased flows of migration due to globalisation have forced these jurisdictions to struggle with providing for and protecting their citizens while simultaneously accommodating thousands of new entrants each year. The standard response to these problems has been to implement restrictive immigration policies via laws that both prevent entry and increase deportation, ultimately resulting in more detention. With the rise of immigration detention, civil society and the international community have moved to support policies in favour of the use of alternatives to detention over physical custody in detention centres. Rather than scale back on restrictive policies and embrace a more integrative approach to immigration, many states have expanded their detention capacity and view detention as an integral part of deportation policy, even where there has been no empirical evidence that the use of detention deters irregular migration.[1]

Statistics on detention in the USA are not regularly maintained by the state. The last 'official' release of statistics by the government was in 2015, when US Immigration and Customs Enforcement (ICE) reported that 307,310 people were detained across the 111 immigration detention centres. The report notes that, though this is the total for the year, the average daily population is much lower, around the 29,000 mark.[2] Additional statistics were obtained from ICE through a Freedom of Information Act request by the National Immigrant Justice

[1] Michael B Flynn, 'From Bare Life to Bureaucratic Capitalism: Analyzing the Growth of the Immigration Detention Industry as a Complex Organization' (2016) 8 *Contemporary Readings in Law and Social Justice* 70.

[2] Department of Homeland Security (DHS), 'Immigration Enforcement Actions 2013' (09/2014) 6. The DHS has not published detention statistics since 2013. However, a draft report for 2014 uncovered by César Cuauhtémoc García Hernández tells us that 425,728 people were detained that year: CC García Hernández 'Immigration Detention Populations Appear to Have Dropped in FY 14 & FY 15', *Crimmigration* (28 January 2016). Statistics on detention were not included in the final published report for 2014: DHS, 'ICE Enforcement and Removal Operations Report 2014' (19 December 2014). More recent statistics on housing of detainees shows that in 2015, ICE 'housed' 307,310 detainees. See US Department of Justice, 'Report and Recommendations Concerning the Use of Restrictive Housing' (January 2016) 88 www.justice.gov/dag/file/815551/download.

Center, which revealed that the average daily population in detention centres for fiscal year 2018 was 39,322.[3] Early on in his presidency, Donald Trump expressed his preference for detention by signing an executive order increasing detention space near the border with Mexico,[4] and stating that detention is the most efficient way to enforce immigration law at the borders to the USA.[5] Since then, he has engaged in a policy of prosecuting all unlawful border crossings, which has resulted in the separation of migrant families and the detention of thousands of children, and has continued despite global criticism. He has also altered the detainee risk assessment process by removing the option of a recommendation for release from the digital risk assessment tool used by ICE.[6] Finally, at the time of writing, it was revealed by the American Immigration Council that the administration had increased its detention bed capacity to 48,000 despite having funding for only 40,500 beds.[7]

In the UK, the number of people being detained has decreased. In 2017, 27,300 people were detained across 11 detention centres, compared to 28,900 in 2016.[8] Detention has been the subject of a number of official inquiries over recent years, examining all aspects of detention, including the process by which detention determinations are made, the conditions of detention and whether an expedited appeals process should be applied to people in detention.[9] Despite the existence of so many inquiries and consultations, little legislative and policy change has resulted from their recommendations.[10] However, at the time of

[3] TT Cullen, 'ICE Released Its Most Comprehensive Immigration Detention Data Yet. It's Alarming' (13 March 2018) https://immigrantjustice.org/staff/blog/ice-released-its-most-comprehensive-immigration-detention-data-yet. An Excel file of the statistics is available to download from that link.

[4] Executive Order, 'Border Security and Immigration Enforcement Improvements' 25 January 2017, Section 5,.

[5] Homeland Security Memorandum, 'Implementing the President's Border Security and Immigration Enforcement Improvements Policies', 20 February 2017, p 2.

[6] K Evans and R Koulish, 'Under Trump, ICE No Longer Recommends Release for Immigrants in Detention', *Crimmigration* (26 July 2018) http://crimmigration.com/2018/07/26/under-trump-ice-no-longer-recommends-release-for-immigrants-in-detention/.

[7] K Shepherd, 'Government Quietly Increases ICE Detention to 48,000 Beds during the Shutdown', *Immigration Impact* (31 January 2019) http://immigrationimpact.com/2019/01/31/increases-ice-detention-beds-shutdown/.

[8] SJ Silverman and M Griffiths, 'Immigration Detention in the UK', Migration Observatory (3 July 2018) https://migrationobservatory.ox.ac.uk/resources/briefings/immigration-detention-in-the-uk/.

[9] See, eg Joint Inquiry by the All Party Parliamentary Group on Refugees & the All Party Parliamentary Group on Migration, 'The Report of the Inquiry into the Use of Immigration Detention in the United Kingdom' (March 2015); Ministry of Justice, 'Response to Its Consultation on Proposals to Expedite Appeals by Immigration Detainees' (April 2017); S Shaw, 'Review into the Welfare in Detention of Vulnerable Persons', Cm 9186 (January 2016); S Shaw, 'Assessment of Government Progress in Implementing the Report on the Welfare in Detention of Vulnerable Persons: A Follow-Up Report to the Home Office', Cm 9661 (July 2018); House of Commons Home Affairs Committee, 'Immigration detention', Fourteenth Report of Session 2017–2019, HC 913 (March 2019).

[10] As a result of the first Shaw review cited in the previous note, administrative working practice has been altered to introduce the concept of a 'gatekeeper function', 'case progression panels' and a new Adults at Risk policy. In addition, a new policy of automatically reviewing bail eligibility at four months of detention for those not subject to deportation was introduced by the Immigration Act 2016.

writing, the Parliament's Joint Committee on Human Rights had published a report on immigration detention that recommended ending the practice of indefinite detention and replacing it with a 28-day limit.[11]

Figures from the EU as a whole are more difficult to obtain. A 2014 study gave a figure of 92,575 for 23 EU Member States in 2013.[12] However, there are signs that the use of detention in Europe is beginning to decrease in some Member States, such as Malta[13] and the Netherlands.[14] Although it is not clear exactly what has contributed to the decreased use of detention in these Member States, one commentator has suggested that the Return Directive has played a role.[15] This is significant in light of statistics from the EU indicating that 533,395 irregular migrants were ordered to leave the EU in 2015.[16]

Several factors have contributed to the rise in use of detention for immigration enforcement purposes in the modern day. For example, an expansion of the legal grounds for detention, including an increase in the use of mandatory detention, has contributed to making the use of detention the norm rather than the exception it once was, most markedly in the USA. Indeed, Bosworth and Kaufman argue that 'the non-citizen ... is the next and newest "enemy" in an American war on crime',[17] and Demleitner writes of mass arrests of non-citizens in the context of fighting the war on terrorism.[18] Linking immigration with security

[11] House of Commons and House of Lords Joint Committee on Human Rights, 'Immigration Detention', Sixteenth Report of Session 2017–19, HC 4484; HL Paper 278 (February 2019).

[12] European Migration Network, 'The Use of Detention and Alternatives to Detention in the Context of Immigration Policies: Synthesis Report' (2014) 9.

[13] In early 2016, Malta introduced a new migration strategy that eliminated the automatic detention of irregular migrants: see Asylum Information Database, 'Malta: New Migration Strategy Ends Automatic Detention of Irregular Entrants', *Asylum in Europe* (8 January 2016) www.asylumineurope.org/news/08-01-2016/malta-new-migration-strategy-ends-automatic-detention-irregular-entrants; press release from Maltese Ministry for Home Affairs and National Security: www.gov.mt/en/Government/Press Releases/Pages/2015/Dec/30/pr152933eng.aspx.

[14] Statistics provided by the Global Detention Project on detention in the Netherlands demonstrate that detention has gone from 8,585 in 2008 to 2,176 in 2015: www.globaldetentionproject.org/countries/europe/netherlands. A similar trend can be seen in Germany, with detention at 8,366 in 2009 and 4,812 in 2013: www.globaldetentionproject.org/countries/europe/germany. In addition, 'data on Germany and the Netherlands indicate that the numbers of persons taken in immigration detention actually diminished considerably over the last years: in Germany from around 9,000 in 2008 and 5,000 in 2012 to less than 2,000 in 2015; in the Netherlands from over 6,000 in 2011 to 2,200 in 2015. This sharp reduction can be explained by a mix of more active national courts guided by the ECJ case law on the Returns Directive and the Dublin Regulation, the campaigns of active NGOs and, probably, also budgetary reasons': K Groenendijk, 'Book Review: The Human Rights of Migrants and Refugees in European Law, by Cathryn Costello. (Oxford University Press, 2015)' (2017) 54 *Common Market Law Review* 943, 944.

[15] Groenendijk (ibid) 944.

[16] European Commission, 'Communication from the Commission to the Parliament and the Council on a More Effective Return Policy in the European Union – A Renewed Action Plan', COM(2017) 200 final (2 March 2017) 2.

[17] M Bosworth and E Kaufman, 'Foreigners in a Carceral Age: Immigration and Imprisonment in the United States' (2011) 22 *Stanford Law and Policy Review* 429, 431.

[18] NV Demleitner, 'Immigration Threats and Rewards: Effective Law Enforcement Tools in the "War" on Terrorism?' (2002) 51 *Emory Law Journal* 1059.

has impacted the way in which the state considers whether detention is justified. This is so in relation to policies of automatic detention and deportation of non-citizen ex-offenders, but also in relation to the way that decision makers evaluate whether release is legitimate: criminal history plays a large role in this regard.

Indeed, it is clear that immigration and security are linked in the minds of policymakers in the three jurisdictions under evaluation here. The recent actions by the US Government discussed above indicate that immigration is viewed as a national security issue. This perspective was confirmed by President Trump in his 2019 State of the Union address, when he said 'The lawless state of our southern border is a threat to the safety, security, and financial well-being of all Americans' and continued to push for 'a strong security wall'.[19] In the UK, a White Paper published by the Home Secretary at the end of 2018 pledges to deliver an immigration system that will 'enhance the security and safety' of the British people and features a section on strengthening border security. Similarly, the EU Commission has expressed its desire to achieve a Europe that is 'open and secure', a feat that is partially realised through the continued development of a common migration policy.[20] The goal of a secure Europe has been complicated by a substantial influx of migrants and refugees, largely from Syria, Iraq and Afghanistan, into EU territory since 2015. Framing immigration issues as related to security encourages states to view detention as an obvious solution to the immigration security problem. It may also serve as a basis for states to enact sweeping laws with minimal due process guarantees. This makes judicial review all the more important.[21]

In addition, a number of practical and strategic factors play a role in the perpetuation of immigration detention, such as the lobbying power of private prison operators,[22] the perceived need of the state to restore credibility to the immigration system and fundamental difficulties surrounding the capability of immigration officials to make informed decisions about who should be detained.[23] In fact, in late 2016, the Department of Homeland Security (DHS)

[19] President Donald J Trump, State of the Union address, 5 February 2019, www.whitehouse.gov/briefings-statements/remarks-president-trump-state-union-address-2/.

[20] European Commission, Communication from the Commission to the European Parliament, the Council, the European Economic and Social Committee and the Committee of Regions, 'An Open and Secure Europe: Making It Happen', COM(2014) 154 final (11 March 2014).

[21] M Kumm, 'Democracy Is Not Enough: Rights, Proportionality and the Point of Judicial Review' New York University School of Law Public Law & Legal Theory Research Paper Series, Working Paper No 09-10 (2009) 26.

[22] Flynn (n 1) 80–84; M Olivares, 'Intersectionality at the Intersection of Profiteering & Immigration Detention' (2016) 94 *Nebraska Law Review* 963; PL Torrey, 'Rethinking Immigration's Mandatory Detention Regime: Politics, Profit and the Meaning of "Custody"' (2015) 48 *University of Michigan Journal of Law Reform* 879.

[23] In the UK, Thomas suggests that a number of factors contribute to the quality of agency decision-making, many of which ring true especially in the context of immigration decisions. Common problems in immigration decision-making at the agency level include a failure to follow relevant procedure or policy, or apply the correct rules, evidentiary errors (including collection and evaluation) and providing improper reasons for decisions. See R Thomas, 'Administrative Justice, Better Decisions and Organisational Learning' (2015) 1 *Public Law* 111, 114.

announced new contracts with private suppliers for nearly 3,000 additional beds in detention facilities.[24] This is in stark contrast to the trends in Europe noted above.

In the meantime, repeated efforts have been made by the state legislatures to reduce the opportunities available to detainees to challenge their detention and obtain release. Effectively, detainees are faced with applying for immigration bail, which does not result in a finding of illegality but does allow temporary release, or challenging the lawfulness of detention through judicial review (including applications for a writ of habeas corpus). These latter options can be time-consuming and costly.

However, in the absence of meaningful legislative reform, the importance of judicial review cannot be overstated. Judicial review of state action is a key principle of the rule of law, which aims to hold the government to account. Deeks refers to this as the 'observer effect' – that is, the idea that judicial oversight and the threat of judicial intervention keeps policy and law in line.[25] Though in many cases judicial discretion has been removed or reduced through increased use of mandatory detention and legislative provisions which explicitly strip the courts of their jurisdiction, where their jurisdiction remains, there is room for the judiciary to take a 'rights-protecting' stance.[26] As national law and policy become more restrictive in this regard, it is for the courts to fill the gaps left by the law and act, where possible, to preserve and protect detainees' right to liberty. Though there have been landmark cases on detention in recent years in all three jurisdictions, the impact of those cases in practice has remained largely unexamined until now.

The use of detention as a tool of immigration enforcement is a manifestation of the growing tendency of states to criminalise immigration law. This phenomenon, now known as 'crimmigration'[27] among immigration and criminal law scholars writing in this field, features an array of legal provisions ultimately aimed at ensuring that undesirable non-citizens can be removed from the territory. Bosworth and Guild suggest that shifting motivations behind criminal legal theory account for the new model of criminalisation in the context of immigration.[28] They argue that the move away from rehabilitation to deterrence and incapacitation in the criminal law context can also be seen in the context of immigration law.[29] Based on this new understanding of immigration regulation,

[24] CC García Hernández, 'In 1 Week, Private Prisons Announce New Contracts for 3000 Immigration Detention Beds', *Crimmigration* (20 December 2016).

[25] AS Deeks, 'The Observer Effect: National Security Litigation, Executive Policy Changes, and Judicial Deference' (2013) 82 *Fordham Law Review* 827.

[26] Rayner Thwaites employs this term in his book *The Liberty of Non-Citizens: Indefinite Detention in Commonwealth Countries* (Hart Publishing, 2014).

[27] JP Stumpf, 'The Crimmigration Crisis: Immigrants, Crime and Sovereign Power' (2006) 56 *American University Law Review* 368.

[28] M Bosworth and M Guild, 'Governing through Migration Control' (2008) 48 *British Journal of Criminology* 703.

[29] ibid, 704.

they highlight a number of examples of criminalisation in the immigration context, including an increased use of detention.[30]

A number of scholars, predominantly from the USA, have written prolifically on the subject of criminalisation, and have identified a number of characteristics of the phenomenon, including the following, which are relevant to this book.[31] First, there is an overlap in the substance of the law, for example by creating immigration consequences for crimes, such as deportation or detention. Koulish has commented that mandatory detention is a component of criminalisation.[32] Secondly, the discretion that had previously been entrusted to traditional decision makers regarding the decision whether to exclude or deport immigrants has been removed and replaced with categorical decision-making by the Executive. Finally, the nation's focus on the fight against terrorism has led to the formulation of criminalisation.[33]

These effects are illustrated not only by many of the cases considered in this book, but by the description of the evolution of law and policy on the use of detention in chapters two and three.

[30] ibid, 707–08.

[31] JP Stumpf, 'The Process is the Punishment in Crimmigration Law' in K Franko Aas and M Bosworth (eds), *The Borders of Punishment: Migration, Citizenship and Social Exclusion* (Oxford University Press, 2013); JP Stumpf, 'Doing Time: Crimmigration Law and the Perils of Haste' (2011) 58 *UCLA Law Review* 1705; JP Stumpf, 'Fitting Punishment' (2009) 66 *Washington and Lee Law Review* 1683; SH Legomsky, 'The New Path of Immigration Law: Asymmetric Incorporation of Criminal Justice Norms' (2007) 28 *Immigration and Nationality Law Review* 679; JP Stumpf, 'Penalizing Immigrants' (2006) 18 *Federal Sentencing Reporter* 264; Stumpf, 'The Crimmigration Crisis' (n 27) 1726–28. See also Demleitner (n 18) 1060, 1088 fn 151, suggesting that because deportation is typically at stake, non-citizens are easily coerced and likely to provide false information; D Kanstroom, 'Criminalizing the Undocumented: Ironic Boundaries of the Post-September 11th "Pale of Law"' (2004) 29 *North Carolina Journal of International Law and Commercial Regulation* 639, 654. In addition, Koh writes of the use of stipulated orders of removal in the USA: JL Koh, 'Waiving Due Process (Goodbye): Stipulated Orders of Removal and the Crisis in Immigration Adjudication' (2013) 91 *North Carolina Law Review* 475. The process is set out in Title 8, s 1003.25(b) of the Code of Federal Regulations (2012) (on the emergency of stipulated removal orders). Medina discusses the specifics of this phenomenon in the context of US national marriages to non-citizens: MI Medina, 'The Criminalization of Immigration Law: Employer Sanctions and Marriage Fraud' (1997) 18 *Immigration and Nationality Law Review* 643, 657. In the UK context, Aliverti identifies three main elements of criminalisation in Britain which have manifested largely in the past two decades: A Aliverti, 'Making People Criminal: The Role of the Criminal Law in Immigration and Enforcement' (2012) 16 *Theoretical Criminology* 417; A Aliverti, 'Exploring the Function of Criminal Law in the Policing of Foreigners: The Decision to Prosecute Immigration-Related Offences' (2012) 29 *Social and Legal Studies* 511.

[32] R Koulish, *Immigration and American Democracy: Subverting the Rule of Law* (Routledge, 2010) 49.

[33] Stumpf, 'The Crimmigration Crisis' (n 27) 385–86; JP Stumpf, 'States of Confusion: The Rise of State and Local Power Over Immigration' (2008) 86 *North Carolina Law Review* 1557. See also TA Miller, 'Blurring the Boundaries between Immigration and Crime Control after September 11' (2005) 25 *British Columbia Third World Law Journal* 81; TA Miller, 'Citizenship & Severity: Recent Immigration Reforms and the New Penology' (2003) 17 *Georgetown Immigration Law Journal* 611 (2003).

II. IMMIGRATION DETENTION IN LITERATURE

Immigration detention has been the subject of much academic scholarship covering a range of themes. By way of an overview of the context in which this book sits, in general, detention is often one aspect of larger pieces focused more on immigration law and policy as a whole, usually in relation to deportation, or as part of a more generalised discussion of immigration adjudication, and how such adjudication differs from other areas of civil or administrative law.[34]

Where detention forms the basis of discussion, it appears in three main types of writing. First, detention is frequently discussed in relation to specific cases or contexts. For example, academics have studied the detention of asylum seekers,[35] the conditions inside immigration detention centres,[36] mandatory detention,[37] detention in the context of national security and terrorism,[38] and detention in police stations or during immigration raids.[39]

Secondly, some work considers detention in the context of access to justice and human rights. This work tends to single out specific aspects of procedural safeguards, rather than assessing the overall availability of access to justice in the context of immigration detention. Within this collection of work, one sees

[34] See, eg T Golash-Boza, *Due Process Denied: Detentions and Deportations in the United States* (Routledge, 2012); J Bleichmar, 'Deportation as Punishment: A Historical Analysis of the British Practice of Banishment and its Impact on Modern Constitutional Law' (1999) 14 *Georgetown Immigration Law Journal* 115; A Bloch and L Schuster, 'At the Extremes of Exclusion: Deportation, Detention and Dispersal' (2005) 28(3) *Ethnic and Racial Studies* 491; JE Family, 'Beyond Decisional Independence: Uncovering Contributors to the Immigration Adjudication Crisis' (2010) 59 *University of Kansas Law Review* 541; MJ Gibney, 'Asylum and the Expansion of Deportation in the United Kingdom' (2008) 43(2) *Government and Opposition* 146; Koh (n 31); SH Legomsky, 'Restructuring Immigration Adjudication' (2010) 31 *Immigration and Nationality Law Review* 503; H Motomura, 'The Curious Evolution of Immigration Law: Procedural Surrogates for Substantive Constitutional Rights' (1992) 92 *Columbia Law Review* 7; PH Schuck, 'The Transformation of Immigration Law' (1984) 84 *Columbia Law Review* 1.

[35] See, eg H O'Nions, 'No Right to Liberty: The Detention of Asylum Seekers for Administrative Convenience' (2008) 10 *European Journal of Migration and Law* 149; D Stevens, 'The Law's Approach to Detention of Asylum Seekers: Help or Hindrance?' University of Warwick School of Law Legal Studies Research paper, No 2010-21 (2010).

[36] See, eg Mary Bosworth, who has written a number of articles concerning conditions of detention, including *Inside Immigration Detention* (Oxford University Press, 2014); Bosworth and Kaufman (n 17); M Bull et al, 'Sickness in the System of Long-Term Immigration Detention' (2013) 2 *Journal of Refugee Studies* 47; M Dow, *American Gulag: Inside US Immigration Prisons* (University of California Press, 2004).

[37] See, eg S Bhargava, 'Detaining Due Process: The Need for Procedural Reform in "*Joseph*" Hearings after *Demore v Kim*' (2006–2007) 31 *New York University Review of Law and Social Change* 51; CM Fialho, 'Rethinking Pre-removal Immigration Detention in the United States: Lessons from Europe and Proposals for Reform' (2012) 31 *Refugee Survey Quarterly* 69.

[38] See, eg Demleitner (n 18); E Guild, *Security and Migration in the 21st Century* (Polity Press, 2009); BA Hepple, 'Aliens and Administrative Justice: The Dutschke Case' (1971) 34 *The Modern Law Review* 501; Miller, 'Blurring the Boundaries' (n 33).

[39] CN Lasch, 'Enforcing the Limits of the Executive's Authority to Issue Immigration Detainers' (2008–2009) 35 *William Mitchell Law Review* 164; SS Wadhia, 'Under Arrest: Immigrants' Rights and the Rule of Law' (2007–2008) 38 *University of Memphis Law Review* 853.

scholarship relating to the right to be heard[40] or the right to counsel,[41] though there has also been work that considers more generally the impact of human rights regimes on immigration detention.[42] There are also pieces considering the constitutional legitimacy of detaining non-citizens.[43]

The third, and final, type of writing is the scholarship most closely related to this book – that is, in-depth examinations of the process of detention. Wilsher has written about the law, history and politics of immigration detention, with a particular focus on the UK, USA and EU.[44] Similarly, Thwaites has examined detention in Commonwealth countries.[45] Legomsky has examined immigration case law, primarily of superior courts, with a focus on immigration and asylum law.[46] There is also much academic discourse in the USA concerning the immigration courts or tribunals, or the jurisprudence of the Supreme Court.[47]

[40] See, eg KJ Kimball, 'A Right to be Heard: Non-citizens' Due Process Right to In-Person Hearings to Justify their Detentions prior to Removal' (2009) 5 *Stanford Journal of Civil Rights and Civil Liberties* 159; SH Legomsky, 'The Detention of Aliens: Theories, Rules and Discretion' (1999) 30 *The University of Miami Inter-American Law Review* 531.

[41] See, eg IV Eagly and S Shafer, 'A National Study of Access to Counsel in Immigration Court' (2015) 164 *University of Pennsylvania Law Review* 1; SH Legomsky, 'Transporting *Padilla* to Deportation Proceedings: A Due Process Right to Effective Assistance of Counsel' (2011) 31 *St Louis U Public Law Review* 43; M Noferi, 'Cascading Constitutional Deprivation: The Right to Appointed Counsel for Mandatorily Detained Immigrants Pending Removal Proceedings' (2012) 18 *Michigan Journal of Race and Law* 63.

[42] See, eg G Cornelisse, 'Case Note Case C-357/09 PPU, Proceedings Concerning Said Shamilovich Kadzoev (Huchbarov) Judgment of the Court (Grand Chamber) of 30 November 2009' (2011) 48 *Common Market Law Review* 3; G Cornelisse, *Immigration Detention and Human Rights: Rethinking Territorial Sovereignty* (Martinus Nijhoff, 2010); G Cornelisse, 'Immigration Detention and the Territoriality of Universal Rights' in N De Genova and N Peutz (eds), *The Deportation Regime: Sovereignty, Space and the Freedom of Movement* (Duke University Press, 2010); C Costello, 'Human Rights and the Elusive Universal Subject: Immigration Detention under International Human Rights and EU Law' (2012) 19 *Indiana Journal of Global Legal Studies* 257; B Kessler, 'In Jail, No Notice, No Hearing ... No Problem? A Closer Look at Immigration Detention and the Due Process Standards of the International Covenant on Civil and Political Rights' (2009) 24 *American University International Law Review* 571.

[43] See, eg M-C Caloz-Tschopp, 'On the Detention of Aliens: The Impact on Democratic Rights' (1997) 10 *Journal of Refugee Studies* 165; W Chelgren, 'Preventive Detention Distorted: Why It Is Unconstitutional to Detain Immigrants without Procedural Protections' (2011) 44 *Loyola Los Angeles Law Review* 1477; A Kalhan, 'Rethinking Immigration Detention' (2010) 110 *Columbia Law Review Sidebar* 42; FW Sayed, 'Challenging Detention: Why Immigrant Detainees Receive Less Process Than 'Enemy Combatants' and Why They Deserve More' (2011) 111 *Columbia Law Review* 1833.

[44] D Wilsher, *Immigration Detention: Law, History, Politics* (Cambridge University Press, 2012). He also discusses the applicability of national, regional and international standards for the protection of liberty in 'The Administrative Detention of Non-Nationals Pursuant to Immigration Control: International and Constitutional Law Perspectives' (2004) 53 *International and Comparative Law Quarterly* 897.

[45] Thwaites (n 26).

[46] SH Legomsky, *Immigration and the Judiciary: Law and Politics in Britain and America* (Clarendon Press, 1987).

[47] See, eg S Benesch, 'Due Process and Decision-Making in U.S. Immigration Adjudication' (2007) 59 *Administrative Law Review* 557; LB Benson, 'As Old as the Hills: Detention and Immigration' (2010) 5 *Intercultural Human Rights Law Review* 11; JM Chacón, 'A Diversion of Attention? Immigration Courts and the Adjudication of Fourth and Fifth Amendment Rights' (2010) 59

In the UK, two retired immigration tribunal judges have offered reflections on their time on the bench.[48] Silva examines US courts of appeals judgments on detention from a selection of US circuits.[49] Finally, Peitzke considered the behaviour of courts in the Ninth and Fifth Circuits in relation to judging the lawfulness of prolonged detention.[50] Each of these has served as a vital source of inspiration for this book. However, though they all include an evaluation of case law, their focus tends to be on senior courts, rather than courts of first instance.

Beyond the field of immigration, there is much academic discourse concerning the use of preventive detention as a legitimate tool for law enforcement.[51] Detention is typically employed where the state wishes to protect its citizens from a perceived danger, to prevent criminal activity or to ensure that people do not flee where they have to face proceedings of some kind. It is a means of weeding out those deemed undesirable by society. However, scholars have pointed out that the traditional rationales for using detention (deterrence and punishment) have little place in the context of immigration detention, especially where the detained individual has already been subject to penal sanctions.[52] Overall, it demonstrates that preventive detention is replete with difficulties, not just in the context of immigration law, but in relation to other forms of preventive detention, which casts yet another shadow on the practice of mass preventive detention in the field of immigration.

Duke Law Journal 1563; Eagly and Shafer (n 41); Kessler (n 42); Kimball (n 40); Legomsky (n 40); GL Neuman, 'Habeas Corpus, Executive Detention, and the Removal of Aliens' (1998) 19 *Immigration and Nationality Law Review* 307; JP Stumpf, 'Civil Detention and Other Oxymorons' (2014) 40 *Queens Law Journal* 55. Scholarly work focusing on specific federal circuits includes M Firmacion, 'Protecting Immigrants from Prolonged Pre-removal Detention: When 'It Depends' Is No Longer Reasonable' (2014) 42 *Hastings Constitutional Law Quarterly* 601; M Harman, 'Indefinite Detention of Excludable Aliens: An International Crisis on American Soil' (2000) 7 *Southwestern Journal of Law and Trade in the Americas* 193; T Silva, 'Toward a Constitutionalized Theory of Immigration Detention' (2013) 32 *Yale Law and Policy Review* 227.

[48] G Care, *Migrants and the Courts: A Century of Trial and Error?* (Ashgate, 2013); J Hanratty RD, *The Making of an Immigration Judge* (Quartet, 2016).

[49] Silva (n 47).

[50] M Peitzke, 'The Fate of "Unremovable" Aliens before and after September 11, 2001: The Supreme Court's Presumptive Six-Month Limit to Post-Removal-Period Detention' (2002) 30 *Pepperdine Law Review* 769.

[51] See, eg A Ashworth and L Zedner, *Preventive Justice* (Oxford University Press, 2015); LI Appleman, 'Justice in the Shadowlands: Pretrial Detention, Punishment, & the Sixth Amendment' (2012) 69 *Washington and Lee Law Review* 1297, 1336–49; DJ Baker, 'Punishment without a Crime: Is Preventive Detention Reconcilable with Justice?' (2009) 34 *Australian Journal of Legal Philosophy* 120; LS Pershan, 'Selective Incapacitation and the Justifications for Imprisonment' (1984) 12 *New York University Review of Law and Social Change* 385.

[52] M Noferi, 'Mandatory Immigration Detention for US Crimes: The Noncitizen Presumption of Dangerousness' in MJ Guia et al, *Immigration Detention, Risk and Human Rights* (Springer, 2016) 234–36.

Moving away from the detention literature, scholarly attention has been paid to theories of judicial reasoning and decision-making in general.[53] Similarly, many scholars and former judges have examined the organisation and functioning of US federal district courts[54] and the Court of Justice of the EU (CJEU),[55] but there is no consideration of judging in the Administrative Court, other than by reference to judicial review procedure.[56]

What is lacking from this wealth of literature is an in-depth analysis of judicial review of immigration detention in courts of first instance. During my research for this book, this absence was acknowledged by a federal district magistrate judge, who commented that few consider the activities of the lower courts. This is certainly borne out in the literature. It is only through examination of practice at all levels that we can understand whether the current legal framework is fit for purpose.

III. ISSUES EXPLORED

The use of detention as a tool of immigration enforcement is not new. Although the power to detain is provided by law, details regarding its implementation are typically scarce. In the USA and the UK, the judiciary has filled this gap by providing standards with which to determine the legality of detention in certain situations. At the EU level, the power to detain is provided by legislation, but that legislation also sets forth standards of legality for interpretation by the EU Member States and for the CJEU, which is often asked for interpretive assistance

[53] See, eg C Guarnieri and P Pederzoli, *The Power of Judges* (Oxford University Press, 2002); T Bingham, *The Business of Judging* (Oxford University Press, 2000); O Raban, *Modern Legal Theory & Judicial Impartiality* (The Glass House Press, 2003); N MacCormick, *Legal Reasoning and Legal Theory* (Oxford University Press, 1994).

[54] See, eg VR Walker, 'The Most Efficient Finder of Fact: The Federal District Judge' (2015) 69 *University of Miami Law Review* 385; JB Weinstein, 'The Roles of a Federal District Court Judge' (2011) 76 *Brook Law Review* 439; DS Law, 'Appointing Federal Judges: The President, the Senate, and the Prisoner's Dilemma' (2005) 26 *Cardozo Law Review* 479; EC Surrency, *History of the Federal Courts* (Oceana Publications, 2002); KL Lyles, *The Gatekeepers: Federal District Courts in the Political Process* (Praeger, 1997); RA Posner, *The Federal Courts* (Harvard University Press, 1996); S Goldman, 'Federal Judicial Recruitment' in JB Gates and CA Johnson (eds), *The American Courts. A Critical Assessment* (Congressional Quarterly Press, 1991) 189.

[55] See, eg Nl Fennelly, 'Legal Interpretation at the European Court of Justice' (1996) 20 *Fordham International Law Journal* 656; A Grimmel, '"This Is Not Life As It Is Lived Here": The Court of Justice of the EU and the Myth of Judicial Activism in the Foundational Period of Integration through Law' (2014) 7 *European Journal of Legal Studies* 56; G Beck, *The Legal Reasoning of the Court of Justice of the EU* (Hart Publishing, 2012); A Arnull, *The European Union and its Court of Justice*, 2nd edn (Oxford University Press, 2006); J Bengoetxea, *The Legal Reasoning of the European Court of Justice: Towards a European Jurisprudence* (Clarendon Press, 1993); H Rasmussen, *On Law and Policy in the European Court of Justice: A Comparative Study in Judicial Policymaking* (Martinus Nijhoff, 1986).

[56] See, eg S Nason, 'The Administrative Court, the Upper Tribunal and Permission to Seek Judicial Review' (2012) 21 *Nottingham Law Journal* 1. This work will be discussed in ch 4 below.

by the Member States. The judiciary, and its power of judicial review, therefore plays an important role in each of these jurisdictions when it comes to safeguarding liberty. This role is perhaps even more important when one considers that other opportunities for release, for example, through immigration bail, are typically dependent upon the judgment of administrative authorities or specialised immigration courts, which are, in some cases, part of the Executive. Moreover, courts and tribunals competent to hear bail applications are not empowered to make a judgment as to the lawfulness of detention in a manner similar to that which occurs in the context of judicial review proceedings.

Given the absence of literature on the important role of courts of first instance in relation to immigration detention, this book therefore examines the extent to which judicial review offers a meaningful safeguard for the liberty of immigration detainees. This question necessarily requires the consideration of several sub-issues, such as the review powers of courts, where judgments reviewing detention sit within the constitutional framework, which standards the courts apply when reviewing detention and the impact (if any) of judicial structure and role on case outcomes.

Two of the most important sub-issues considered in this book are the quality of the immigration law at the judges' disposal and the role that fundamental rights plays in each jurisdiction. As will be explored more deeply in chapter six, the notion that the law be of sufficient quality is a component part of the rule of law requirement of legality. This requires not only that the state act in conformity with the law, but that the law itself possess certain qualities, such as accessibility, foreseeability and consistency. As will be revealed elsewhere in this book, the quality of the law on detention in the UK, USA and EU varies and thus indirectly impacts the way that judges assess the lawfulness of detention, thereby resulting in varied case outcomes.

Linked to quality of law is the role played by fundamental rights principles, such as the right to liberty. This book outlines in chapter two the legislative history of each jurisdiction's detention laws in an effort to understand the extent to which lawmakers considered the fundamental rights implications of laws permitting the (sometimes indefinite) detention of non-citizens. Though this subject is examined more thoroughly in chapters two and six, my research suggests that there is a link between the immigration law drafted with fundamental rights principles in mind and positive detention case outcomes.

IV. APPROACH OF THIS BOOK

This book approaches the above issues through a comparative forensic evaluation of first-instance case law in the UK (England and Wales, specifically), USA and EU. The 191 cases selected demonstrate how these jurisdictions are grappling with immigration detention and liberty. In addition, I interviewed a selection of judges and practitioners for clarification of concepts and to obtain a sense of how the relevant players perceive what is happening in practice. Of the 191 cases, 63 are from the UK Administrative Court, 110 are from the US district courts of the Second Circuit and 18 are from the CJEU.

A. Chosen Jurisdictions

The jurisdictions examined were chosen for personal and practical reasons. At the personal level, I studied law in the USA and qualified as a lawyer there. I then moved to the UK (London) to pursue a master's degree in EU law, and later a PhD in law, and remained in the UK for 13 years. These three jurisdictions are therefore the subject of my legal practice as an academic.

At the practical level, the UK and USA are sensible comparisons because, as Wilsher indicates in *Immigration Detention*, both 'developed some of the first recognizably modern systems of immigration control'.[57] Until well into the nineteenth century, both states had largely functioned without formal immigration controls. In fact, the UK took pride in its tradition of equal protection of liberty and its record in granting asylum.[58] When initial attempts to regulate the entry of non-citizens were made, both countries encountered the tension between protecting their nationals and risking the erosion of liberties by allowing the Executive to regulate immigration. Following World War I, both nations experienced shifts in attitude towards immigration, partly based on economic fears and concerns about allowing the entry of certain 'undesirables' (eg those viewed as potentially anarchistic or a threat to the health of the local population).[59] From those basic concerns, immigration control has fluctuated and evolved, in both countries, into a centralised system administered by the Executive, with immigration detention as the centrepiece. In addition, neither country has a maximum time limit for detention.

Both the UK and the USA have also traditionally emphasised supremacy and national sovereignty. The USA is arguably more isolated in its interpretation of, and relationship to, international law. Although it is a member of the UN and the Organization of American States, it has developed an immigration detention policy that is effectively free of international legal influence and is very inward-looking. The UK has had a similar history, but temporarily chose to sacrifice some of its sovereignty to participate as a Member State of the Council of Europe and the EU. As such, its immigration law and immigration policy are impacted to a certain extent by European law.

Though neither the UK nor the USA has a statutory maximum period of detention, courts in both jurisdictions evaluate the legality of detention according to a test of reasonableness. In the USA, this test was developed by

[57] Wilsher (n 44) 8.
[58] ibid 5.
[59] ibid 45–54.

the US Supreme Court (USSC) in 2001,[60] while in the UK, the test was created by the Administrative Court 18 years earlier, in 1983.[61] The US test, while not establishing a bright line maximum, considers that there is a presumptively reasonable period of detention of six months, which has arguably had the unintended consequence of becoming a default minimum. The Administrative Court has not gone down this path; instead, it continues to assess the reasonableness of any period of detention in light of a number of principles. These tests are important because judicial interpretation of them comprises the majority of content in the judgments evaluated in this book.

In contrast to the UK and the USA, the EU has had comparatively short involvement in the field of immigration. The EU shares its competence in immigration with the Member States, but it has chosen to uniformly regulate (or harmonise) procedures with respect to the return of third-country nationals staying illegally in the territory of a Member State. In doing so, the EU has adopted the Return Directive, which sets forth rules on the detention of third-country nationals in return proceedings. Although only in force in the Member States since 2010, the applicable legislation has already generated important case law at the European level.

B. Substance of the Cases

This book focuses on cases in which the legality of *ongoing* detention is challenged. It does not consider whether the initial decision by the state to detain is lawful. The judgments take on two main forms: (i) those concerning the length of time the individual has been in detention in light of the likelihood of his or her removal; and (ii) those concerning individuals in mandatory detention who have had no opportunity to challenge their detention. In the context of the EU, because there are so few cases in which the legality of detention under the Return Directive is considered, all of the case law to date under the Return Directive is included in this analysis, most of which touches on the issue of detention in some way. Though those cases do not necessarily fall within the two categories just specified, there are many shared characteristics in terms of judicial evaluation. Details of the cases are included in chapter five of this book. However, it is vital at this stage to emphasise that the majority of the judgments examined involve cases of prolonged detention where detainees have not secured release through administrative processes, such as bail or bond, which will be discussed in chapter four. In fact, given that the average length of detention in

[60] *Zadvydas v Davis* (2001) 533 US 678.

[61] *R (Hardial Singh) v Governor of Durham Prison* [1983] EWHC 1 (QB). The detail of this case are discussed in ch 6, s I below.

the USA in 2015 was 34.4 days,[62] and that in the UK, in the fourth quarter of 2017, 78 per cent of detainees were held for less than two months,[63] it would appear that in most cases, the work done in relation to assessing the appropriateness of detention occurs at the administrative level, and not in the judiciary. Therefore, the findings in this book should not be considered as representative of all detention cases.

This book excludes consideration of cases concerning detention of vulnerable people, such as pregnant women, the mentally ill, asylum seekers or cases linked to terrorism, including where the detainee is a terror suspect. The result is that most of the cases examined involve the detention of non-citizens who have been convicted of crimes and are therefore liable to removal or deportation.

Finally, this book does not include cases of detention at state borders, for example, in airports or other temporary accommodation facilities at borders.

C. Courts Examined

The UK and the USA both have a system of immigration courts that determines a number of issues, including whether a detainee is eligible for bail. However, the legality of detention is not considered by these courts – legality is only assessed by the judiciary through judicial review or habeas corpus proceedings. In the UK, this takes place in the Administrative Court, while in the USA, it occurs in the federal district courts. Within the USA, I have chosen to consider cases arising from the New York (NY) federal district courts within the Second Circuit. The Second Circuit was very strongly impacted by reforms to immigration law in 1996, which led to a massive increase in immigration challenges[64] and more non-citizens being subject to automatic deportation and detention. By mid-2004, immigration cases accounted for 44 per cent of the Circuit's case load.[65] This did not even include the cases concerning habeas review of immigration detention in the NY federal district courts. In the UK, the Administrative Court was chosen because it is the court competent to determine the legality of immigration detention in England and Wales.

With regard to the EU, because the focus is on the Return Directive, an EU legislative instrument, as opposed to legislation from individual Member States,

[62] US Department of Justice, 'Report and Recommendations Concerning the Use of Restrictive Housing' (January 2016) http://www.justice.gov/dag/file/815551/download. These are the most recent statistics on detention length released by the US Government.

[63] Silverman and Griffiths (n 8).

[64] Chapter 4, s III.B below.

[65] SH Legomsky and CM Rodríguez, *Immigration and Refugee Law and Policy*, 5th edn (Foundation Press, 2009) 758–60, citing the Commission on Federal Courts, 'The Surge of Immigration Appeals and Its Impact on the Second Circuit Court of Appeals' (2004).

the CJEU is the court of inquiry. Though not empowered to make findings on legality, the CJEU is the ultimate authority when it comes to interpretation of the Return Directive and its provisions on detention. The CJEU is a constitutional court and therefore cannot be compared directly with the federal district courts or the Administrative Court, especially when it comes to evaluating the way in which the courts refer to fundamental rights principles, as will be discussed in chapter six. The CJEU is part of a system of co-operation wherein national courts refer questions of interpretation of EU law to the CJEU and are responsible for ensuring that the interpretation is given effect in national proceedings. In this way, the CJEU is more akin to the USSC or the UK Supreme Court. The CJEU cases in this book illustrate the types of national courts that refer cases to the CJEU, as well as the type of interpretive questions they have. The Administrative Court is one such national court that may refer questions to the CJEU, though it has not done so with regard to the EU Return Directive because the UK does not take part in the Directive. However, the main point to emphasise is that, like the federal district courts and the Administrative Court, the CJEU is part of a judicial system that is frequently asked to rule on the lawfulness of detention. Though it cannot always be fairly compared to the UK and US courts examined in this book, the extent to which it may serve as a model for those courts is addressed in chapters five to seven. Thus, this book only draws upon discussion of the CJEU and its case law, where it can be usefully compared to the other two jurisdictions.

D. Time Period under Evaluation

Cases were selected based on the years in which key legislative provisions affecting detention were adopted. In the USA, this was 1996, when the Illegal Immigration Reform and Immigrant Responsibility Act (IIRIRA)[66] and the Antiterrorism and Effective Death Penalty Act (AEDPA)[67] entered into force. In the UK, 1999 saw the entry into force of the Immigration and Asylum Act,[68] which extended the grounds for detention in the Immigration Act 1971 (1971 Act)[69] to allow detention where there are 'reasonable grounds to suspect' that a person might be removable, even without a formal removal decision being made. Finally, in the context of the EU, this book focuses on case law coming from the CJEU since the entry into force of the Return Directive in 2010. No cases issued after 31 December 2016 are included. Beyond the cases, this book does not include information after 1 January 2019.

[66] Pub L No 104-208, Div C, 110 Stat 2009-546.
[67] Pub L No 104-132, 110 Stat 1214.
[68] Immigration and Asylum Act 1999, c 33, which received Royal Assent on 11 November 1999.
[69] Immigration Act 1971, c 77, which received Royal Assent on 28 October 1971.

V. STRUCTURE OF THE BOOK

This book consists of eight chapters, including the introduction (chapter one) and conclusion (chapter eight). Following this introduction, chapter two concerns the historical and constitutional context of immigration detention, tracing early uses of detention in the chosen jurisdictions to its use today. It also examines each jurisdiction's relationship with the right to liberty. Chapter three provides an overview of the relevant state players who have the power to detain and to supervise detention, and reviews the applicable legislative frameworks for detention in each jurisdiction. Chapter four illustrates the character of judicial proceedings available in each jurisdiction to review the lawfulness of detention. Chapter five marks the beginning of the case law analysis and focuses on the standards of review employed by each court to determine the legality of detention. It sets out the common components of each set of standards and examines them in detail from a comparative perspective. Chapter six then focuses on how the judges in each jurisdiction use the law at their disposal in judicial review proceedings. It considers issues such as the role that precedent plays, what place (if any) fundamental rights principles play in the assessment of legality and the quality of the law on detention itself. Chapter seven moves from the law to the judges, and discusses the varied role of the judge and the extent to which judges defer to the state when it comes to immigration detention. Finally, the book concludes that the extent to which fundamental rights form part of the legal fabric in a jurisdiction can have a significant impact on various aspects of judicial review of immigration detention.

2

Liberty and the Historic Context of Immigration Detention

I. INTRODUCTION

BEFORE EXAMINING THE specifics of how immigration detention is managed in each jurisdiction, this chapter looks at how the right to liberty is protected by each jurisdiction generally, and how, within the context of immigration detention, liberty has been treated legislatively and judicially.

The right to liberty and to be free from arbitrary detention is perhaps the oldest and most recognised human right.[1] The UK, USA and EU each enshrine the right to liberty in their constitutions. However, the right to liberty is far from absolute. Deprivations of liberty by the state are permissible in certain circumstances.[2] A key component in determining whether a particular deprivation is acceptable is the concept of proportionality. Proportionality is a key organising principle of law and has worldwide application.[3] In the immigration context, the state's right to determine who can enter its territory and its decision to detain particular individuals must be proportionate to a stated legal objective.[4] Thus, when judicially reviewing immigration detention, the courts are primarily tasked with determining whether detention has been used proportionately. The courts engage in this determination largely through balancing competing interests. For example, the courts examined in this book balance the detainee's right to liberty against concerns such as community safety or combating unlawful immigration. The way the courts engage in this balance in practice is discussed in detail in chapter five. This chapter will break from the format of the rest of the book by examining on a geographical basis the way each

[1] WJ Hopkins, 'Piercing the Veil: Executive Detention and Judicial Deference' (2005) 8 *Yearbook of New Zealand Jurisprudence* 239, 241.

[2] M Kumm, 'Democracy Is Not Enough: Rights, Proportionality and the Point of Judicial Review' New York University School of Law Public Law & Legal Theory Research Paper Series, Working Paper No 09-10 (2009).

[3] E Engle, 'The History of the General Principle of Proportionality: An Overview' (2012) 10 *Dartmouth Law Journal* 1, 3.

[4] M Flynn, 'Immigration Detention and Proportionality', Global Detention Project Working Paper No 4 (2011).

jurisdiction safeguards the right to liberty for immigration detainees by reference to key legislative and judicial developments.

Immigration detention, particularly in the UK and USA, has had a long history associated with war. What originally began as wartime powers to detain enemies of the state evolved into general detention powers to detain those considered by the state to be undesirable and therefore ineligible to reside in the territory. In such circumstances, the right to liberty was often sacrificed for national security. By contrast, the EU has only relatively recently begun to regulate the entry and exit of non-EU nationals across its external borders, including through the use of immigration detention. Its framework benefits from a strong tradition of protection of fundamental rights that was quite influential in the adoption of legal measures in this field.

Though not by any means a comprehensive historical analysis of immigration detention in the UK, USA and EU, this chapter is aimed at demonstrating how such a fundamental right – the right to liberty – is impacted when the subject is a non-citizen.

II. THE UNITED KINGDOM

A. The Impact of Europe on Liberty

The Magna Carta of 1215 enshrined the right to liberty and freedom from executive detention in its text, making it perhaps the oldest recognised human right in the UK, and in all common law legal systems modelled on the British system.[5] The immigration bail guidance for tribunal judges in England and Wales recognises the primacy of the right to liberty when it states that 'Liberty is a fundamental right of all people and can only be restricted if there is no reasonable alternative. This principle applies to all people in the UK, including foreign nationals.'[6]

In addition to this grand national tradition of liberty, the UK derives its human rights framework from European memberships: the UK is a Member State of the Council of Europe, and will remain a Member State of the EU until its formal withdrawal. To the extent that EU legislation applies in the UK, it is also limited by the EU Charter of Fundamental Rights and the general principles of the EU law developed by the CJEU. However, the UK has chosen not to take part in the Return Directive, nor does it take part in recast

[5] T Bingham, 'Personal Freedom and the Dilemma of Democracies' (2003) 52 *International and Comparative Law Quarterly* 841, 842.

[6] Judge Clements, President of the First-tier Tribunal (Immigration and Asylum Chamber), Presidential Guidance Note No 1 of 2018, 'Guidance on Immigration Bail for Judges of the First-tier Tribunal (Immigration and Asylum Chamber)' (15 January 2018).

versions of asylum legislation that regulate detention.[7] Therefore, the influence of Europe over immigration detention largely emanates from the European Convention on Human Rights (ECHR)[8] and the European Court of Human Rights (ECtHR).

Article 5(1)(f) ECHR limits the purposes for which people may be detained under immigration law, and provides certain procedural protections for those subject to detention:

> Everyone has the right to liberty and security of the person. No one shall be deprived of his liberty save in the following cases and in accordance with a procedure prescribed by law: … the lawful arrest or detention of a person to prevent his effecting an unauthorized entry into the country or of a person against whom action is being taken with a view to deportation or extradition.

Immigration detention under Article 5(1)(f) ECHR can therefore only be resorted to for two purposes: to prevent unauthorised entry and pending deportation. Regarding the former, the ECtHR has held that until an individual is granted leave to enter or remain, he or she is considered unauthorised and can therefore be detained without the state having to demonstrate that it is necessary, for example, to prevent the person from absconding.[9] Therefore there is no requirement under the ECHR to consider alternative measures or to conduct an individualised assessment of the appropriateness of detention.[10] Consequently, as Cornelisse has pointed out, the ECtHR has not been able to improve the situation in states which impose detention without reference to individual circumstances.[11] Somewhat confusingly, there is case law from the European Court holding that detention may be considered disproportionate if it is not used as a last resort.[12] This implies the existence of a necessity requirement, though that is not officially the case. Regardless, it seems to be required at the national level. This is borne out somewhat by the UK's detention policy discussed below in section B and in some of the cases discussed in chapters five to seven.[13]

The second purpose of detention under Article 5(1)(f) relates to deportation. All that is required is that 'action is being taken with a view

[7] Directive 2013/32/EU of the European Parliament and of the Council on common procedures for granting and withdrawing international protection (recast) [2013] OJ L180/60.

[8] Signed 4 November 1950; entry into force 3 September 1953.

[9] *Saadi v UK* [2006] ECHR 732; *Chahal v UK* [1996] ECHR 54, 112; *Bozano v France* [1986] ECHR 16, 60.

[10] *Chahal* (ibid).

[11] G Cornelisse, 'The Constitutionalisation of Immigration Detention: Between EU Law and the European Convention on Human Rights', Global Detention Project Working Paper No 15 (October 2016) 6. She makes the same argument in her book, *Immigration Detention and Human Rights: Rethinking Territorial Sovereignty* (Martinus Nijhoff, 2010).

[12] *Litwa v Poland* [2000] ECHR 141.

[13] The Joint Committee on Human Rights in the UK Parliament has stressed that 'Detention should only be used in necessary and proportionate': House of Commons and House of Lords Joint Committee on Human Rights, 'Immigration Detention', Sixteenth Report of Session 2017–19, HC 4484; HL Paper 278 (February 2019) para 28.

toward deportation'.[14] However, deportation proceedings must actually be in progress, and removal must be likely and realistic.[15] This requires that the authorities pursue deportation proceedings with 'due diligence'.[16]

Article 5 includes a proportionality requirement: detention must be proportionate to its aim. This ensures the provision of appropriate safeguards for detained individuals. However, there is no maximum limit on detention under the ECHR. Instead, the ECHR requires that the length of the detention corresponds to the reason for detention,[17] and that it must not exceed that which is reasonably required to achieve its purpose.[18] The meaning of 'reasonably' is to be determined on a case-by-case basis.[19]

Article 5(4) provides that anyone who is detained has the right to challenge the lawfulness of the detention before a court that is empowered to order release. This is the habeas corpus provision of the ECHR.[20] The ECtHR held in *Chahal v UK*[21] that the court proceedings must include hallmarks of judicial procedure, such as the right to legal representation, adequate notice[22] and independent review by a court with the power to take a legally binding decision.[23] Article 5(4) also requires equality of arms between the parties and an adversarial procedure.[24] Finally, detained individuals must be capable of challenging their detention 'speedily'. Whether proceedings satisfy that requirement is decided on a case-by-case basis, and the Court has found periods ranging from, for example, 17 days to six months to be excessive.[25] One scholar has read Article 5(4) to require periodic reviews of immigration detention, although whether this is indeed the case is unclear from the case law.[26]

[14] *Chahal* (n 9) 113.

[15] ibid. The requirement of proceedings actually being in progress was first present in *Kolompar v Belgium* [1992] ECHR 59, 39. See also *Quinn v France* [1995] ECHR 9, 48.

[16] *Chahal* (n 9) 113.

[17] *Amuur v France* [1996] ECHR 25, 43. For example, if someone is being detained pending examination upon entry and the examination is concluded within seven days, to continue to detain the person beyond that time may be considered disproportionate.

[18] *Saadi v UK* [2008] ECHR 80. The length must not be excessive: see *Chahal* (n 9) 113. *Kolompar* (n 15) 36. Protocol 7 to the ECHR contains additional procedural safeguards for application to the expulsion of aliens, but the UK did not ratify this Protocol.

[19] In *Saadi v UK* [2008] (ibid), the Court held that a period of seven days was not unreasonable in the context of fast-track asylum claims, but it did not explain its reasoning. However, this process of detention has since been struck down domestically by the Court of Appeal in *R (Detention Action) v First-tier Tribunal (Immigration and Asylum Chamber), Upper Tribunal (Immigration and Asylum Chamber* [2015] EWCA Civ 840.

[20] JL Murdoch, 'Article 5 of the European Convention on Human Rights' (Council of Europe, 2002) 86.

[21] *Chahal* (n 9).

[22] ibid 130. Note that this case involved national security matters and closed proceedings, which led to the creation of the Special Immigration Appeals Commission in the UK.

[23] *Dougoz v Greece* [2001] ECHR 213.

[24] *Chahal* (n 9).

[25] *Aden Ahmed v Malta* [2013] ECHR 720, 115 and cases cited therein.

[26] IA Macdonald and R Toal, *Macdonald's Immigration Law and Practice*, 8th edn (LexisNexis Butterworths, 2012) 8.68. Macdonald and Toal cite *Toth v Austria* [1991] ECHR 72, *Lamy v Belgium* [1989] ECHR 5 and *A, X and Y* [2002] EWCA Civ 1502 in support of this contention.

The ECHR contains a provision on fair trial rights (Article 6), but the ECtHR has held that these provisions do not apply to immigration cases because they are an administrative matter.[27] This is routinely endorsed by the Court, which explained in *Megyeri v Germany* that the

> judicial proceedings referred to in Article 5(4) need not always be attended by the same guarantees as those required under Article 6(1) for civil or criminal litigation. None the less, it is essential that the person concerned should have access to a court and the opportunity to be heard either in person or, where necessary, through some form of representation.[28]

It would seem, therefore, that detention proceedings must only abide by the requirements of Article 5. However, there is some authority which suggests that, even though Article 6 fair trial rights do not apply to decisions about the entry and residence of aliens, they do apply to the determination of the substantive right to liberty, at least with regard to the requirement of equality of arms.[29] In *A, X and Y*,[30] the Court of Appeal of England and Wales held that, although the issuing of a certificate of suspected international terrorism under the Anti-Terrorism, Crime and Security Act 2001 did not attract Article 6 rights, detention under the Act did. However, the applicability of Article 6 to immigration detention is somewhat cast into doubt by the fact that Article 5 has its own set of procedural protections. Moreover, the recent case of *MA v Cyprus* reiterated the conclusion in *Megyeri*.[31]

The UK Human Rights Act 1998[32] incorporates most of the rights contained in the ECHR and applies to acts of public authorities. Prior to the incorporation of ECHR rights into domestic law via the 1998 Act, there was no method for individuals to assert their ECHR rights before the UK courts. There is a duty under section 3(1) of the Human Rights Act to interpret primary and subordinate legislation in line with Convention rights as far as possible. Under section 2, UK courts are required to take ECtHR case law into account when making their decisions, and generally the case law is followed if the issue has been the subject of 'clear and constant jurisprudence'.[33]

[27] *Uppal and Singh v UK* App no 8244/78 (Commission decision, 2 May 1979). This was confirmed by the Grand Chamber in *Maaouia v France* [2000] ECHR 455.

[28] *Megyeri v Germany* [1992] ECHR 49, 22. This was underscored by the UK in the case of *Raynor v SSHD* [2007] EWHC 1028 (Admin) 53–84.

[29] Macdonald and Toal (n 26) 8.73. See also JN Stefanelli, 'Disclosure in Immigration Bail Proceedings: Ensuring Equality of Arms' (2016) 30 *Journal of Immigration Asylum and Nationality Law* 301.

[30] *A, X and Y* (n 26).

[31] *MA v Cyprus* [2013] ECHR 717, 161.

[32] Human Rights Act 1998, c 42 received Royal Assent on 9 November 1998.

[33] *R (Alconbury Developments Ltd) v Secretary of State for the Environment* [2001] UKHL 23, 26.

B. Detention in the United Kingdom

In the mid-nineteenth century, Britain was renowned for its positive treatment of non-nationals, which was due in no small part to the availability of the habeas corpus remedy.[34] However, this attitude soured during the French Revolution, when fears of foreign-led insurgency and uprising on British soil led to parliamentary debate on the merit of passing entry restriction laws.[35] Still, it was not until the Aliens Act 1905 that the UK Parliament adopted the sort of immigration law that exists today. While these laws were debated, detention was never discussed separately from the issue of deportation, and was viewed simply as a tool for implementing immigration powers,[36] though Silverman points out that, even as early as 1906, the House of Commons had questioned whether detention could be considered an acceptable tool for migration control.[37] Despite these concerns, restrictive immigration law grew, being driven, in part, by a realisation that Britain was an outlier compared to American and European efforts to control immigration.[38] In fact, the UK remains an outlier in the sense that it is the only European state without a maximum length of detention prescribed by law, despite recommendations that a maximum should be adopted.[39]

The power of detention under the Aliens Act was rarely used, mostly because there was little difficulty achieving removal.[40] During and after World War I, detention was used on a more frequent basis, and for longer lengths of time.[41] World War I saw the first mass internment of non-citizens under the Aliens Restriction Act 1914, which gave the Executive wartime powers to deny entry to, deport and detain non-citizens.[42] The Executive's power to deport and detain established by this legislation remains in force today, despite

[34] T Erskine May, *The Constitutional History of England Since the Accession of George III*, vol III (Corsby and Nichols, 1862) 50.

[35] D Wilsher, *Immigration Detention: Law, History, Politics* (Cambridge University Press, 2012) 5–6.

[36] ibid 6.

[37] SJ Silverman, '"Regrettable but Necessary?' A Historical and Theoretical Study of the Rise of the UK Immigration Detention Estate and Its Opposition' (2012) 40 *Politics and Policy* 1131, 1140.

[38] Wilsher (n 35) 36.

[39] House of Commons Home Affairs Committee, 'Immigration detention', Fourteenth Report of Session 2017–2019, HC 913 (March 2019), recommending a 28-day limit; Joint Committee on Human Rights, 'Report on Immigration Detention' (n 13), recommending a 28-day limit; Joint Inquiry by the All Party Parliamentary Group on Refugees & the All Party Parliamentary Group on Migration, 'The Report of the Inquiry into the Use of Immigration Detention in the United Kingdom' (March 2015) 33 (recommending a 28-day limit). See also the UK National Preventive Mechanism Seventh Annual Report (January 2017) 25, calling for a time limit in general.

[40] Wilsher (n 35) 43.

[41] ibid 45. The Aliens Restriction Act 1914 was originally intended as a temporary measure, but was renewed yearly until 1971. For more detail on the development of immigration law through to the 1990s, see A Bloch and L Schuster, 'At the Extremes of Exclusion: Deportation, Detention and Dispersal' (2005) 28(3) *Ethnic and Racial Studies* 491, 494.

[42] Wilsher (n 35) 46.

its origin as a temporary emergency power.[43] Farbey and Sharpe argue that 'Perhaps because of the wartime origins and phrasing of the power [to deport], the courts have been hesitant, and at times wholly unwilling, to interfere with its exercise'.[44] They further point out that the Executive's power to detain was 'defined in a time of emergency, and its exercise … contested in cases full of political overtone'.[45] Post-war deportation cases demonstrated a greater willingness on the part of judges to assert control over the detention power, but in practice it was not very effective.[46]

In the UK, the concept of territorial sovereignty has served as a justification for exclusive executive control of immigration.[47] The House of Lords, quoting from Oppenheim's *International Law* in the *Saadi* case, expressed the sentiment that 'every state is by reason of its territorial supremacy competent to exclude aliens from the whole, or any part, of its territory'.[48] The ECtHR has echoed this on several occasions holding that 'a State has the right to control the entry of non-nationals into its territory'.[49] The state therefore has the power to decide who can enter the UK and who must leave it. It does so on the basis of legislation, but it also uses a vast array of policy guidance to implement the powers granted by law. This is known as a prerogative power of the state, and it has influenced the development of detention case law because it impacts the extent to which the courts consider certain issues as justiciable. Today, it is rare that an issue will be wholly immune from judicial review, even if it is within the prerogative power of the state.[50] The courts will instead make a judgment regarding the extent to which they should defer (if at all) to the state on certain matters. This is certainly borne out in the UK cases that are discussed in chapter seven.

By contrast, the internment of non-citizens under the Aliens Act in the early twentieth century was met with deferential judicial response, especially if the non-citizen was linked in some way to the enemy state.[51] In 1920, what is now the Queen's Bench had occasion to consider the detention of Mr Venicoff, a Russian living in Britain for more than 30 years, who had been accused of activities contrary to the public policy of the state.[52] He applied for habeas

[43] Immigration Act 1971, s 3(5); see also Sch 2.

[44] J Farbey and RJ Sharpe (with S Atrill), *The Law of Habeas Corpus*, 3rd edn (Oxford University Press, 2011) 132.

[45] ibid 133.

[46] ibid 134.

[47] For a background to the concept of the prerogative, see *R (Alvi) v SSHD* [2012] UKSC 33, paras 25–33.

[48] *R (Saadi) v SSHD* [2001] EWCA Civ 1512, 38.

[49] *Abdulaziz, Cabales and Balkandali v UK* [1985] ECHR 7, 67.

[50] See, eg *Council of Civil Service Unions v Minister for the Civil Service* [1985] AC 374, [1984] UKHL 9.

[51] Wilsher (n 35) 47, 53. Wilsher notes that wartime powers of internment were extended under a new Aliens Order in 1919, Art 12(1), which was made under the statutory authority of the Aliens Restriction Act 1914.

[52] *R (Venicoff) v Inspector of Leman Street Police Station* [1920] 3 KB 72.

corpus, arguing that he had not been given a fair hearing on the facts of the case. In dismissing the claim, the then King's Bench stated

> The Legislature in its wisdom took from the Courts during the war the power of inquiry into the facts of particular cases where orders were made under the Defence of the Realm Acts or the Aliens Order, and left the matter entirely to the judgment of the Home Secretary.[53]

Immigration powers, therefore, were viewed at that time as being within the prerogative powers of the state and not a matter for the judiciary.

Things continued along this vein until the *Ahsan* case in 1969, which involved a group of Commonwealth citizens who had entered the UK unlawfully and were detained for two months by the time of their habeas case.[54] The Queen's Bench, emphasising a presumption in favour of liberty, held that the state bore the burden of proving that the individuals should be subject to removal.[55] However, the presumption of liberty for British subjects who were considered to have a special status in the UK was short-lived. Just a few years later, in *Azam*, the House of Lords eliminated any distinction between British subjects and non-citizen aliens in its refusal to interpret the 1971 Act as permitting them to settle in the UK, despite an allegedly unlawful entry before the entry into the force of the 1971 Act.[56] They were therefore, in the eyes of the Court, legitimately detained and subject to expulsion. Then, in *Hassan*, the Queen's Bench held that immigration detainees bore the burden of proving the illegality of detention in order to succeed on a habeas claim.[57]

III. THE UNITED STATES

In his famous essay 'On Liberty', John Stuart Mill discusses the necessity of liberty as a limit on the state's power and the power of the 'tyranny of the majority'. He wrote that the limit manifests itself in two forms: fundamental rights and democracy. But even Mill acknowledged that the fundamental right of liberty was not absolute and that, in some circumstances, it could be curtailed. In particular, Mill spoke of limited liberty for those he labelled 'barbarians' or those from 'backward states of society in which the race itself may be considered as in its nonage'.[58] Thus, even in 1859, the grant of liberty in the USA seemed to depend partly on nationality.

[53] ibid 79. See also Wilsher (n 35) 54.
[54] *R (Ahsan) v Governor of Brixton Prison* [1969] 2 QB 222.
[55] ibid 241.
[56] Wilsher (n 35) 83, discussing *Azam v Secretary of State* [1974] AC 1.
[57] *R (Hassan) v Governor of Risley* [1976] 1 WLR 971, 978–79.
[58] JS Mill, *On Liberty, Utilitarianism and Other Essays* (Oxford University Press, 2015) 13.

The right to liberty is enshrined in the Due Process Clause of the Fifth Amendment to the Constitution, which states that 'No person shall be … deprived of life, liberty, or property, without due process of law'.[59] The US concept of due process is rooted in English constitutional law,[60] and applies to judicial and non-judicial proceedings, including decisions to detain by the Executive. The Due Process Clause informs the development of all detention law and policy, and has informed judicial practice, particularly with regard to the limits placed on detention.

The use of immigration detention has been part of the Executive's system for immigration regulation since the USA began using deportation to rid itself of unwanted non-citizens (typically, this included the physically or mentally ill, morally corrupt or destitute). Indeed, Benson suggests that the use of detention as a practical means of regulating non-citizens is 'as old as the hills'.[61] The first notable use of detention was in the late eighteenth century, and was in connection with the deportation of Irish and French revolutionaries. This was mostly effected under the 1798 Alien and Sedition Acts, a collection of statutes that allowed the state to protect itself, through deportation, from organised rebellion against the US Government.[62] The third act gave the state the power to arrest, restrain, secure and remove any non-citizens within the territory from nations with which the USA was at war. The concern of possible harm from revolutionaries continued into the early twentieth century.[63]

The first federal act exclusively aimed at regulating immigration was passed in 1882,[64] but it was considered inadequate because it failed to address the problem of border officers becoming overwhelmed with the number of non-citizens seeking entry into the USA, and their inability to properly inspect each individual at the border to determine whether they were undesirable.[65] Thus, immigration detention arose out of practical necessity, and was formally introduced in the Immigration Act of 1891.[66] The 1891 Act mandated that all non-citizens

[59] US Constitution, Amend V.

[60] DJ Galligan, *Due Process and Fair Procedures: A Study of Administrative Procedures* (Clarendon Press, 1996) ch 6.

[61] LB Benson, 'As Old as the Hills: Detention and Immigration' (2010) 5 *Intercultural Human Rights Law Review* 11.

[62] The four acts were: (i) An Act to Establish an Uniform Rule of Naturalization (Naturalization Act); (ii) An Act Concerning Aliens; (iii) An Act Respecting Alien Enemies; and (iv) An Act for the Punishment of Certain Crimes against the United States (Sedition Act). They are available online at www.loc.gov/rr/program/bib/ourdocs/Alien.html.

[63] For an interesting overview of Communism-related terrorism in the USA and its relation to immigration law, see Benson (n 61) 26–35. Although most of these statutes expired two years following their enactment, the third remains in force today.

[64] Immigration Act 1882 (An act to regulate immigration), Session I, ch 376; 22 Stat 214, 47th Congress, 3 August 1882. Prior to this, immigration was dealt with by the states.

[65] Wilsher (n 35) 9–10.

[66] An act in amendment to the various acts relative to immigration and the importation of aliens under contract or agreement to perform labor (Immigration Act 1891), Session II, ch 551; 26 Stat 1084, 51st Congress, 3 March 1891.

be inspected upon entry either on board the vessels on which they arrived or in the territory of the USA, in which case they would be detained until the inspection occurred.[67] The 1891 Act also indicated that arrival on the territory for purposes of inspection did not count as an official entry: 'such removal shall not be considered a landing during the pendency of such examination'.[68] This 'entry fiction' became a key component in the way that detainees were treated as detention developed in the USA. Just one year later, another federal statute provided for mandatory detention in case of doubt as to whether the non-citizen should be admitted.[69]

The Constitution does not specifically give the US Federal Government the power to regulate immigration. This left the matter open to interpretation by the courts, which determined, through a series of landmark cases, that the US Federal Government had 'plenary power' to regulate immigration.[70] Plenary power, like prerogative powers, impacts the extent to which certain issues are amenable to judicial review in the courts. In the immigration context, plenary power is important because it can be invoked to restrict non-citizens' ability to raise due process claims before the courts. Van Marle has called plenary power an example of anti-intellectualism that had very little breakthrough.[71] Even when there was a liberalisation in the case law of the mid-twentieth century, the Supreme Court still hung tight to the doctrine, holding in *Knauff v Shaughnessy* that 'Whatever the procedure authorized by Congress is, it is due process as far as an alien denied entry is concerned'.[72] US district courts and the Supreme Court have treated detention as a necessary part of the removal process and, for nearly 100 years from the beginning of its use, did not question the practice in any meaningful way. The Supreme Court's general position was that 'detention is necessarily a part of [the] deportation procedure. Otherwise aliens arrested for deportation would have opportunities to hurt the United States during the pendency of deportation proceedings.'[73]

Because deportation is part of the state's immigration, and therefore plenary, powers, detention was considered non-justiciable for quite some time. However, it did not go without challenge in the courts. In 1892, in *Nishimura Eiku v US*,[74] a Japanese detainee under suspicion of becoming a public charge was ordered to be deported. Ms Eiku challenged the facts underlying the accusation of

[67] Immigration Act 1891, s 8.

[68] ibid.

[69] Immigration Act of 3 March 1893 (27 Statutes-at-Large 570).

[70] Legomsky explains that this conclusion was refined by Supreme Court case law, which took place in five distinctive stages. See SH Legomsky, *Immigration and the Judiciary: Law and Politics in Britain and America* (Clarendon Press, 1987) 180–217.

[71] Presentation by Karin Van Marle, Queen Mary University of London, half day workshop on 'Diversity and Legal Reasoning', 23 November 2016.

[72] (1950) 338 US 537, 544.

[73] *Carlson v Landon* (1952) 342 US 524, 541.

[74] *Nishimura Ekiu v United States* (1892) 142 US 651.

destitution, and argued that she was detained without due process of the law. The Court first demonstrated, through a showing of precedent, that

> An alien immigrant, prevented from landing by any such officer claiming authority to do so under an act of Congress and thereby restrained of his liberty, is doubtless entitled to a writ of habeas corpus to ascertain whether the restraint is lawful.[75]

It then recalled that it may be possible for Congress to authorise the courts to review the facts upon which a judgment of entry or deportation was made.[76] However, in this context, the Court held that Congress imbued the power to make determinations as to entry in its executive officers, who have the final say regarding who enters and who must leave, and that the judiciary did not have the power to contradict a decision of the Executive in that regard unless the inspection official did not act within his authority.[77] After determining that the official was correctly appointed and was given the power to determine whether Ms Ekiu could enter the USA, the Court concluded that it could not review the decision itself, and therefore it could not order the release of Ms Ekiu.[78] It did not consider whether it might still have the power to review the constitutionality of Ms Ekiu's detention based on due process grounds.

The following year, the Supreme Court rendered a judgment that motivated judicial intervention in immigration matters for many years. *Fong Yue Ting* involved several detainees who petitioned for their release through a writ of habeas corpus.[79] They were to be deported for failing to register and demonstrate their entitlement to reside in the USA under the Geary Act of 1892.[80] Upon reaffirming the Executive's plenary power over immigration,[81] the Court stated that deportation is concerned with 'the removal of an alien out of the country simply because his presence is deemed inconsistent with the public welfare, and without any punishments being imposed or contemplated'.[82] Because the Court framed deportation as a non-criminal device, it concluded that constitutional due process protections were inapplicable, and that therefore the petitioners were unable to challenge their detention. The Supreme Court explicitly extended its holding in *Fong Yue Ting* to detention in *Wong Wing v US*[83] when it held:

> Proceedings to exclude or expel would be vain if those accused could not be held in custody pending the inquiry into their true character, and while arrangements were being made for their deportation. Detention is a usual feature in every case of arrest

[75] ibid 660.
[76] ibid.
[77] ibid.
[78] ibid 664.
[79] *Fong Yue Ting v United States* (1893) 149 US 698.
[80] Session I, ch 60, 52nd Congress, 5 May 1892. This was an exception of the 1882 Chinese Exclusion Act (An act to inaugurate certain treaty stipulations relating to Chinese), Session I, ch 126, 22 Stat 58, 47th Congress, approved 6 May 1882.
[81] *Fong Yue Ting* (n 79) 705–08.
[82] ibid 709.
[83] *Wong Wing v US* (1896) 163 US 228.

> on a criminal charge, even when an innocent person a [*sic*] wrongfully accused, but it is not imprisonment in a legal sense.[84]

However, in *Wong Wing*, the detention attracted due process protection because it consisted of hard labour imposed prior to deportation, and was therefore considered to be a criminal punishment.[85]

Detention continued to be used frequently as a routine part of the deportation process, and it continued to be challenged before the courts. In the 1950s, it was employed as a means of dealing with Communism and the Cold War, and gave rise to challenges focused solely on detention, rather than detention in conjunction with deportation. In *Mezei*, the indefinite detention of a non-citizen at the border after a refusal of admission was permitted.[86] Despite the fact that his removal could not be effected, the Supreme Court held that because he had not technically entered the USA, he was not entitled to constitutional protection.[87] This treatment even extended to lawfully admitted non-citizens in certain contexts, such as the fight against Communism, which purportedly allowed unreviewable detention in relation to individuals suspected of being Communists.[88] These Cold War-era cases allowed the Executive to detain whole classes of people without individual review of suitability for detention, a practice which is still employed today with regard to foreign national offenders after the changes made to immigration law by the AEDPA and IIRIRA.[89]

IV. THE EUROPEAN UNION

The EU has a long tradition of respect for fundamental rights, which largely began with the CJEU. Bast argues that 'When it comes to fundamental rights, the Court of Justice has never accepted the notion of Member States' autonomy'.[90] Prior to the Treaty of Amsterdam in 1999, no explicit reference to respect for human rights was contained in the Treaties. However, the CJEU would often consider human rights in its assessment of the compatibility of national law with EU law. To do this, it would use Article 220 of the Treaty Establishing the European Community (EC Treaty), which obligated the Court to ensure that the law is observed in the interpretation and application of the Treaty. The rights included in the ECHR played an important role in this case law,[91] as all

[84] ibid 235.
[85] ibid 238.
[86] *Shaughnessy v United States ex rel Mezei* (1953) 345 US 206.
[87] ibid 215.
[88] *Carlson* (USSC).
[89] See ch 4, s III.B below.
[90] J Bast, 'Of General Principles and Trojan Horses – Procedural Due Process in Immigration Proceedings under EU Law' (2010) 11 *German Law Journal* 1006, 1010.
[91] Case 36/75 *Rutili* [1975] ECR 1219 was the first case which explicitly referenced the ECHR. See also Joined Cases C-20/00 and C-64/00 *Booker Aquaculture* [2003] ECR I-7411: 'fundamental

of the EU Member States are party to the ECHR. Article 6(3) of the Treaty of Lisbon has cemented the important role of fundamental rights in the EU legal order, stating that 'Fundamental rights, as guaranteed by the [ECHR] ... shall constitute general principles of the Union's law'.[92] The Treaty of Lisbon also obliges the EU itself to become a signatory to the ECHR.[93] Indeed, the CJEU has confirmed that part of its role is to ensure that fundamental rights (including those provided by the ECHR and its case law) are protected.[94]

In 2000, the EU developed its own Charter of Fundamental Rights (the Charter), which became legally binding with the entry into force of the Treaty of Lisbon in December 2009. The Charter includes fundamental rights derived from the case law of the CJEU and from the Declaration on Fundamental Rights of the European Parliament of 1989.[95] It also includes the rights guaranteed in the ECHR, including the right to liberty, which is enshrined in Article 6. It requires that interpretation of rights corresponding to the ECHR must at least be in conformity with the case law of the ECtHR,[96] but it permits EU law to provide a higher level of protection.[97] The Charter applies to the acts of EU institutions and bodies, and to the Member States only when they are implementing EU law.[98] Precisely when EU law is being implemented for purposes of Charter application was the subject of the *Åkerberg* judgment of the CJEU, which held that 'the requirement to respect fundamental rights defined in the context of the Union is only binding on the Member States when they act in the scope of Union law'.[99]

Following *Åkerberg*, in *Siragusa* the CJEU provided more clarity regarding when national law comes within the scope of the Charter. In particular, the Court stated that it was necessary to determine

> whether [national] legislation is intended to implement a provision of EU law; the nature of that legislation and whether it pursues objectives other than those covered by EU law, even if it is capable of indirectly affecting EU law; and also whether there are specific rules of EU law on the matter or capable of affecting it.[100]

rights form an integral part of the general principles of law, whose observance the Court ensures ... The [ECHR] has special significance in that respect' (para 65). This includes the former European Commission on Human Rights.

[92] Consolidated version of the Treaty on European Union [2012] OJ C326, 13-390.

[93] ibid Art 6(2).

[94] Case C-465/07 *Elgafaji* [2009] ECR I-921, para 28.

[95] European Parliament, Resolution adopting the Declaration of fundamental rights and freedoms [1989] OJ C120/51.

[96] Charter of Fundamental Rights of the European Union [2012] OJ C326/391, Art 52(3).

[97] ibid Art 52(4).

[98] ibid Art 51(1).

[99] Case C-617/10 *Åkerberg Fransson* [ECR TBC], para 20. Note that subsequent cases have illustrated that it is not always obvious when states are acting within the scope of EU law. See, eg Case C-40/11 *Iida v Stadt Ulm* [ECR TBC].

[100] Case 206/13 *Siragusa v Regione Sicilia – Soprintendenza Beni Culturali e Ambientali di Palermo* [ECR TBC], para 25.

The fact that the national law is on a subject covered by EU, on its own, is not enough to trigger application of the Charter.[101] Moreover, in the past, the CJEU has held that EU fundamental rights were inapplicable to cases where the relevant EU law did not impose any obligations on the Member States with regard to the issue before the Court.[102] However, the CJEU indicated that the Charter might be nonetheless applicable where there is a risk that fundamental rights will be infringed by EU-level or Member State action.[103] This is so because of 'the need to avoid a situation in which the level of protection of fundamental rights varies according to the national law involved in such a way as to undermine the unity, primacy and effectiveness of EU law'.[104]

Whether or not the Charter is applicable in the EU cases under consideration in this book is not a topic of discussion in any of the judgments. It is quite apparent from the Directive that EU law is applicable any time a Member State makes a determination that a third-country national is illegally present on its territory, and so too is the Charter. Moreover, the subject matter of the Return Directive implicates an array of fundamental rights, which counsels even more favourably towards the application of the Charter in light of the CJEU's desire to maintain the 'uniformity, primacy and effectiveness' of EU law.[105] Yet, the Charter itself is only mentioned explicitly in five judgments.[106]

In addition to the fundamental rights set forth in the Treaties and the Charter, the CJEU has developed a number of general principles that have become an important interpretive aid, especially in cases where there is a gap in the law or where the law is ambiguous or unclear, though this is not a prerequisite for the use of these principles.[107] Among them are respect for fundamental rights as recognised in EU law and the principle of effectiveness, or *effet utile*, which has been the subject of much academic commentary.[108] Effectiveness has been employed by the Court in a number of circumstances, often to protect the rights of EU nationals. For example, in *Francovich*, the Court held that

> the full effectiveness of [EU] rules would be impaired and the protection of the rights which they grant would be weakened if individuals were unable to obtain redress

[101] ibid para 26.

[102] Case C-144/95 *Maurin* [1996] ECR I-2908, paras 11–12.

[103] *Siragusa*, para 31.

[104] ibid para 32.

[105] ibid.

[106] Case C-383/13 PPU *G and R* [ECR TBC]; Case C-146/14 PPU *Mahdi* [ECR TBC]; Case C-166/13 *Mukarubega* [ECR TBC]; Case C-249/13 *Boudjilda* [ECR TBC]; Case C-554/13 *Zh and O* [ECR TBC]. In addition, the least referenced source in these cases is the Treaty of Lisbon, which is typically only mentioned in relation to the preliminary reference procedure or the urgent procedure (see eg *G and R*, paras 22–24; Case C-534/11 *Arslan* [ECR TBC], para 33).

[107] T Tridimas, *The General Principles of EU Law* (Oxford University Press, 2006).

[108] See, eg D Curtin, 'Directives: The Effectiveness of Judicial Protection of Individual Rights' (1990) 27 *Common Market Law Review* 709; S Mayr, 'Putting a Leash on the Court of Justice – Preconceptions in National Methodology v *Effet Utile* as a Meta-Rule' (2012) 5 *European Journal of Legal Studies* 3; U Sadl, 'The Role of *Effet Utile* in Preserving the Continuity and Authority of European Union Law: Evidence from the Citation Web of the Pre-accession Case Law of the Court

> when their rights are infringed by a breach of [EU] law for which a Member State can be held responsible.[109]

In the context of criminal law, effectiveness has been used, for example, to ensure that national criminal measures do not disproportionately interfere with free movement.[110] These cases make clear the important and expanding role of the principle of effectiveness in the jurisprudence of the CJEU.[111]

Most recently, the Court has deployed the principle of effectiveness in the context of immigration law. Its judgments demonstrate an attempt to ensure that national law does not impair the effective functioning of the Return Directive. In so doing, many of these judgments have had an indirectly positive impact on the fundamental rights of individuals, especially immigration detainees. This will be explored more in relation to the case law.

Unlike the UK and USA, because the EU immigration framework is comparatively new, all of its case law can be considered modern. Key detention cases have therefore been reserved for discussion in chapters four to seven.

V. CONCLUSION

The right to liberty is a fundamental principle which can be found in each of the legal systems examined in this book. As Ashworth and Zedner point out, the state's role in protecting liberties is in tension with its obligation to protect its citizens from harm.[112] In an attempt to provide security to its citizens so that they may exercise their liberties without undue restraint, the state often restricts liberties, for example, through the use of preventive detention.[113] Striking the appropriate balance in law between liberty and protection is challenging, and in many cases may be done incorrectly. Indeed, Friedman and Stumpf have

of Justice of the EU' (2015) 8 *European Journal of Legal Studies* 18; V Skouris, '*Effet Utile* versus Legal Certainty: The Case-Law of the Court of Justice on the Direct Effect of Directives' (2006) 17 *European Business Law Review* 241.

[109] Joined Cases C-6 & 9/90 *Francovich and Bonifaci v Italy* [1991] ECR I-5357, para 33. See also Case 6/64 *Costa v ENEL* [1964] ECR 585; Case 41/74 *Van Duyn v Home Office* [1974] ECR 1337, para 12, using effectiveness to extend direct effect to directives; Case 14/83 *Von Colson and Kamann v Land Nordrhein-Westfalen* [1984] ECR 1891, establishing the concept of indirect effect.

[110] Case 203/80 *Casati* [1981] ECR 2595, para 27.

[111] On the use of effectiveness in the context of criminal law, see S Melander, 'Effectiveness in EU Criminal Law and Its Effects on the General Part of Criminal Law' (2015) 5 *New Journal of European Criminal Law* 274; V Mitsilegas, 'The Changing Landscape of the Criminalisation of Migration in Europe' in M João et al (eds), *Social Control and Justice: Crimmigration in the Age of Fear* (Eleven International Publishing, 2013) 98–100; P Craig, 'The ECJ and *Ultra Vires* Action: A Conceptual Analysis' (2011) 48 *Common Market Law Review* 395, 401; E Herlin-Karnell, 'Effectiveness and Constitutional Limits in European Crim Law' (2014) 5 *New Journal of European Criminal Law* 267; E Herlin-Karnell, 'An Exercise in Effectiveness?' (2007) 18 *European Business Law Review* 1181.

[112] A Ashworth and L Zedner, *Preventive Justice* (Oxford University Press, 2015) 6–10, 251–66.

[113] ibid 6.

persuasively argued that there is an imbalance that prioritises immigration enforcement over the enforcement of civil rights.[114] Similarly, Harman suggests that a further 'conflict occurs when [courts try] to balance rights appropriately afforded to persons in the Constitution [such as in the Due Process Clause] and those rights that should only apply to citizens of the United States'.[115]

The next chapter will explore how the modest use of immigration detention during times of war or conflict evolved into a routine and sometimes indispensable part of the modern detention framework of each jurisdiction. It will look in some detail at their legislative development, before outlining the governing legal provisions implicated by the case studies examined in later chapters. Contemporary judicial intervention is, of course, the main subject of this book and will be explored in depth in chapters four to seven.

[114] B Friedman and J Stumpf, 'Advancing Civil Rights through Immigration Law: One Step Forward, Two Steps Back?' (2002) 6 *New York University Journal of Legislation and Policy* 131.

[115] M Harman, 'Indefinite Detention of Excludable Aliens: An International Crisis on American Soil' (2000) 7 *Southwestern Journal of Law and Trade in the Americas* 193, 202.

3

Current Legal Frameworks

I. INTRODUCTION

THE PREVIOUS CHAPTER outlined the historical development of the law on immigration detention with a view to focusing here on the beginnings of the modern legal framework for managing immigration detention in each jurisdiction. This chapter first considers how the current legal framework developed and considers what, if any, concerns were expressed regarding the inclusion of detention powers within the modern immigration enforcement system. It then moves on to provide an overview of the authorities responsible for immigration enforcement. Finally, it outlines the relevant statutory provisions and non-statutory guidance that governs the implementation of immigration detention today.

II. ORIGINS OF THE MODERN SYSTEMS

A. United Kingdom

The origin of the modern immigration detention system in the UK can be traced to the 1960s, when Britain struggled with how to treat citizens of its Commonwealth who had previously been considered British subjects with the right to enter the UK. This period saw the clawing back of entry rights for Commonwealth citizens under the Commonwealth Immigrants Acts of 1962 and 1968, and by the time the 1971 Act was adopted, most Commonwealth citizens had to obtain permission to enter the UK. Detention of Commonwealth citizens prior to deportation was commonplace.

The 1971 Act is a general law which regulates all manner of immigration-related issues, including detention. Its aim was to integrate the law relating to Commonwealth citizens and all other non-citizens in a single instrument.[1] Parliamentary debate surrounding the Act did not focus much on the issue of detention as a separate matter, other than discussing a proposed amendment

[1] A Samuels, 'The United Kingdom Immigration Act 1971' (1972) 11 *University of Western Australia Law Review* 54 1973, 54.

requiring that detainees be brought before a magistrate every seven days to determine whether the detention was still lawful.[2] This seems to be in contrast to debate in the 1950s questioning whether detention was consistent with the nation's liberal values.[3] The amendment did not make it into the Act.[4] A 1972 overview of the Act reserved any mention of detention until the final paragraph: 'The Act also contains a wide range of criminal offences and increased penalties in relation to the immigration laws and confers powers of arrest, search and detention upon constables and immigration officers.'[5] The Immigration Acts of 2014 and 2016 represent recent amendments to the 1971 Act, but do not touch on detention powers.[6]

The use of immigration detention increased through the 1980s, when rising numbers of asylum seekers were requesting refuge in the UK, but at that time, most people were being detained in prisons rather than purpose-built facilities.[7] In the 1990s, a large policy shift occurred. The number of asylum applications in Britain began to rise in the 1980s, but hit a high in the mid-1990s, when Labour was in power.[8] The increase, in addition to delays in the examination process and what was considered a failure to remove enough applicants, led to a general feeling that the government was soft on immigration and that many asylum applications were fraudulent. This asylum 'crisis' led to the enactment of restrictive immigration laws, including the Immigration and Asylum Appeals Act 1993, which permitted detention of asylum seekers pending their claims, and the Asylum and Immigration Act 1996, which strengthened powers to detain asylum seekers. Then, in 1998, the government published 'Fairer, Faster and Firmer – A Modern Approach to Immigration and Asylum',[9] which addressed concerns that the asylum process was moving too slowly and that the system was being abused by false asylum claims. Though detention was still viewed as only used in 'a relatively small number of cases and as a last resort',[10] the White Paper suggested that better procedural protections would be offered to detainees, such as the right to receive written reasons for their detention at the outset of detention and monthly thereafter, and a higher level of judicial involvement in the

[2] *Hansard*, HC, Vol 819, cols 712–29 (17 June 1971). The amendment at issue was named Amendment 127. See also *Hansard*, HL, Vol 323, cols 1009–86 (3 August 1971).

[3] SJ Silverman, '"Regrettable but Necessary?' A Historical and Theoretical Study of the Rise of the UK Immigration Detention Estate and Its Opposition' (2012) 40 *Politics and Policy* 1131, 1140.

[4] *Hansard*, HL, Vol 323, cols 1105–44 (3 August 1971).

[5] JM Evans, 'Immigration Act 1971' (1972) 35 *The Modern Law Review* 508, 524 (footnotes omitted).

[6] The 2014 Act does not regulate detention, but the 2016 Act includes provisions on immigration detention bail. However, neither will be given separate attention in this book.

[7] M Bosworth, *Inside Immigration Detention* (Oxford University Press, 2014) 22.

[8] MJ Gibney, 'Asylum and the Expansion of Deportation in the United Kingdom' (2008) 43(2) *Government and Opposition* 146, 155.

[9] Secretary of State for the Home Department, 'Fairer, Faster and Firmer – A Modern Approach to Immigration and Asylum' Cm 4018 (1998).

[10] *Hansard*, HC, Vol 326, cols 37–129 (22 February 1999) (according to then-Secretary of State, Jack Straw).

detention process.[11] However, this was likely because the UK was in the process of passing the Human Rights Act, which incorporated rights from the European Convention on Human Rights (ECHR).[12]

From 1997 to 2009, the Labour Government passed seven pieces of legislation regulating immigration matters, and the detention estate was expanded dramatically.[13] Over 80 new immigration offences were created as a result of this legislation.[14] Also during this time, the practice of mandatory detention of asylum seekers upon entry became commonplace, and was even approved by the ECtHR, subject to certain considerations linked to whether the detention was reasonable in all the circumstances.[15] In 2006, another 'crisis' revealed that over a thousand foreign national offenders were released from UK prisons at the end of their sentences without being considered for deportation.[16] As a result, the government enacted the UK Borders Act 2007, which required the deportation and detention of foreign nationals who had either been sentenced to more than one year in prison or convicted of certain crimes.[17]

Parliamentary debate in the context of the Labour Government era of immigration legislation more markedly focused on detention as a separate issue, especially in the House of Lords. However, concern was almost always limited to asylum seekers, largely because the perceived crisis was what fuelled the development of this legislation. Particularly regarding what would become the Immigration and Asylum Act 1999, a number of Lords were concerned that no maximum duration of detention would be prescribed by law and accordingly suggested that a provision for automatic bail hearings be included.[18] Although eventually such a provision was included, it was repealed by the Nationality, Immigration and Asylum Act 2002 (NIAA 2002).[19] Debate surrounding the NIAA 2002 again emphasised the lack of a maximum time limit and stressed

[11] Secretary of State for the Home Department (n 9) 12.7–12.10.

[12] Signed in Rome, 4 November 1950.

[13] Bosworth (n 7) 33.

[14] A Aliverti, 'Making People Criminal: The Role of the Criminal Law in Immigration and Enforcement' (2012) 16 *Theoretical Criminology* 417; A Aliverti, 'Exploring the Function of Criminal Law in the Policing of Foreigners: The Decision to Prosecute Immigration-Related Offences' (2012) 29 *Social and Legal Studies* 511.

[15] Immigration Act 1971, sch 2, para 21. Clayton points out that this detention was considered 'relaxed' by the Home Office because it applied to asylum seekers who did not fall within the scope of the normal detention powers because they were not at risk of absconding. See G Clayton, *Textbook on Immigration and Asylum Law*, 7th edn (Oxford University Press, 2016) 530. The ECtHR case was *Saadi v UK* [2008] 47 EHRR 17.

[16] See, eg 'How the Deportation Story Emerged' *BBC News* (London, 9 October 2006) http://news.bbc.co.uk/1/hi/uk_politics/4945922.stm; 'Clarke Insists "I Will Not Quit"' *BBC News* (London, 25 April 2006) http://news.bbc.co.uk/1/hi/uk_politics/4944164.stm; MJ Gibney, 'Deportation, Crime, and the Changing Character of Membership in the United Kingdom' in K Franko Aas and M Bosworth (eds), *The Borders of Punishment: Migration, Citizenship and Social Exclusion* (Oxford University Press, 2013).

[17] UK Borders Act 2007, c 30, received Royal Assent on 30 October 2007, s 32.

[18] *Hansard*, HL, Vol 605, cols 1193–284 (20 October 1999).

[19] Nationality, Immigration and Asylum Act 2002, c 41, s 68(6).

that the UN Working Group on Arbitrary Detention and the United Nations High Commissioner for Refugees (UNHCR) had criticised UK practice in this regard.[20] There was also concern expressed about the intention to increase the number of detention spaces available in detention estates from 2,700 to 4,000.[21] Much discussion was also focused on what was perceived by some parliamentarians as the poor quality of reasons for detention provided by the government.[22] Particular criticism of the requirement to give reasons was voiced because of its general nature and the risk that it could become a tick list used in every case.[23] Debate surrounding the development of the UK Borders Act 2007 centred on the provisions relating to automatic deportation and detention. In particular, there was concern that the UK Borders Bill did not include a specific time frame within which the Secretary of State must decide whether the provisions on automatic deportation apply to a specific individual.[24] Some Lords were concerned that there was a possibility for prolonged periods of detention while such a determination was being considered. They were not alone in this concern.[25]

Unfortunately, many of these concerns were dismissed by the majority, and attempts to provide some additional safeguards through legislation failed. Opposition to these proposals expressed concern that, for example, a maximum duration would motivate detainees to exhaust all routes of judicial redress (whether or not with merit) so as to purposely reach the maximum and achieve release. It was felt that at that stage, they could then abscond and elude immigration authorities.[26] Consequently, even today there is no maximum duration of detention, no automatic review of detention through a bail hearing or otherwise, and no set time limit for the Secretary of State to determine the applicability of the automatic deportation and detention provisions under the 2007 Act.[27]

Immigration policy continues to be controversial. In fact, the UK's decision to withdraw from the EU may be partly based on fears that the UK is being overwhelmed by immigration as a result of EU membership, while others consider that the UK's obligation to respect human rights (particularly the right to family life) because of its Council of Europe membership has permitted foreign national offenders to remain in the UK when they would otherwise have been deported. Moreover, the UK Parliament engaged in a review of its detention

[20] *Hansard*, HL, Vol 636, cols 1087–181 (24 June 2002).

[21] ibid.

[22] *Hansard*, HL, Vol 639, cols 412–82 (10 October 2002).

[23] ibid.

[24] *Hansard*, HL, vol 692, UK Borders Bill Second Reading (13 June 2007).

[25] House of Lords, House of Commons Joint Committee on Human Rights, 'Legislative Scrutiny: Sixth Progress Report', Thirteenth Report of Session 2006-07, HL Paper 105, HC 538 (21 May 2007).

[26] See, eg *Hansard*, HL, Vol 606, cols 724–800 (2 November 1999); *Hansard*, HL, Vol 637, cols 1048–84 (15 July 2002).

[27] As to the lattermost, the UK Borders Act 2007, s 34(1) states that a deportation order must be 'made at a time chosen by the Secretary of State'.

practice in 2015, which included examination of available procedural safeguards against detention.[28] Despite recommendations that, among other things, there should be automatic judicial review of detention orders and a maximum period of detention,[29] none of these suggestions were adopted.

In addition, 'Operation Nexus', a joint enforcement initiative between the police and the Home Office, aims at targeting 'high harm'[30] foreign nationals for detention and deportation, based on a decision by the Home Office that their presence is not conducive to the public good. As Nason critically points out, in practice, this means that individuals can be held responsible for criminal conduct within the context of a deportation hearing, even absent a criminal conviction.[31] The system is based on referrals to immigration enforcement by police forces in England and Wales (at the time of writing, it did not apply to Scotland, though it is intended to do so). None of the detention cases in this book are Nexus cases, but the operation of this policy illustrates the indirect way in which the use of detention has been increased in the UK.

B. United States

Detention in the USA is carried out under the authority of the Immigration and Nationality Act 1952 (INA),[32] which has been amended a number of times since its entry into force. At the time the Act was being debated in Congress, the average detention population in the eight detention facilities in the country was 1,473, though there was space for a maximum 3,343.[33] Joint Congressional hearings on the Act in its Bill form demonstrated that discussion of detention was largely focused on carrier liability for costs of detaining non-citizens on board vessels at ports, awaiting decisions on admissibility.[34] However, that does not mean that detention did not merit discussion beyond costs. For example,

[28] All Party Parliamentary Group on Refugees & the All Party Parliamentary Group on Migration, 'The Report of the Inquiry into the Use of Immigration Detention in the United Kingdom' (March 2015).

[29] ibid 48–53.

[30] This is defined as 'cases where [a foreign national offender's] conduct incurs significant adverse impact, whether physical, emotional or financial, upon individuals or the wider community'. See Home Office, 'Operation Nexus – High Harm', version 1.0 (15 March 2017) 5.

[31] N Nason, 'Home Office Belatedly Issues Guidance on Operation Nexus' (freemovement.org.uk, 24 April 2017) www.freemovement.org.uk/home-office-belatedly-issues-guidance-operation-nexus/. See also *R (V) v Asylum and Immigration Tribunal & Anor* [2009] EWHC 1902 (Admin); Home Office (ibid).

[32] Immigration and Nationality Act 1952, Pub L 82-414, 66 Stat 163, enacted 27 June 1952. Although passed in 1952, it has been amended many times. See www.uscis.gov/iframe/ilink/docView/SLB/HTML/SLB/act.html.

[33] US Senate Report 81-1515, Serial Set No 11373 (20 April 1950), 915.

[34] See, eg Joint Hearings before the Subcommittees of the Committees on the Judiciary, 82nd Congress, First Session on S 716, HR 2379 and HR 2816, bills to revise the laws relating to immigration, naturalization and nationality, 6–9, 12–16, 20–21 March and 9 April 1951: 9 March 1951, 168, 189; 14 March 1951, 312 et seq; 16 March 1951, 458.

Mr Stanley H Lowell, speaking on behalf of the Americans for Democratic Action, expressed

> grave doubts that the kind of legislation in which we are interested, based on concepts of justice and equal treatment, can be drawn in this period of world tension, which is reflected in politically exploited hysteria and confusion in this country.[35]

Others discussed a concern that the Attorney General would interpret the power to detain under the Act as giving him 'uncontrolled discretion to detain aliens', which he had apparently done in relation to detention powers under the Internal Security Act, passed in 1950.[36] Several people from the Association of Immigration and Nationality Lawyers attempted to include a provision in the Act which would permit detention only where there was a risk of absconding or a danger to the public.[37] The necessity or appropriateness of using detention as a means of immigration enforcement was not discussed at all, but rather seemed to be a given.[38] In any event, the INA led to a decrease in the use of detention in favour of alternatives, such as parole.[39] It also created a removal period of six months, which operated as a de facto maximum duration of detention.[40] This largely remained the state of things until the 1980s, when three main incidents led to a resurgence in the use of immigration detention. First was the sudden influx of Cuban citizens after Fidel Castro gave blanket permission to Cuban nationals to exit Cuba.[41] Second, and occurring nearly simultaneously, was the arrival of thousands of Haitians to the USA.[42] Third was the arrival of South American civil war exiles.[43] This dramatic increase in the number of arrivals at US borders led to a policy of mandatory detention to deal with the increased volume of non-citizens applying for asylum.[44] It became difficult to keep track of the people

[35] ibid 14 March 1951, 413–14.

[36] ibid 680.

[37] ibid.

[38] It is important to note that I was unable to locate the text of debates within the Senate and House separately, so I am unable to comment as to whether this issue was addressed in those discussions.

[39] D Wilsher, *Immigration Detention: Law, History, Politics* (Cambridge University Press, 2012) 64.

[40] INA, s 242(c).

[41] ME Sartori, 'The Cuban Migration Dilemma: An Examination of the United States' Policy of Temporary Protection in Offshore Safe Havens' (2003) 15 *Georgetown Immigration Law Journal* 319.

[42] M Lennox, 'Refugees, Racism, and Reparations: A Critique of the United States' Haitian Immigration Policy' (1993) 45 *Stanford Law Review* 687, 701–03. See M Dow, *American Gulag: Inside US Immigration Prisons* (University of California Press, 2004) ch 3, focusing on the treatment of Haitians inside Krome detention centre in Miami. Legomsky and Rodríguez also discuss the general US policy of detaining Haitians in particular: SH Legomsky and CM Rodríguez, *Immigration and Refugee Law and Policy*, 5th edn (Foundation Press, 2009) 1056–58.

[43] DM Hernández, 'Pursuant to Deportation: Latinos and Immigrant Detention' in JA Dowling and JX Inda (eds), *Governing Immigration Through Crime: A Reader* (Stanford University Press, 2013) 207–10.

[44] The Refugee Act of 1980 (Pub L 96–212, 94 Stat 102) amended the Immigration and Nationality Act of 1965 and gave asylum seekers the right to claim entry via a work authorisation.

who were released on parole, and the government claimed that many individuals were failing to appear at their removal hearings.[45] By the early 1990s, the government felt that it had an asylum 'crisis' on its hands, fuelled by media portrayals of non-citizens allegedly destroying documents, applying for asylum, earning work authorisation and then disappearing within the USA.[46] As a result, detention facilities were expanded, and detention began to be used a means of deterrence, largely against asylum seekers.[47]

Crime became linked with immigration in 1988, when certain types of criminal offences deemed 'aggravated felonies' resulted in mandatory detention and deportation.[48] In 1996, the situation worsened. The AEDPA was borne out of the Oklahoma City bombing in 1995 and a specific desire to address what were thought of as 'deficiencies in criminal law' regarding appeals.[49]

Though primarily concerned with anti-terrorism and criminal law enforcement, the AEDPA had several far-reaching effects on immigration law. Specifically regarding detention, the AEDPA has further criminalised migration by expanding the category of crimes qualifying as aggravated felonies, which led to a corresponding increase in the number of non-citizens liable to immigration detention because they qualified for automatic deportation. At the time, President Clinton remarked that he hoped that the AEDPA, among other things, would serve as a mechanism for the expeditious deportation of 'alien terrorists'.[50] Moreover, there was no maximum duration of detention specified for mandatory detainees. This led, in some instances, to detainees being termed 'lifers' because no other countries would receive them upon removal from the USA.[51] In response to some concern over foreign national offenders' and terror suspects' increased exposure to automatic deportation, Republican Senator Hatch reiterated that deportation is not a criminal process during which the individual might be incarcerated – it is instead 'simply' the removal of these individuals from the USA.[52] There was no mention of immigration detention being part of the deportation process.

In tandem, the IIRIRA focused on the expedited apprehension and removal of undocumented immigrants, and specifically addressed immigration detention.

[45] LB Benson, 'As Old as the Hills: Detention and Immigration' (2010) 5 *Intercultural Human Rights Law Review* 11, 46.

[46] DA Martin, 'Making Asylum Policy: The 1994 Reforms' (1995) 70 *Washington Law Review* 725, 738.

[47] Benson (n 45) 44.

[48] Anti-Drug Abuse Act of 1988, Pub L 100-690, 102 Stat 4181, enacted 18 November 1988 and codified in 2000 under 8 USC §1326.

[49] Senate Report, Vol 141, No 88, 104th Congress, 1st Session, S7479. At that time, the AEDPA was referred to as the Comprehensive Terrorism Prevention Act of 1995.

[50] Congressional Record, Vol 141, No 88, 104th Congress, 1st Session, S7497.

[51] DA Martin, 'Graduated Application of Constitutional Protections for Aliens: The Real Meaning of *Zadvydas v Davis*' (2001) *Supreme Court Review* 47, 63.

[52] Senate Report, Vol 141, No 88, 104th Congress, 1st Session, S7480.

The IIRIRA was intended to enhance border enforcement through increasing the resources for border protection, and it sought to ensure that all foreign national offenders would be detained once released from serving their criminal sentences, and not released until they could be removed. It also created an expedited process for removing those attempting to enter the USA illegally. Such people would not be allowed to appeal, but instead would be deported immediately. It was felt that these provisions were 'in the national interest' and necessary to 'achieve control over [the] borders ... over illegal immigration and the misuse of ... generous public support and welfare programs that so burden the taxpayers'.[53]

The IIRIRA created a host of new federal immigration crimes, but it also responded in part to the problem of lifers by imposing a 90-day removal period for all non-citizens subject to a final deportation order.[54] While that seems positive at first glance, the IIRIRA provided for detention beyond the 90-day period for certain non-citizens subject to deportation: those deportable for having committed certain crimes and those deemed by the Attorney General to be dangerous or a flight risk. It was still possible, however, for these people to be granted supervised release at the discretion of the Attorney General, but only in exceptional circumstances.[55]

This is how the law relating to immigration detention in the USA remains today. Born out of necessity, detention was first used as a means to deal with the physical inspection of non-citizens upon arrival, but evolved into an essential part of immigration enforcement, especially once the authorities began linking immigration to crime in the 1980s. Immigration detention is viewed as an indispensable part of immigration enforcement and is largely justified on the basis of a need to ensure presence, either to determine whether someone should be removed or to ensure that removal occurs once it has been ordered. It was so tied to enforcement that, for many years, it was not considered as a separate process in need of an independent evaluation. Indeed, scholars have remarked that the power to deport has been mistakenly conflated with the power to detain.[56]

[53] Senate Report, Vol 142, No 127, 104th Congress, 2nd Session, S10573.

[54] INA, s 241(a)(1)(A). The IIRIRA also eliminated a prior distinction between exclusion proceedings (for those who were deemed inadmissible) and deportation proceedings (for those who were on the territory but were being removed to another country) in favour of using the combined 'removal proceedings'.

[55] INA, s 241(a)(6). The IIRIRA also changed the terminology by eliminating use of the terms 'exclusion' and 'deportation' proceedings and merging them into 'removal proceedings'.

[56] D Cole, 'In Aid of Removal: Due Process Limits on Immigration Detention' (2002) 51 *Emory Law Journal* 1003, 1038; S Bhargava, 'Detaining Due Process: The Need for Procedural Reform in "*Joseph*" Hearings after *Demore v Kim*' (2006–2007) 31 *New York University Review of Law and Social Change* 51, 64; JP Stumpf, 'Civil Detention and Other Oxymorons' (2014) 40 *Queens Law Journal* 55.

C. European Union

The EU shares legislative competence with the Member States over legal and illegal migration, integration and readmission.[57] After the entry into force of the Treaty of Amsterdam, the EU legislated quite actively, adopting six measures between 1999 and 2005 with the purpose of achieving a Common European Asylum System (CEAS) and establishing minimum standards across the Member States with regard to qualification for refugee status and the procedures thereof, and a number of other related aims.[58] This included a provision which permitted Member States to detain asylum seekers where necessary 'for legal reasons or reasons of public order'.[59] During this period, discussions began regarding the need for common standards concerning irregular (ie what would be termed 'illegal' or 'unlawful' in the USA or UK) migration in the Member States, particularly with regard to conditions for the admission and residence of third-country nationals into the Member States – a subject for which the Commission felt it had a role to play, especially in light of diverging views in the Member States.[60]

After developing a directive concerning the mutual recognition of expulsion decisions,[61] the Commission published a Green Paper on the return policy of

[57] Treaty on Functioning of the European Union [2012] OJ C326/47, Art 4.

[58] Regulation 604/2013/EU of the European Parliament and of the Council of 26 June 2013 establishing the criteria and mechanisms for determining the Member State responsible for examining an application for international protection lodged in one of the Member States by a third-country national or a stateless person (recast) [2013] OJ L180/31; Regulation 603/2013/EU of the European Parliament and of the Council on the establishment of 'Eurodac' for the comparison of fingerprints for the effective application of Regulation (EU) No 604/2013 establishing the criteria and mechanisms for determining the Member State responsible for examining an application for international protection lodged in one of the Member States by a third-country national or a stateless person and on requests for the comparison with Eurodac data by Member States' law enforcement authorities and Europol for law enforcement purposes, and amending Regulation (EU) No 1077/2011 establishing a European Agency for the operational management of large-scale IT systems in the area of freedom, security and justice (recast) [2013] OJ L180/1; Directive 2001/55/EC of the Council of the European Union on minimum standards for giving temporary protection in the event of a mass influx of displaced persons and on measures promoting a balance of efforts between Member States in receiving such persons and bearing the consequences thereof [2001] OJ L212/12; Directive 2013/32/EU of the European Parliament and of the Council on common procedures for granting and withdrawing international protection (recast) [2013] OJ L180/60 (EU Asylum Procedures Directive 2013/32); Directive 2011/95/EU of the European Parliament and of the Council on minimum standards for the qualification and status of third-country nationals or stateless persons as refugees or as persons who otherwise need international protection and the content of the protection granted (recast) [2011] OJ L337/9.

[59] Directive 2003/9/EC of 27 January 2003 laying down minimum standards for the reception of asylum seekers [2003] OJ L31/18, Art 7(3) (EU Reception Conditions Directive 2003/9).

[60] European Commission, 'Communication on a Community Immigration Policy', COM(2000) 757 final.

[61] Directive 2001/40/EC of the Council on the mutual recognition of decisions on the expulsion of third-country nationals [2001] OJ L149/34.

illegal immigrants.[62] 'Return' was defined in the Green Paper as 'the preparation or implementation aiming at the way back to the country of origin or transit, irrespective of the question, whether the return takes place voluntarily or forced'.[63] The Green Paper stressed that migration played a role in the economic and social development of the EU,[64] and that a return policy was needed 'to safeguard the integrity of the legal and humanitarian admissions system',[65] to 'ensure that admission policy [was] not undermined and to enforce the rule of law'.[66]

The Green Paper dedicated a separate section to a discussion of detention and its role as a coercive measure used to enforce removals.[67] After acknowledging that coercive measures significantly limit personal liberty, the Green Paper identified two purposes for the use of immigration detention: (i) to identify the person and obtain the requisite travel documents; and (ii) to prevent the person from absconding prior to removal.[68] The Green Paper also suggested the creation of minimum standards regarding detention orders, which would cover issues relating to the competence of the responsible authorities, preconditions for detention, identification of classes of persons who should not be detained and mechanisms for judicial oversight.[69] It was also thought necessary to harmonise the varying statutory time limits for detention in the Member States. Prior to this, the EU had only addressed the possibility of detention in two pieces of legislation, concerning, respectively, procedures relating to asylum applications and conditions for the reception of asylum seekers.[70] However, neither regulated the actual implementation of detention, a matter which was left to the Member States.[71]

The Green Paper provided an overview of human rights instruments that would be applicable to return legislation.[72] The emphasis was on the ECHR and the Charter, highlighting provisions on the prohibition of torture,[73] the

[62] European Commission, 'Green Paper on a Community Return Policy on Illegal Immigrants', COM(2002) 175 final.

[63] ibid Annex I.

[64] ibid 5.

[65] ibid 6.

[66] ibid 7.

[67] ibid 14–15.

[68] ibid 14.

[69] ibid 14. The Green Paper also foresaw the development of minimum standards related to the conditions of detention.

[70] Directive 2005/85/EC of 1 December 2005 on minimum standards on procedures in Member States for granting and withdrawing refugee status [2005] OJ L326/13; EU Reception Conditions Directive 2003/9, Art 7.

[71] These directives have since been recast and include more specific regulation of detention. See Directive 2013/32/EU of the European Parliament and of the Council of 26 June 2013 on common procedures for granting and withdrawing international protection (recast), Art 26; Directive 2013/33/EU of the European Parliament and of the Council of 26 June 2013 laying down standards for the reception of applicants for international protection (recast), Arts 8–11.

[72] European Commission (n 62) 10.

[73] ECHR, Art 3; Charter of Fundamental Rights of the European Union [2012] OJ C326/391, Art 4 (EU Charter).

right to liberty[74] and integrity of the person,[75] fair trials,[76] family life,[77] the right to an effective remedy,[78] collective expulsions and non-refoulement,[79] and children's rights.[80] The Green Paper reiterated the fact that fundamental rights are a foundation for the EU and therefore that the returns policy must 'be fully respectful' of them.[81]

The Commission published its Communication on the results of the Green Paper's public consultation the following October, in support of a return policy, including the use of immigration detention and the adoption of minimum standards thereof.[82] Three years later, a proposal for a directive was tabled by the Commission.[83] The document stressed that the proposal was highly scrutinised in terms of its compatibility with fundamental rights at the EU and international levels, and that procedural safeguards were given much attention.[84] Chapter IV of the proposal focused on detention, or 'temporary custody', as it was called in the proposal. The Explanatory Memorandum at the start of the proposal indicated that detention was to be used as a last resort, and in full consideration of the principle of proportionality.[85] It was also intended to be used only if necessary to prevent absconding, and where other less coercive means were not available. The proposed provisions listed examples of alternatives, such as reporting requirements and paying a financial guarantee.[86] Although there was much discussion of procedural safeguards with respect to removal orders, protections associated with detention included that: (i) custody orders be issued by judicial authorities, or in urgent cases, by administrative authorities, the latter situation requiring judicial confirmation within 72 hours; (ii) temporary custody orders were to be reviewed by a judicial authority at least once a month; and (iii) custody was actually supposed to be temporary in nature, ie it was to be limited to six months.[87]

What followed were three years of intense negotiation of the proposal. The UK, in particular, decried the rights-protecting provisions, claiming that

[74] ECHR, Art 5.

[75] EU Charter, Art 3.

[76] ECHR, Art 6; EU Charter, Art 47.

[77] ECHR, Art 8.

[78] ECHR, Art 13; EU Charter, Art 47.

[79] EU Charter, Art 19.

[80] Ibid, Art 24.

[81] European Commission (n 62) 10.

[82] European Commission, 'Communication from the Commission to the Council and the European Parliament on a Community Return Policy on Illegal Residents', COM(2002) 564 final (14 October 2002) 20.

[83] Proposal for a Directive of the European Parliament and of the Council on common standards and procedures in Member States for returning illegally staying third-country nationals, COM (2005) 391 final (1 September 2005).

[84] ibid 5.

[85] ibid 7.

[86] ibid draft Art 14(1).

[87] ibid draft Arts 14(2)–(4).

the proposal was actually aimed at protecting those unlawfully present, rather than enhancing the removal process.[88] The discussion of detention focused on three main issues: (i) the grounds for detention; (ii) judicial supervision of detention; and (iii) the appropriate maximum period of detention.[89] Acosta clearly illustrates the complicated back and forth between the European Council Presidency, the Justice and Home Affairs Council and the European Parliament during the amendment process.[90] The Finnish Presidency suggested a number of compromises relating to detention. It extended the grounds of detention to include situations where there was a risk that the removal process would be impaired, and it increased the maximum period of detention, which could be between four and eight months, or even longer where there were delays in obtaining the necessary paperwork or where the detainee was not co-operating. It also suggested that administrative authorities could order detention in any case, not only those that were urgent. The subsequent German Presidency in February 2007 sought to 'drain the proposal of all its significance', including with regard to detention.[91] It kept the maximum period of detention of six months, but permitted an extension of an additional 12 months, which remains in the final Return Directive today, and it agreed with the Finnish Presidency's suggested scope of the grounds for detention.[92] However, it felt that any safeguards, including reviewing the legality of detention, should be left to the Member States' national frameworks.[93]

Unlike the Council Presidencies, amendments to the proposal presented by the Parliament in September 2007 were more protective of rights. Parliament suggested that any detention ordered by an administrative authority required judicial review within 48 hours. The initial period of detention was set at three months, but an extension of up to 18 months, as suggested by the Finnish Presidency and endorsed by the German, was possible where there was a lack of co-operation or a difficulty in obtaining travel documents. However, their amendments provided that detention must be terminated if removal was not possible. The EU Council's position was markedly different. Rather than being used as a last resort, the Council suggested that detention was necessary to ensure the proper functioning of the return process, unless alternative measures could be applied.[94] It also permitted detention to carry on indefinitely, as long as there were reasonably regular reviews of detention.[95]

[88] A Baldaccini, 'The EU Directive on Return: Principles and Protests' (2010) 28 *Refugee Survey Quarterly* 114, 125.

[89] D Acosta, 'The Good, the Bad and the Ugly in EU Migration Law: Is the European Parliament Becoming Bad and Ugly? (The Adoption of Directive 2008/115: The Return Directive)' (2009) 11 *European Journal of Migration and Law* 19, 27.

[90] ibid 28–37.

[91] ibid 29.

[92] ibid 30.

[93] ibid.

[94] ibid 32.

[95] ibid.

As Acosta points out, by the end of March 2008, most issues were settled, including detention, and the Council had backtracked somewhat from its harsh position. Detention was permissible where there was a risk of absconding, or where the individual was impairing his or her removal. Judicial review of administratively ordered detention was to occur as soon as possible from the start of detention. Finally, the maximum period of detention was set at an initial six months, extendable by another 12 months in specified circumstances.

The Return Directive was finally adopted in 2008, and entered into force in 2009.[96] That year also saw the entry into force of the Treaty of Lisbon, which included in Article 79(1) of the Treaty on the Functioning of the EU (TFEU) the objective of developing a 'common immigration policy aimed at ensuring … the prevention of, and enhanced measures to combat, illegal immigration'.

The UK and Denmark chose not to take part in the Return Directive as per specific arrangements made at the time of their accession to the EU. Among the various statements of principle in its preamble, the Directive indicates in Recital 13 that coercive measures should be 'expressly subject to the principles of proportionality and effectiveness with regard to the means used and objectives pursued', and in Recital 24 that the Directive respects fundamental rights and principles recognised by the EU. Respect for fundamental rights is reiterated in Article 1, which states that the Directive is concerned with common standards for the return of illegally staying third-country nationals 'in accordance with fundamental rights'.

The Directive applies to third-country nationals staying illegally on the territory of a Member State, but it permits the Member States to exclude from its scope third-country nationals who are being returned because they have committed a qualifying crime under national law.[97] Its aim is to establish 'an effective removal and repatriation policy, based on common standards, for persons to be returned in a humane manner and with full respect for their fundamental rights and dignity'.[98] Therefore, Article 6 mandates the Member States to issue a return decision once they have determined that a third-country national is illegally staying, as defined in Article 3(2).

In addition to detention, the Directive harmonises standards in a number of areas relating to return. For example, Article 7 requires Member States to provide illegally staying third-country nationals with a period for voluntary departure of between seven and 30 days, and a possibility for extension in certain cases. Article 11 requires removal decisions to be accompanied by an

[96] Directive 2008/115/EC of the European Parliament and of the Council on 16 December 2008 on common standards and procedures in Member States for returning illegally staying third-country nationals.

[97] ibid Art 2. Art 2(2) also allows the exclusion of individuals from the Directive based on other grounds not relevant to the discussion here.

[98] ibid recital 2.

entry ban in cases where voluntary departure has not been granted, or where a removal order has not been respected. The length of the ban is not to exceed five years, and should be determined by reference to all the circumstances in the individual case. However, the five years can be exceeded in cases of serious threat to public policy, public security or national security. Finally, Chapter III provides a number of procedural safeguards applicable in the return context, such as the obligation to issue the return decision in writing, with reasons in fact and in law under Article 12(1), the right to an effective remedy to appeal or review the return decision in Article 13(1), and the right to legal advice and linguistic assistance in Article 13(3).

In March 2014, the Commission published a communication on the EU Return Policy, which included an implementation report of the Return Directive.[99] At the time, seven Member States were yet to fully transpose the Directive, despite the December 2010 deadline. The first section of the implementation report focuses on detention.[100] Several items are noteworthy, particularly the statement that implementation is greatly varied.[101] On the positive side, the report indicates an increase in the availability of alternatives to detention, and that there has been an improvement regarding available grounds for detention and certainty as to the meaning of 'risk of absconding'.[102] However, it seems that there is a wide disparity of interpretation of 'reasonable intervals' with regard to the periodic review of detention.[103] Perhaps most importantly, although there has been an overall reduction on the maximum duration of detention in the Member States, it has been raised in eight states to 18 months.[104] The implementation report did not go into detail regarding the procedural safeguards available to detainees under Article 15 of the Directive.

The Return Directive garnered much criticism, especially from international organisations. Several members of the UN Human Rights Council were particularly concerned with the provisions concerning detention. They felt that the maximum duration of 18 months was 'excessive' and emphasised that irregular migrants are not criminals, and as such should not be subject to detention at all.[105] They also pushed for a greater level of procedural protection concerning judicial review of the legality of immigration detention, recommending that

[99] Communication from the Commission to the Council and the European Parliament on EU Return Policy, COM(2014) 199 final (28 March 2014).

[100] ibid 14–21.

[101] ibid 14.

[102] ibid 15.

[103] ibid 14.

[104] ibid 16. Twelve Member States have either decreased or implemented a limit where one had not previously existed.

[105] OHCHR, 'UN Experts Express Concern about Proposed EU Return Directive' (2008) www.ohchr.org/en/NewsEvents/Pages/DisplayNews.aspx?NewsID=8440&LangID=E - sthash.vuMAfFKS.dpuf.

clear time limits be implemented in the Member States. In addition to concerns at the UN level, there were some strong reactions from Latin American leaders, who feared that the Return Directive would have a negative impact on their nationals living abroad, and also from regional organisations, such as the Organization of American States, MERCOSUR and the Union of South American Nations.[106]

In 2013, the UN Special Rapporteur on the Human Rights of Migrants, François Crépeau, issued a report which concluded that the EU Member States use detention as a means of migration control in the EU and do not seek the application of alternatives, despite the fact that they are obliged to do so.[107] Moreover, the report points out that in the time following the entry into force of the Return Directive, the use of detention actually flourished within the Member States and in countries at the EU's borders, and was often funded by the EU.[108] It was his view that the EU's persistence in viewing irregular immigration as being linked to security and crime is 'fundamentally at odds with a human rights approach'.[109] The Special Rapporteur is clearly disappointed in the immediate aftermath of the Directive, especially as the EU is uniquely placed to standardise practice regarding irregular migration in a way that is respectful of human rights.[110]

Another active critic of practice under the Return Directive has been the EU Agency for Fundamental Rights (FRA). The FRA acts as an advisory body to the EU institutions regarding Member State practice, and also plays a role in the development of EU legislation. In 2010, the FRA published a report specifically looking at the detention of third-country nationals.[111] It reviewed Member State practice in light of the Return Directive, and specifically criticised the 18-month maximum, which it considered 'a serious interference with a person's right to liberty' that should be used sparingly.[112] It also pointed out that, in light of the 18-month maximum, some Member States that had previously imposed lower maximum time limits had increased them to correspond to the 18 months in the Directive.[113]

Scholars have also spoken out against the Return Directive, particularly with regard to its 18-month detention maximum, its provision for lengthy entry bans

[106] D Acosta Arcarazo, 'Latin American Reactions to the Adoption of the Return Directive' (CEPS, 2009) 3–4.

[107] UN Human Rights Council, 'Report of the Special Rapporteur on the Human Rights of Migrants, François Crépeau: Regional Study: Management of the External Borders of the European Union and Its Impact on the Human Rights of Migrants', A/HRC/23/46 (2013) paras 47–48.

[108] ibid paras 49–50.

[109] ibid para 31.

[110] ibid para 22.

[111] EU Agency for Fundamental Rights, 'Detention of Third-Country Nationals in Return Procedures' (2010).

[112] ibid 34.

[113] ibid 33.

and its case law.[114] But Majcher also points out that, even though the Directive admonishes states to turn to detention only where alternatives cannot effectively be applied, the Directive does not obligate Member States to actively assess whether alternatives can feasibly be applied.[115] She also criticises the Directive's failure to provide for a clear presumption in favour of release, and the fact that it does not require automatic judicial review of detention.[116]

Not all of the academic opinion has been negative, however. In writing about the right to liberty in the context of EU criminal law, Mancano has commented that, in comparison to the protections afforded by the ECHR and the ECtHR, the right to liberty under the EU Charter carries enhanced safeguards.[117] Writing primarily about immigration detention, Costello points out how protection afforded by the Return Directive and the CJEU case law has surpassed that of the ECHR and ECtHR.[118] The Directive's framework has brought a necessity test into the process of determining whether someone should be detained, whereas such a test was explicitly rejected by the ECtHR in the *Saadi* case.[119] Like the UN Special Rapporteur, Costello feels that the EU occupies a unique position in the field of immigration in that the EU has the 'capacity not only to penetrate the domestic legal order, but also to shift aside other domestic norms and make way for its own "full effectiveness"'.[120] Indeed, the concept of 'effectiveness' plays a prominent part in CJEU case law under the Directive, and will be explored in detail in chapter six. Moreover, it is worth noting that the imposition of a maximum, though 18 months in duration, is nevertheless innovative at the regional level and has been resisted by the ECtHR in its case law.

When viewing the Return Directive on its own, and within the context of its initial embodiment as a proposal, it is not difficult to understand the criticism. EU involvement in this area of immigration law did have great potential in the sense that it might have developed a legal instrument which adopted the highest possible standard of protection for human rights. However, the political will

[114] See, eg Baldaccini (n 88); A Baldaccini, 'The Return and Removal of Irregular Migrants under EU Law: An Analysis of the Return Directive (2009) 11 *European Journal of Migration and Law* 1; Acosta Arcarazo (n 106) 7; on criticism of the European Parliament in the adoption of the Directive, see Acosta (n 89); G Cornelisse, 'Case Note Case C-357/09 PPU, Proceedings Concerning Said Shamilovich Kadzoev (Huchbarov) Judgment of the Court (Grand Chamber) of 30 November 2009' (2011) 48 *Common Market Law Review* 3; R Raffaelli, 'Case Note: The *Achughbabian* Case: Impact of the Return Directive on National Criminal Legislation' [2012] *Diritto Penale Contemporaneo* 176; R Raffaelli, 'The Returns Directive in Light of the *El Dridi* Judgment' (2011) 3 *Perspectives on Federalism* 32.

[115] I Majcher, '"Crimmigration" in the European Union through the Lens of Immigration Detention', Global Detention Project Working Paper No 6 (2013) 8.

[116] ibid 8.

[117] L Mancano, 'The Right to Liberty in European Union Law and Mutual Recognition in Criminal Matters' (2016) 18 *Cambridge Yearbook of Legal Studies* 215.

[118] C Costello, 'Human Rights and the Elusive Universal Subject: Immigration Detention under International Human Rights and EU Law' (2012) 19 *Indiana Journal of Global Legal Studies* 257.

[119] ibid 300. *Saadi* (n 15) is the case in the ECtHR which rejects necessity as a condition.

[120] Costello (n 117) 298.

of the Member States meant that a compromise had to be reached. Thus, the Return Directive is, in a sense, a mixed instrument – partly aimed at creating and ensuring the operation of an efficient removal process, but also aimed at respecting human rights in the implementation of that process, including with regard to the use of detention. Although it is unclear at present in which direction the case law will evolve, there is potential, as indicated later in this book, for it to take on a distinctly human rights-protecting approach, whether or not such approach is direct.

Detention is touched upon in two other pieces of legislation in the context of immigration and asylum. Article 8 of the Asylum Reception Conditions Directive permits detention when it has been determined in an individual case that it is necessary, and that alternatives to detention would not suffice.[121] It also provides an exhaustive list of six grounds for detention of asylum seekers under the Directive.[122] Article 9 includes a number of procedural guarantees for detainees, including the right to written reasons for detention, the possibility for speedy judicial review of detention, the right to free legal assistance and a requirement that administrative procedures relevant to detention be undertaken by the state with due diligence. Article 10 regulates the conditions of detention, and Articles 11 and 12 regulate the detention of vulnerable people and families, respectively.

The Asylum Procedures Directive also refers to the use of detention, though it does not itself provide a legal basis to detain. Article 26 requires that Member States provide for the possibility of speedy judicial review of detention.[123] Both Directives unequivocally state that individuals are not to be detained for the sole reason that they are applying for asylum or other forms of international protection.[124]

III. DETENTION AUTHORITIES

Immigration enforcement is the role of the state, often through specialised branches of government departments with authority over internal matters. In both the UK and the USA, the immigration authorities consist of several departments in charge of various aspects of immigration enforcement, such as visas or border controls. The situation differs in the EU because the EU shares

[121] EU Reception Conditions Directive 2013/33, Art 8(2).

[122] ibid Art 8(3).

[123] EU Asylum Procedures Directive 2013/32.

[124] EU Asylum Reception Conditions Directive 2013/33, Art 8(1); EU Asylum Procedures Directive 2013/32, Art 26(1). Liberty is addressed by the EU outside the context of immigration law in a number of legislative instruments, including the European Arrest Warrant Framework Decision 2002/584/JHA, the Framework Decision on the mutual recognition of criminal judgment imposing custodial sentences or measures involving the deprivation of liberty 2008/909/JHA and the Framework Decision on the mutual recognition of decisions on supervision measures imposed as alternatives to detention 2009/829/JHA.

competence over immigration matters with the Member States.[125] Therefore, though the EU regulates some aspects of detention in its legislation, it does not manage the day-to-day implementation of detention in the Member States. In this section, there is consequently no discussion of authorities at the EU level.

A. United Kingdom

Immigration and asylum policy is regulated by three bodies in the Home Office, the head of which is the Secretary of State for the Home Department (SSHD).[126] UK Visas and Immigration (UKVI) manages decisions on entry and stay, citizenship applications and asylum applications. Immigration Enforcement is tasked with preventing abuse of the system and ensuring that immigration is in line with government policy. Border Force is tasked with overseeing immigration and customs controls.

In addition to the Home Office structure, there are two immigration and asylum chambers within the First-tier and Upper Tribunals. The tribunals handle agency decisions (eg visa refusals, asylum refusals and deportation decisions), rather than decisions to detain, although the First-tier Tribunal has jurisdiction to consider bail applications.[127] Decisions from the Immigration and Asylum Chamber of the First-tier Tribunal are appealable to the same Chamber in the Upper Tribunal, and Upper Tribunal decisions can be appealed to the Court of Appeal.

B. United States

The Department of Justice (DOJ) and the Department of Homeland Security (DHS) have concurrent jurisdiction over immigration detention. Prior to the

[125] Though the Member States' national authorities manage their own borders, the EU established the European Border and Coast Guard in 2016 to ensure 'integrated border management at the external borders' of the EU. The establishing Regulation does not manage any aspects of immigration detention. See Regulation 2016/1624/EU of the European Parliament and of the Council of 14 September 2016 on the European Border and Coast Guard and amending Regulation 2016/399/EU of the European Parliament and of the Council and repealing Regulation No 863/2007/EC of the European Parliament and of the Council, Council Regulation No 2007/2004/EC and Council Decision 2005/267/EC.

[126] These two departments were formerly together in one department called the UK Border Agency, which split in 2013 after the Home Secretary assessed performance by the Border Agency as poor.

[127] Some scholars have suggested that agency decision-making, including on whether or not to detain, has suffered in quality, not just in the Home Office, but in many other agencies. See, eg R Thomas, 'Administrative Justice, Better Decisions and Organisational Learning' (2015) 1 *Public Law* 111; Independent Chief Inspector of Borders and Immigration, 'The Effectiveness and Impact of Immigration Detention Casework' (2012) ch 4; Administrative Justice & Tribunals Council, 'Right First Time' (2011); Administrative Justice & Tribunals Council, 'Right First Time' (2011); L Weber and L Gelsthorpe, 'Deciding to Detain: How Decisions to Detain Asylum Seekers Are Made at Ports of Entry' (Institute of Criminology, University of Cambridge, 2000).

entry into force of the Homeland Security Act of 2002,[128] the sole authority was the DOJ. The Attorney General, through the now-defunct Immigration and Naturalization Service (INS), had the power to detain non-citizens pending deportation under the INA.[129] Once the Homeland Security Act passed in 2002, however, the INS was disbanded and the job of regulating detention was given to the DHS and the Secretary of Homeland Security.[130]

Like the UK Home Office, there are two immigration departments within the DHS: Customs and Border Protection (for border enforcement), and Immigration and Customs Enforcement (ICE) (for enforcement in the interior of the USA, including immigration detention).[131] Within the DOJ, the Executive Office for Immigration Review (EOIR) is responsible for immigration adjudication. It encompasses three units: the Office of the Chief Immigration Judge (which comprises a number of immigration courts throughout the USA), the Board of Immigration Appeals (BIA) and the Office of the Chief Administrative Hearing Officer.[132] Decisions of the BIA can be appealed to the federal Courts of Appeal, though, as will be discussed in chapter four, their judicial review powers have been extensively limited by the IIRIRA and AEDPA.

C. European Union

Authorities within the EU context do not closely mirror the UK and USA because of the shared competence over migration between the EU and the Member States.[133] This means that both are able to legislate in this area as much as they wish, but the Member States can only act if the EU has not. Thus, in the field of irregular migration, the EU has chosen to harmonise only provisions relating to the return of illegally staying third-country nationals. Because its legal form is the directive, the Member States are only bound to the result to be achieved, and can choose their own methods of implementation.[134]

In Article 15, the Return Directive sets out a framework for the detention of illegally staying third-country nationals that must be implemented by the Member States. Subject to these requirements, the Member States retain the

[128] Pub L 107-296, 116 Stat 2135, enacted 25 November 2002.

[129] INA, s 236(a) reads: 'On a warrant issued by the Attorney General, an alien may be arrested and detained pending a decision on whether the alien is to be removed from the United States.'

[130] ibid ss 441, 451, 471. However, the Congressional Research Service has pointed out that, effectively, the language of the INA has remained such that both the DOJ and DHS have authority over immigration law, and highlights that this issue is by no means clear. See Congressional Research Service, 'Immigration-Related Detention: Current Legislative Issues' (12 January 2012) 2.

[131] The US Citizenship and Immigration Services deals with applications for immigration benefits, eg visas, work permits, but that is not relevant to this book.

[132] Details of each of these units are available on the EOIR website: www.justice.gov/eoir/eoir-organization-chart.

[133] See section II.C above.

[134] TFEU, Art 288.

competence to regulate detention in other circumstances. Because this book is concerned with the activity of the EU as a whole, individual Member State practice under Article 15 is not considered. Rather, this book considers judgments of the CJEU in response to preliminary references from national courts concerning the application of the Directive. The details of this are discussed below.

IV. GROUNDS FOR DETENTION

Each legislative instrument considered in this book includes a number of grounds upon which a decision to detain can be based. These grounds typically relate to aspects of entry and removal. For example, individuals can be detained upon arrival to determine whether they may lawfully be granted entry, or they may be detained after a removal or deportation order has been entered against them while travel arrangements are made. When a state determines that detention is appropriate, it is typically based on an assessment that the individual poses a risk of flight or harm to the community. In the context of the EU Return Directive, the grounds for detaining are necessarily limited to the return process. This section sets out the grounds for detention and some concerns regarding risk, but discussion of how these provisions operate in practice is reserved until chapter five.

A. United Kingdom

The power to detain is set out in Schedules 2 and 3 of the 1971 Act, and in the UK Borders Act 2007. They empower immigration officers and the SSHD to order detention in a number of circumstances. Schedule 2, section 16 addresses situations of removal and allows detention pending: (i) examination by an immigration officer or a medical inspector; (ii) a decision whether to grant or deny entry; and (iii) removal (ie once the order has been made). The latter power allows for the possibility of detention where there are 'reasonable grounds' to suspect that a person might be removable, prior to a formal removal decision being made.

Schedule 3, section 16 concerns deportation and detention, and permits the detention of individuals: (i) for whom there has been made a recommendation for deportation by a court pending the making of a deportation order (this is mandatory unless the court or SSHD directs otherwise); (ii) following notice of a decision to make a deportation order; and (iii) where a deportation order is in force, pending removal.[135]

[135] Within Sch 3, there are more detailed grounds for detention. For example, para 2(1) permits detention where a recommendation for deportation has been made by a court; para 2(2) covers detention where a person has been given notice that a deportation order may be made against

Finally, sections 32 and 36 of the UK Borders Act 2007 permit detention of those who have served a period of imprisonment of at least 12 months: (i) while the Secretary of State determines whether the automatic deportation provisions in section 32 apply; (ii) once the Secretary of State determines that they do; and (iii) while the deportation order is pending. Once the deportation order is made, section 36(2) requires the SSHD to exercise the detention power unless he or she determines that detention is inappropriate.[136]

B. United States

It can be difficult to tease out the relevant legal framework for detention in the USA, especially regarding how to challenge detention, and the procedures and standards that apply. To aid in this endeavour, this section will focus on the main statutory and regulatory structure surrounding detention. The governing statute is the INA, which was codified in Title 8 of the United States Code (USC) and implemented through regulations in Title 8 of the Code of Federal Regulations (CFR).[137] This book will refer to the provisions as numbered in the INA.

The INA gives the DHS the authority to detain non-citizens in several circumstances, including: (i) detention pending a decision on removal; and (ii) detention pending removal once a final removal order has been issued. However, it should be noted that, though not considered in this book, special detention regimes exist for asylum seekers,[138] juveniles,[139] detention pending a decision on admissibility (at the borders)[140] and the use of immigration detainers by local law enforcement agencies.[141] Non-citizens who are in the USA lawfully may be

him or her by the Secretary of State; and para 2(3) permits detention once a deportation order is in force. See *R (Qaderi) v SSHD* [2008] EWHC 1033 (Admin) 24.

[136] As noted above, arriving asylum seekers who do not fall within any of those categories will be detained automatically pending a determination of their claim. However, as that is outside the scope of this book, it will not be discussed.

[137] The USC should be considered the law, whereas the CFR consists of implementing regulations. This book refers to the provisions in the INA and, where relevant, the CFR.

[138] INA, s 235(b)(1)(B)(iii)(IV); ICE, 'Parole of Arriving Aliens Found to Have a Credible Fear of Persecution or Torture', Directive No 11002.1 (2009), effective 4January 2010, paras 4.4, 6.2.

[139] 8 CFR 1236.3(a)–(d); EOIR Benchbook, 'Bond/Custody' (2008) s E(5)(b) www.justice.gov/eoir/vll/benchbook/tools/Bond Guide.htm.

[140] INA, s 235(b)(2)(A).

[141] A detainer is essentially a form that is issued to local law enforcement agencies by ICE informing the local agencies that ICE intends to take custody of a non-citizen that was apprehended by local law enforcement or released into their custody following completion of a criminal sentence. A non-citizen may be held by local law enforcement for up to 48 hours (not including weekends and holidays) until ICE can take custody. If ICE is unable to take custody of the non-citizen, he or she must be released. See INA, ss 103(a)(3), 287(d)(3); 8 CFR 287.7(d). Some states' local law agencies have questioned the legitimacy of this regime. See, eg *Galarza v Szalczyk* (3d Cir 2013) 745 F3d 634, in which the Court of Appeals for the Third Circuit held that detainers are not mandatory and that therefore local law enforcement may be held liable for the wrongful detention of non-citizens. In addition, under President Trump, ICE issued a new detainer form for use by local police which provides for a broader scope for use of detainers for any non-national who ICE believes may be subject to removal.

subject to detention if, for example, they have breached conditions of entry, or if they have committed crimes that qualify them for removal. Status as a permanent resident does not change this.

(i) Detention Pending a Final Removal Order

Section 236 of the INA provides the general power to detain non-citizens pending a decision on removal from the USA. The detention power under section 236(a) is discretionary. The DHS may release the non-citizen on bond (see chapter four, section III.B), and has 48 hours to make this determination after apprehension of the non-citizen.[142] The determination of whether release is appropriate differs according to what type of detention is at issue, but at its root is whether the individual poses a danger or a risk of flight. For example, eligible non-citizens who have not yet received a final order of removal to obtain release must demonstrate to the satisfaction of the Attorney General that they do not pose a danger to people or property, and that they are likely to appear for any future proceedings.[143]

Section 236(c) provides that 'criminal aliens' must be detained pending a decision on removal. The arrival of mandatory detention for aggravated felons began to complicate what had once been a relatively straightforward framework: generally, anyone who was inadmissible was subject to indefinite detention and anyone who was removable could only be detained for six months.[144] This clear dividing line began to blur in 1988, when the Anti-Drug Abuse Act created the concept of mandatory pre-removal order detention for individuals convicted of aggravated felonies, which subjected all non-citizens to detention without a six-month limit, whether they were excludable or deportable.[145] Because this spawned several legal challenges, especially by non-citizens with permanent resident status, an amendment was passed in 1991 which allowed for the release of aggravated felons with permanent residence after an individualised hearing on whether they are a flight risk or a danger to the community.[146] But that

See ICE Detainer Policy at www.ice.gov/detainer-policy. See also J Rivas, 'ICE Quietly Updates Rule to Make it Easier to Detain Even More Migrants' (fusion.net, 24 March 2017) http://fusion.net/ice-quietly-updates-rule-to-make-it-easier-to-detain-ev-1793859312. *cf* the discussion on Operation Nexus in the UK in s II.A above.

[142] 8 CFR s 287.3(d). That provision contains an exception that provides DHS with 'an additional reasonable period of time' in an emergency or extraordinary circumstance.

[143] INA, s 236(c)(2); 8 CFR 236.1(c)(8).

[144] Martin (n 51) 52, 59.

[145] The Anti-Drug Abuse Act of 1988, s 7343, Pub L No 100-690, 102 Stat 4181, 4470, added this provision through a new s 242(a)(2) of the INA.

[146] Immigration Act of 1990, s 504(a), Pub L No 101-649, 104 Stat 4978, 5049. This again amended s 242(a)(2) of the INA: 'The Attorney General shall release from custody an alien who is lawfully admitted for permanent residence on bond or such other conditions as the Attorney General may prescribe if the Attorney General determines that the alien is not a threat to the community and that the alien is likely to appear before any scheduled hearings.' This provision can now be found in s 241(a)(6) of the INA.

progress was reversed in 1996 with the expansion in the AEDPA of the concept of aggravated felony, a repeal of the 1991 amendment providing for a review of permanent residents subject to detention and a return to the indefinite detention as enacted in 1988.[147]

Today, the mandatory detention provisions provide that the following non-citizens must be detained pending a decision on removal: (i) those convicted of certain crimes, including aggravated felonies as defined in section 101(a)(43) of the INA;[148] and (ii) those inadmissible or deportable on grounds of terrorism.[149] These provisions are also applicable to applicants at the border.

(ii) Detention Following a Final Removal Order

Once a final removal order has been issued, non-citizens must be detained during the 90-day removal period under section 241(a) of the INA.[150] This is known as post-removal order detention. A removal order becomes final, and the 90-day removal period begins, once 30 days have elapsed from its issue and the non-citizen has not filed a petition for review.[151] Where the non-citizen has filed for review and the court has issued a stay of removal, the removal order becomes final on the date of the court's final order.[152] Where a non-citizen is in federal custody (ie not for immigration purposes), the removal order will become final once he or she is released.[153] The DHS has an agreement with the Second Circuit according to which it will cease attempting to effect removal of a non-citizen if that non-citizen has a motion for a stay of removal pending with the Second Circuit.[154] This is treated as the equivalent of a court-ordered stay of removal and can therefore affect the date upon which a removal order becomes final. This is considered in more detail in chapter five, section VII.B.

Celaya argues that detention during the 90-day removal period is constitutionally suspect because of deficient procedural safeguards. There is no requirement of necessity, the burden of proof to demonstrate that detention is improper is on the individual detainee and there is little opportunity to challenge this type of detention.[155] Indeed, these concerns also apply to mandatory pre-removal order detention, and will be discussed in chapters five to seven.

[147] AEDPA, s 440(c), amending INA, s 242(a)(2).
[148] INA, s 236(c)(1)(A) through (C).
[149] ibid s 236(c)(1)(D).
[150] See also 8 CFR 241.3(a).
[151] INA, ss 241(a)(1)(B)(i), 242(b)(1).
[152] ibid s 241(a)(1)(B)(ii).
[153] ibid s 241(a)(1)(B)(iii).
[154] See, eg *Agoro v District Director of ICE* 2010 WL 9976 (SDNY) 2; *Mathews v Philips* 2013 WL 5288166 (WDNY) 3; *Charran v Philips* 2014 WL 296429 (WDNY) 6.
[155] GA Celaya, 'US Immigration Detention: Policy and Procedure from a Human Rights Perspective' (2010) 5 *Intercultural Human Rights Law Review* 177.

Detention often continues beyond the 90-day removal period.[156] Indeed, this is the basis for the majority of habeas applications considered in Celaya's thesis and will be explored in more detail in several parts of this book.

C. European Union

The Return Directive rejected the proposal's use of the term 'temporary custody' and instead named Chapter IV 'Detention for the Purpose of Removal'. Therefore, in the context of the Directive, individuals can only be detained if they are the subject of return procedures. The first paragraph on detention in the Directive makes clear that detention is only to be used where 'other sufficient but less coercive measures can be applied effectively in a specific case'.[157] This means that detention is a last resort and a determination of whether detention is appropriate must depend on the individual's specific circumstances. The Directive provides that detention is permissible where there is a risk of absconding or where the third-country national impedes the return or removal process.[158]

V. NON-STATUTORY GUIDANCE ON DETENTION DECISION-MAKING

In addition to legislative management of detention, the UK and US authorities have published non-statutory guidance relating to immigration detention. Whereas, in the UK, this guidance specifically regulates certain aspects of decision-making, in the USA, guidance is confined to addressing conditions in detention centres. In the EU, there is no non-statutory guidance on the operation of the Return Directive, including its detention provisions.

A. United Kingdom

Beyond the statutory footing, the actual implementation of detention is governed by policy guidance, which is largely not subject to parliamentary scrutiny and is frequently updated.[159] Though not formally binding in practice,

[156] INA, s 241(a)(1)(C), (6).
[157] EU Return Directive 2008/115/EC, Art 15(1).
[158] ibid.
[159] The Immigration Rules (www.gov.uk/guidance/immigration-rules) may also be applicable to the framework for entry to and exit from the UK. They provide the details of the powers set out in statutes, and are considered legislation that must be laid before Parliament. However, it is fairly simple for the Immigration Rules to be amended, and hundreds of amendments are made yearly. The Immigration Rules do not cover immigration detention – it is only referred to briefly in relation to the deportation power. See Immigration Rules, Part 13: Deportation, paras 362, 382.

guidance may provide grounds for judicial review if a government official fails to follow published policy.[160] Chapter 55 of the Enforcement Instructions and Guidance (EIG) issued by UKVI addresses initial decisions to detain, and its content is largely derived from statutory and case law at the domestic and European levels. It begins with a presumption in favour of temporary admission or release, though there is no corresponding presumption of release in any immigration statute. This presumption is repeated later in relation to the obligation to consider alternatives to detention, and to examine each case on its own merits. The guidance states that 'there must be strong grounds for believing that a person will not comply with conditions of temporary admission or temporary release for detention to be justified'.[161]

Chapter 55 includes a number of provisions aimed at helping UKVI officials make detention determinations, including a list of acceptable reasons for detention (eg risk of absconding, pendency of removal) and categories of vulnerable people who should not be detained (eg mentally ill, pregnant women, children).[162] It also supplies a number of procedural obligations, such as providing detainees with written reasons for detention and requirements for periodic reviews of continuing detention.[163]

B. United States

Unlike the UK, there is no applicable guidance aimed at assisting immigration officials in the USA in their determinations of whether detention is appropriate where they have discretion to detain. However, at the time of writing, President Trump had signed an executive order that directs the Secretary of Homeland Security to produce guidance for the DHS officials 'regarding the appropriate and consistent use of lawful detention authority under the INA'.[164]

In addition, there is evidence that where officials have the discretion to detain, such discretion is often exercised arbitrarily based on practical concerns,

[160] JN Stefanelli, 'Disclosure in Immigration Bail Proceedings: Ensuring Equality of Arms' (2016) 30 *Journal of Immigration Asylum and Nationality Law* 301, 314.

[161] UK Visas and Immigration, 'Enforcement Instructions and Guidance', ch 55 (EIG ch 55) s 55.3 (last updated 13 January 2015). However, when it comes to the detention of foreign national prisoners following their sentence, the EIG suggests that the presumption in favour of liberty may be trumped by a concern that the public may be harmed as a result of reoffending, or by the risk of absconding, if the person's history suggests this would be a particular risk (s 55.3A).

[162] EIG ch 55, ss 55.1.1, 55.1.3, 55.10. There are also a number of laws and policies relating to the detention of children and families, eg Borders, Citizenship and Immigration Act 2009, c 11, s 55, received Royal Assent on 21 July 2009; EIG ch 55, s 55.9.3. See also Home Office, Detention Services Order 03/2016, 'Consideration of Detainee Placement in the Detention Estate' (April 2016). See also Immigration Act 2016, ss 59–60.

[163] EIG ch 55, s 55.7–8.

[164] Executive Order, 'Border Security and Immigration Enforcement Improvements' (25 January 2017) s 6.

such as available bed space.[165] Consequently, there is a lack of uniformity in detention decisions, which, Gryll argues, makes officials reluctant to release non-mandatory detainees.[166] In addition, since 2013, ICE has employed an automated risk assessment tool to assist it in determining whether detention is appropriate. The tool assigns a public safety and flight risk assessment score, based on the DHS enforcement priorities.[167] The risk assessment is conducted by ICE for all non-citizens entering custody, though it appears it is not used for those who qualify for mandatory detention.[168] The system relies on certain data about the individual at issue being entered into the computerised system. This includes information relating to family ties, criminal record and history of drug or alcohol abuse.[169] The system makes a recommendation, but the ICE official takes the final decision, with confirmation by a superior officer. Very little is publicly available concerning the operation of the risk assessment tool. It has been criticised by some as being weighted in favour of detention, and therefore not resolving the problem of over-detention, which it was designed, in part, to address.[170] In any case, its automated nature leaves no room for qualitative assessment in a way similar to that which is inherently possible in the UK with the EIG, which provides only a list of factors to consider when making the decision to detain. Though the ICE official has the final say, the system does not permit officials to input data in free text fields, which would allow for additional explanation or qualification of the data input into the system.[171]

VI. ADDITIONAL DETENTION PROVISIONS IN THE RETURN DIRECTIVE

While there is no non-statutory guidance on detention in the EU, the Return Directive includes a number of other provisions aimed at safeguarding detainees' rights and providing access to justice. These provisions are important not

[165] S Gryll, 'Immigration Detention Reform: No Band-Aid Desired' (2011) 60 *Emory Law Journal* 1211.

[166] ibid 1232.

[167] M Noferi and R Koulish, 'The Immigration Detention Risk Assessment' (2014) 29 *Georgetown Immigration Law Journal* 45, 60–61.

[168] ibid 63, fn 130.

[169] ibid 63, fn 132.

[170] ibid 60. Noferi and Koulish note that an independent expert for the UNHCR expressed concern that the tool 'risks becoming a bureaucratic, tick-box exercise and may lead only to artificial individual assessments rather than real ones': A Edwards, 'Back to Basics: The Right to Liberty and Security of Person and 'Alternatives to Detention' of Refugees, Asylum-Seekers, Stateless Persons and Other Migrants' (UNHCR, 2011) 80 http://www.refworld.org/docid/4dc935fd2.html. See also R Koulish, 'Immigration Detention in the Risk Classification Assessment Era' (2016) 16 *Connecticut Public Interest Law Journal* 1, looking at the assessment tool in practice in Baltimore, Maryland.

[171] Noferi and Koulish (n 167) 63.

only from a constitutional and fundamental rights point of view, but because some of them are the subject of the case studies discussed in subsequent chapters.

In addition to the detention provisions discussed above, the Directive imposes a due diligence requirement on immigration authorities: detention can only be maintained for as long as removal arrangements are in progress and pursued diligently, and must be as short as possible. The maximum period of detention is 18 months, comprising an initial six-month period that can exceptionally be extended by up to 12 months where removal has not yet occurred due a lack of co-operation by the third-country national, or where there is difficulty obtaining the requisite documents from third countries.[172]

The Return Directive also introduces procedural rules requiring detention to be ordered in writing and for reasons in fact and law to be provided to the third-country national.[173] It permits detention ordered by 'judicial or administrative authorities',[174] but where it is ordered by administrative authorities, Member States may choose whether to provide for 'speedy judicial review of the lawfulness of detention' or to grant third-country nationals the right to take proceedings for such a review, in which case the third-country national must be informed of such right.[175] Periodic reviews of detention must be undertaken at 'reasonable intervals' either at the request of the third-country national or *ex officio*, and a judicial authority need only be involved in the review in cases of prolonged detention.[176] Finally, the Directive makes explicit that where detention is not lawful, the third-country national must be released. Detention will not be considered lawful where appropriate grounds do not exist, or where it appears that removal is no longer reasonably possible.[177] There is no overt statement as to whether a violation of the procedural requirements will result in release.

Unlike the statutory law in the UK and USA, the Return Directive provides a detailed test of the legality of detention. Though Article 15 does not cover every eventuality, for example regarding the procedure applicable to decisions to extend detention, it does provide the CJEU with the main standards which it is required to apply to cases before it. This is in contrast to the UK and USA, where the law is quite vague – providing a basic power to detain in certain circumstances – and does not go into detail concerning how to determine whether continued detention is lawful. Rather, such standards were developed by the courts: in the USA, the Supreme Court, and in the UK, the Administrative Court. This will be discussed in chapter four below.

[172] EU Return Directive 2008/115/EC, Art 15(6).
[173] ibid Art 15(2).
[174] ibid.
[175] ibid.
[176] ibid Art 15(3).
[177] ibid Art 15(5).

VII. CONCLUSION

This chapter has demonstrated the motivations behind the modern use of immigration detention in the UK, USA and EU. The UK and USA share a similar history of modest use during war or in response to other perceived threats which, rather than decreasing in peace time, evolved into something considered so necessary to enforce immigration law that its appropriateness as a means of enforcing immigration law was barely discussed in its own right by Congress or Parliament as immigration legislation developed. It is interesting to contrast the detailed discussion of detention in the development of the Return Directive, which was borne out of a desire to create uniformity among the Member States not only with regard to admission standards, but also with regard to enforcement measures. Indeed, though the EU Member States may identify with the experience of the UK and USA in the context of their domestic detention frameworks, the EU as a legal entity does not have the same history of using detention, and comes from a background where discussion of fundamental rights is a necessary and routine aspect of lawmaking.

The regulation of detention in the three jurisdiction shares similar qualities. The grounds for detention under the legislative frameworks are roughly aimed at ensuring removal and preventing harm. However, the quality of the legal bases for detention differs across the three. In the USA, the legislation provides broad grounds for detention and is accompanied by federal regulations which detail some aspects of detention, but not all. In the UK, a similar system prevails, though the guidance is more detailed and considers explicitly that release should be favoured. Finally, the EU Return Directive aims to not only provide the legal basis for detention of illegally staying third-country nationals, but also detailed standards for implementation.

More importantly, the value of the Return Directive lies in the fact that it places limits on Member State sovereignty over immigration and the criminalisation of immigration.[178] It permits the Member States to implement coercive measures to ensure removal, ranging from granting a period of voluntary return to imposing detention where necessary. However, the Member States must comply with the Return Directive in the implementation of these coercive measures. The principle of the primacy of EU law obliges the Member States to give priority to EU law where it conflicts with national law, the result of which is that Member State policy on detention in the context of returning illegally staying third-country nationals must comply with EU law, including judgments of the CJEU. As Costello points out, this means that the EU has the power to 'penetrate' national legal orders and change them in a way that other

[178] V Mitsilegas, *The Criminalisation of Migration in Europe: Challenges for Human Rights and the Rule of Law* (Springer, 2015).

organisations, such as the Council of Europe, cannot.[179] The value of this should not be underestimated.

The following chapter focuses on modern judicial intervention in the states' immigration powers and examines judgments that have significantly shaped the way the courts evaluate the legality of immigration detention today. Prior to doing so, the chapter provides an overview of the mechanisms for judicial review in each jurisdiction.

[179] Costello (n 117) 298.

4

Judicial Intervention into Detention

I. INTRODUCTION

THOUGH THERE ARE specialised immigration courts in the UK and the USA, judicial review of the legality of detention is conducted in the standard court system. In the UK, review takes place in the Administrative Court through judicial review or habeas corpus, while in the USA, review takes place in the federal district courts through habeas corpus hearings. The situation in the EU is different because the Member States' national courts are responsible for judicial review. However, because this book evaluates the operation of the EU Return Directive at the EU level, the CJEU is the relevant court that evaluates the Member States' implementation of the Return Directive's detention provisions. Ultimately, the nature and functioning of these courts can influence the way in which the lawfulness of detention is assessed. A specific discussion of this is presented in chapter seven.

After providing an overview of those courts and the judges sitting on them, this chapter will review the procedures for judicial review available in each jurisdiction, as well as discuss the status of access to justice for immigration detainees. Finally, the chapter will outline some of the influential case law on immigration detention using the review procedures just described. This discussion is not restricted to cases emanating from the courts under review in this book, but also includes judgments from superior courts that have influenced the development of jurisprudence at the lower levels.

Emphasising judicial intervention is important not only because it is the main line of inquiry in this book, but because it is the role of the courts to ensure that the detention legislation is being applied according to its own terms as well as with respect to constitutional principles. Any gaps left in the statutory law regarding its appropriate implementation must be filled by the courts. This is an important function.

II. COURTS AND JUDGES

The three courts included in this book are quite different from each other. The main point of similarity between the Administrative Court in the UK and the NY federal district courts is that they are competent to hear challenges to the legality of detention and order release if detention is unlawful. After that, the differences abound. The CJEU does not even share that point of comparison because it is not empowered to make legality determinations in this context – it can only give an opinion as to the compatibility of national law with EU law.

None of these courts are specialist courts in the sense that the US immigration courts or the UK immigration tribunals are. They are multi-jurisdictional courts, dealing with varied matters every day, and they have large dockets. That is not to say that they are unable to build up the sort of specialism that comes with time and experience, however.

The judges that sit on these courts are appointed through different processes, which have each attracted criticism at one time or another. The main point of distinction is that the federal district judges are appointed through political process. That is, the President of the USA nominates candidates for approval by Senate majority. In the UK, Administrative Court judges are selected based on merit by a panel of people, including retired judges. Finally, justices of the CJEU are nominated by their home Member State and an independent advisory panel assists in the determination of whether the candidates are suitable.

A. The Administrative Court

The Administrative Court is part of the Queen's Bench Division in the High Court of England and Wales, which is a senior court.[1] The Administrative Court in particular deals primarily with administrative law matters and exercises a supervisory jurisdiction over lower courts and tribunals through judicial review.[2] The Administrative Court also functions as a constitutional court which reviews the powers of public bodies[3] and strives to ensure that individuals are treated fairly by public bodies.[4] In 2018, the Administrative Court received 3,597 judicial review applications, of which 1,793 concerned civil immigration and asylum, including applications for judicial review of detention. Separate statistics on immigration detention cases are not published.[5] At the time the statistics were published, only 538 cases of the whole had been granted permission to proceed.

[1] Senior Courts Act 1981, as amended by the Constitutional Reform Act 2005, c 4, received Royal Assent on 24 March 2005, s 59, sch 11, para 26(1).

[2] Ministry of Justice, 'Types of Cases' www.justice.gov.uk/courts/rcj-rolls-building/administrative-court/types-of-cases.

[3] S Nason, 'Regionalisation of the Administrative Court' (2009) 14 *Judicial Review* 1, para 8.

[4] *Chief Constable of North Wales Police v Evans* [1982] UKHL 10 (Hailsham LC, p 1160).

[5] See Ministry of Justice, 'Civil Justice Statistics Quarterly: October to December 2018' www.gov.uk/government/statistics/civil-justice-statistics-october-to-december-2018.

Administrative Court decisions are appealable to the Court of Appeal and the Supreme Court on points of law. Below the High Court are the magistrates' courts, which deal with the majority of criminal cases; the county courts, which handle most civil claims; and the Crown Court, which handles criminal trials. In addition to being bound by its own prior decisions, the Administrative Court is bound by decisions of the Court of Appeal and the Supreme Court.[6] Its decisions are binding on lower courts; however, because the Administrative Court has original jurisdiction to review the legality of detention, the judgments in this book are not applied by any lower courts. This does not, however, mean that Administrative Court decisions have no reach beyond the parties; rather, its judgments are binding on the Home Office and can impact national detention policy. The impact of the *Hardial Singh* judgment (discussed below) on detention policy is an obvious example. Detention guidance incorporates the *Hardial Singh* principles in a section on limitations on statutory powers to detain.[7]

Since 2005, judges in the High Court have been appointed based on recommendations by an independent Judicial Appointments Commission. Prior to this, they were appointed by the Lord Chancellor, a politically appointed officer of the state who had the dual role of head of the judiciary and member of the Cabinet. This posed obvious problems for the notion of separation of powers and was criticised by many, mostly because candidates were encouraged to apply because of their social and professional connections, which meant that, ultimately, the judiciary was filled with judges from a certain elite social class.[8] Justices of the Administrative Court, though specialised in public law, do not spend their time solely on administrative matters; rather, like all High Court judges, they hear other civil and criminal cases.[9] In addition, deputy High Court judges hear cases in the Administrative Court.[10] These judges are typically senior practitioners who sit part-time, as needed. Most High Court judges are barristers who have the status of Queen's Counsel, indicating their experience in trial advocacy. Though appointment to the Court of Appeal is also a matter of open competition, most judges there are selected from the High Court, based on their experience.[11]

B. Federal District Courts

The US federal district courts are also first instance courts when it comes to judging the legality of immigration detention. Their decisions are appealable

[6] K Malleson, *The Legal System*, 3rd edn (Oxford University Press, 2007) 7.12.

[7] UK Visas and Immigration, 'Enforcement Instructions and Guidance', ch 55 (EIG ch 55) s 55.1.4.1.

[8] S Shetreet and S Turenne, *Judges on Trial: The Independence and Accountability of the English Judiciary* (Cambridge University Press, 2013) 103, 107.

[9] H Woolf et al, *De Smith's Judicial Review*, 7th edn (Sweet & Maxwell, 2013) 16-005.

[10] Senior Courts Act 1981, s 9, as amended by the Crime and Courts Act 2013, sch 14, ss 2–3.

[11] Shetreet and Turenne (n 8) 136. See also the Senior Courts Act 1981, s 10(3)(b).

before the federal courts of appeals and the US Supreme Court, if it grants certiorari. There are 94 district courts across 12 regional circuits, with at least one court in each state (including the District of Columbia).[12] In 2018, there were 1,587 immigration detention habeas cases filed in the federal district courts.[13] Of the 1,587 cases, 131 came from the Second Circuit, and within that, 129 came from the New York federal district courts.[14] Overall, the NY federal district courts saw 4,124 civil cases[15] and 3,220 criminal cases filed during that period.[16]

The district courts originally had jurisdiction over low-level crime and offences relating to admiralty law,[17] importation and trade.[18] The Judiciary Act of 1789 also imbued the federal courts with the power to issue writs of habeas corpus to inquire into the reasons for detention.[19] In 1790, district court jurisdiction was expanded to encompass specific patent and bankruptcy law issues, but they remained primarily criminal law trial courts.[20] Finally, in 1875, federal courts were given original jurisdiction over all cases arising under the Constitution, laws or treaties of the USA.[21] This has been described as 'enormous authority'.[22] Though the regulation of immigration is not specifically vested in Congress by the Constitution, the Supreme Court's creation and application of the plenary power doctrine (discussed in chapter two, section III) has effectively ensured that this is the case. Consequently, federal courts have exclusive jurisdiction over all immigration matters, including determinations of the lawfulness of detention through habeas corpus proceedings. As will be discussed more thoroughly in chapter six, in practice, federal courts are bound by their own precedent. They are also bound by decisions by the Court of Appeals in their circuit and, of course, US Supreme Court judgments.

[12] There is also a federal district court in each of the four USA territories of Puerto Rico, the Virgin Islands, Guam and the Northern Mariana Islands.

[13] Federal Court Management Statistics, Table C-3: US District Courts – Civil Cases Commenced, by Nature of Suit and District, During the 12-Month Period Ending December 31, 2018 www.uscourts.gov/statistics/table/c-3/statistical-tables-federal-judiciary/2018/12/31.

[14] ibid.

[15] ibid.

[16] Federal Court Management Statistics, Table D-3: US District Courts – Criminal Defendants Commenced (Excluding Transfers), by Offense and District, During the 12-Month Period Ending December 31, 2018 www.uscourts.gov/statistics/table/d-3/statistical-tables-federal-judiciary/2018/12/31.

[17] At the time, most district courts were located on the Eastern seaboard. See EC Surrency, *History of the Federal Courts* (Oceana Publications, 2002) 66.

[18] They shared jurisdiction with the circuit courts over alien tort suits where the law of nations or a treaty was involved, where the government was the plaintiff in a suit over $100 or less and suits against consuls. See Judiciary Act 1789, ch 20, 1 Stat 77, s 9.

[19] ibid s 14.

[20] Surrency (n 17) 66.

[21] Judiciary Act 1875, 18 Stat 470. It is beyond the scope of this work to elaborate on the specifics of jurisdiction. Their jurisdiction is set out in Title 28, ch 85 of the United States Code (USC).

[22] KL Lyles, *The Gatekeepers: Federal District Courts in the Political Process* (Praeger, 1997) 12.

Federal district judges are appointed for life and can only be removed in rare circumstances, usually for gross misconduct.[23] Though this is intended to ensure their independence,[24] the appointment process is, for better or worse, political in nature.[25] District judges are nominated by the President, and confirmed by the Senate by a simple majority.[26] However, in practice, if the senior senator from the judge's state is in the same political party as the President, he or she will provide the President with a list of candidates for consideration. If the senior senator is from the opposition party, then the Attorney General will take on this role.[27] Despite this overtly political process, an individual judge's experience and qualifications will also play a role.[28] Federal judges maintain their position during good behaviour,[29] and can only be removed by impeachment.[30]

The number of case filings in the district courts experienced a drastic increase in the 1960s, when they more than tripled.[31] Rather than increase the number of judges on the bench, the position of magistrate judge was created in 1968 to assist the district judges in handling this larger caseload.[32] Magistrate judges are appointed by the district court judges in the district where they will sit, through a selection panel consisting of lawyers and non-lawyers from the community. Once appointed, they sit for a period of eight years, though their term is

[23] RA Posner, *The Federal Courts* (Harvard University Press, 1996) 13, 277; US Constitution, Art II, s IV.

[24] C Guarnieri and P Pederzoli, *The Power of Judges* (Oxford University Press, 2002) 48.

[25] Law suggests that three aspects of the nomination process are worthy of criticism: (i) over-emphasis on the political ideology of candidates; (ii) the appointment of extremist judges; and (iii) 'gridlock' in the timeliness of the appointment process. See DS Law, 'Appointing Federal Judges: The President, the Senate, and the Prisoner's Dilemma' (2005) 26 *Cardozo Law Review* 479, 500.

[26] MC Tolley, 'Legal Controversies over Federal Judicial Selection in the United States' in K Malleson and PH Russell, *Appointing Judges in an Age of Judicial Power* (University of Toronto Press, 2006) 84. This is the result of tradition rather than constitutional mandate.

[27] Posner (n 23) 14.

[28] S Goldman, 'Federal Judicial Recruitment' in JB Gates and CA Johnson (eds), *The American Courts. A Critical Assessment* (Congressional Quarterly Press, 1991) 189.

[29] US Constitution, Art III, s 1.

[30] Some argue that impeachment is not the only method by which to remove federal judges. See S Prakash and SD Smith, 'How to Remove a Federal Judge' (2006) 116 *Yale Law Journal* 72.

[31] Posner (n 23) 59.

[32] ibid 131. Their appointment and powers are regulated under 28 USC, ch 43. Some districts' local rules also regulate the use of magistrate judges. See, eg US District Court for the Western District of New York, Local Rules of Civil Procedure (effective 1 January 2015), Rules 72–73; Local Rules of the US District Courts for the Southern and Eastern Districts of New York (effective 3 September 2013 with amendments), Rules 72.1–72.2. Boyd and Sievert use principal-agent theory to suggest that the decision-making of magistrate judges is influenced by the political ideologies of their district judges. See CL Boyd and JM Sievert, 'Unaccountable Justice? The Decision Making of Magistrate Judges in the Federal District Courts' (2013) 34 *Justice Systems Journal* 249, 251. Singer and Young link bench presence of district judges with procedural fairness, implying that the use of magistrate judges negatively impacts parties' procedural rights. See JM Singer and WG Young, 'Measuring Bench Presence: Federal District Judges in the Courtroom, 2008–2012' (2013) 118 *Penn State Law Review* 243.

often renewed.[33] Magistrate judges conduct a wide range of judicial functions at the behest of the district judges, including presiding over immigration detention habeas cases.[34]

C. Court of Justice of the European Union

Unlike the Administrative Court and the federal district courts, the CJEU is not empowered to make a judgment regarding the legality of detention at the national level, or to order release if detention is unlawful. The CJEU is the highest court in the EU judicial architecture. Below it sits the General Court, and a number of specialised courts, such as the European Civil Service Tribunal, whose decisions are appealable to the General Court. The basic task of the court is to ensure that 'in the interpretation and application of the Treaty the law is observed'.[35] In 2018, the CJEU received 849 cases lodged before it, 568 of which were preliminary references.[36] It is worth noting that the largest share (82) of those preliminary references was in the area of freedom, security and justice, which includes immigration policy (ie cases under the EU Return Directive).[37] Between its entry into force and the time of writing, the Return Directive has been the subject of 27 judgments, with one judgment pending.

The CJEU has jurisdiction over all areas of EU policy except that relating to the Common Foreign and Security Policy, which is a matter for the states acting collectively.[38] In addition to preliminary rulings,[39] the Court is competent to hear infringement actions against Member States and direct actions, eg reviewing the legality of legislative acts of the European institutions.[40]

The CJEU is composed of one judge per EU Member State, nominated by each Member State. The Member States have great discretion in the choice of candidates, though they must be independent 'beyond doubt'.[41] Though there is not a uniform procedure for appointing judges in the Member States, candidates are typically chosen from the national judiciary or are members of the legal profession. Since 2009, an independent advisory panel has provided opinions on

[33] Boyd and Sievert (ibid) 252.

[34] WW Schwarzer, 'Case management in the federal courts' (1996) 15 *Civil Justice Quarterly* 141, 143.

[35] Treaty on European Union, Art 19(1).

[36] Court of Justice of the European Union, 'Annual Report 2018: Judicial Activity' (2019) 121–22 https://curia.europa.eu/jcms/upload/docs/application/pdf/2019-04/_ra_2018_en.pdf.

[37] ibid 123.

[38] Art 275 TFEU.

[39] Art 267 TFEU.

[40] Arts 258–260, 268, 340 TFEU on infringement actions and Arts 263, 265 and 268 TFEU on direct actions.

[41] Art 253 TFEU.

judicial candidates to address concerns regarding objectivity and transparency to the appointments process.[42]

The judges of the CJEU are assisted by eight Advocates General, who provide advisory opinions in some, but not all, of the cases before the Court.[43] Their appointment process is the same as that which applies to the judges because they have equal status at the Court.[44] Their opinions are intended to assist the judges as they deliberate, but they are not binding on the Court. Both the judges and the Advocates General are appointed for a renewable period of six years.[45] In addition to the Advocates General, each judge has three *réferendaires*, who assist the judges with research and may draft judgments and opinions, but do not participate in deliberations.

The Court of Justice is viewed by some as lacking in democratic legitimacy, perhaps owing in part to the way in which its judges are appointed. Some suggest that its legitimacy is tied to concerns over the legitimacy of the EU as a whole,[46] while others have expressed concern that the Court has become activist, straddling the line between judicial decision maker and policymaker.[47] Grimmel argues that feelings of rampant activism are a 'myth' derived from the period during which the CJEU issued its judgments on supremacy and direct effect, and that such behaviour was legitimate in light of the context and the need for the Court to establish a European law autonomy in the early days of the EU.[48] Regardless, reforms in the Treaty of Lisbon have gone some way to addressing such concerns.

Though this book does not, by any means, attempt to offer an in-depth examination of the appointment of judges in these jurisdictions, it is interesting to note the inherently political nature of the federal courts, whose judges are

[42] Art 255 TFEU; Council Decision 2010/124/EU relating to the operating rules of the panel provided for in Article 255 of the Treaty on the Functioning of the European Union (25 February 2010) para 6. See also Third Activity Report of the Panel Provided for by Article 255 of the Treaty on the Functioning of the EU (13 December 2013) SN 1118/2014, 13–15. See also T Dumbrovský, B Petkova and M Van der Sluis, 'Judicial Appointments: The Article 255 TFEU Advisory Panel and Selection Procedures in the Member States' (2014) 51 *Common Market Law Review* 455, 458. There is also a feeling among some that certain states will select candidates who are 'anti-Europe' in an attempt to prevent encroachment by the Court into areas of national competence. See S Kenney, 'The Members of the Court of Justice of the European Communities' (1998) 5 *Columbia Journal of European Law* 101, 128.

[43] Art 252 TFEU.

[44] A Arnull, *The European Union and its Court of Justice*, 2nd edn (Oxford University Press, 2006) 19.

[45] Art 253 TFEU.

[46] See, eg GA Caldeira and JL Gibson, 'The Legitimacy of the Court of Justice in the European Union: Models of Institutional Support' (1995) 89(2) *The American Political Science Review* 356.

[47] See, eg H Rasmussen, *On Law and Policy in the European Court of Justice: A Comparative Study in Judicial Policymaking* (Martinus Nijhoff, 1986).

[48] A Grimmel, '"This Is Not Life As It Is Lived Here": The Court of Justice of the EU and the Myth of Judicial Activism in the Foundational Period of Integration through Law' (2014) 7 *European Journal of Legal Studies* 56, 63.

appointed not only with regard to experience, but also political affiliation. This is seen less in the UK, which only relatively recently established an independent selection panel. The extent to which politics plays a role in the nomination of CJEU judges is unclear, though it has been suggested that, even though the judges are not generally viewed as representing the interests of their home states, they do ensure that the national context is taken into consideration during deliberation on cases.[49] The independence of the judiciary is particularly important in a context such as immigration law, where the law and policy emanates only from the state. The state's ability to exert influence through the appointment of judges who are sympathetic to party ideals may impact the outcome of detention cases either directly or indirectly, especially where the political mood is one of anti-immigration and pro-deportation, as is the case particularly in the USA.

III. JUDICIAL REVIEW PROCEEDINGS

The courts discussed in this book have the competence to make determinations regarding the legality of immigration detention. In the UK and USA, this is undertaken through judicial review or habeas corpus proceedings, where the detainee files a claim against the state, most often seeking release, but sometimes seeking merely the opportunity to apply for bond or bail. The situation differs in the EU, where the Member State courts determine the legality of detention under the Return Directive, but sometimes refer questions of interpretation to the CJEU, which is empowered to issue a preliminary ruling to guide the national courts in their decision-making. This section provides an overview of the nature of these proceedings. A detailed look at how these processes work in practice is reserved for chapters five to seven, as it is the main point of inquiry in this book.

A. Judicial Review and Habeas Corpus in the UK

There is no statutory right to appeal decisions to detain. There are consequently only three ways by which a person in immigration detention can obtain his or her release: applying for bail;[50] seeking judicial review of detention; or

[49] C Cordelli, 'Judicial Appointments to the Court of Justice' (2013) 54(1) *Acta Juridica Hungarica* 24, 28.

[50] Immigration Act 2016, c 19, Sch 10, received Royal Assent on 12 May 2016. Schedule 10, s 11 introduced a new requirement for the Secretary of State to arrange a bail hearing before the First-tier Tribunal (Immigration and Asylum Chamber) after four months of detention and at certain other points as defined in the Schedule.

petitioning for a writ of habeas corpus.[51] Although a successful bail application will result in the release of the individual, it is important to stress that bail proceedings do not address the legality of the detention decision.[52] Rather, bail proceedings address the question of whether, even though there is a legitimate ground to detain the individual, he or she can be released, with particular regard to whether the person poses a risk of harm or reoffending. The bail system has been criticised in relation to a number of technical and procedural irregularities, including the routine failure by the Secretary of State to disclose evidence relating to detainees' behaviour to the detainees and their legal counsel,[53] so the ability to petition for release before the Administrative Court takes on an even greater importance.

As indicated above, applications for bail are not challenges to the legality of detention. To challenge the legality of detention, one must make an application for judicial review or apply for a writ of habeas corpus before the Administrative Court, though primarily the former option is chosen.[54] Chapter 60 of the UKVI EIG applies to judicial reviews and injunctions, and makes clear that detention is subject to judicial review.[55]

Judicial review is a form of discretionary relief, which means that, even where the court has made a finding of unlawfulness, it is not required to grant a remedial order, such as release. This is the opposite of succeeding in habeas corpus review, where a remedy must be granted upon a finding of unlawfulness.

Throughout its relatively short lifespan, judicial review has borne its share of criticism, especially in the context of immigration and asylum, which has been a great source of judicial review claims.[56] In the early 2000s, the government viewed judicial review as a tactic used by some failed asylum seekers to delay their removal from the UK, burdening the Administrative Court with 'last minute and abusive applications'.[57] Changes were made to the judicial review framework that were aimed at processing certain reviews (not of detention) more quickly by introducing paper-based review of decisions by the Immigration and Asylum

[51] In addition, a detained person may file for damages based on a claim of false imprisonment for past periods of detention. See *Lumba (WL) v SSHD* [2011] UKSC 12; *Kambadzi (SK (Zimbabwe) v SSHD* [2011] UKSC 23.

[52] *R (Konan) v SSHD* [2004] EWHC 22 (Admin) 30.

[53] Bail for Immigration Detainees, 'A Nice Judge on a Good Day: Immigration Bail and the Right to Liberty' (2010); JN Stefanelli, 'Disclosure in Immigration Bail Proceedings: Ensuring Equality of Arms' (2016) 30 *Journal of Immigration Asylum and Nationality Law* 301.

[54] Civil Procedure Rules, Pt 54. The Administrative Court is a part of the Queen's Bench Division in the High Court of England & Wales. In practice, many people apply for both judicial review and habeas corpus and, if permission is granted, both will be considered in a 'rolled up' hearing.

[55] EIG, ch 60, s 1.1.

[56] S Nason, 'The Administrative Court, the Upper Tribunal and Permission to Seek Judicial Review' (2012) 21 *Nottingham Law Journal* 1, 4, 10. The formal procedure of an application for judicial review was created in 1967 by Supreme Court Rule O.53, and later confirmed by statute in ss 29–31 of the Supreme Court Act 1981. See R Gordon QC, *Judicial Review and Crown Office Practice* (Sweet & Maxwell, 1999) 1-012.

[57] *Hansard*, HC, col 698 (29 July 2002) (comments by Lord Bassam of Brighton).

Tribunal and limiting the time limit for applying for judicial review to 14 days instead of three months.[58] Additional reforms have been made, further restricting access to judicial review,[59] but it is important to note that none of these reforms touched upon judicial review of immigration detention. This includes the transfer of jurisdiction in most immigration and asylum cases to the Upper Tribunal Immigration and Asylum Chamber.

The Administrative Court has jurisdiction to hear applications for review of the lawfulness of detention against the Secretary of State for the Home Department. Before proceeding to a full hearing on the claim, the applicant must be given permission to bring a judicial review claim. Applications for permission will generally succeed if the applicant has a 'sufficient interest' in the claim,[60] and if the judge considers that the applicant's case is arguable (ie that there is a realistic prospect of success).[61] This usually consists of the judge undertaking a cursory paper-based review of the claim and making a judgment as to its likely outcome should it proceed to a full hearing.[62] If permission is granted, a hearing will take place at which the Secretary of State bears the burden of proving that detention is lawful.[63] Judicial review claims can include consideration of whether there has been a breach of Article 5 ECHR, and damages may be awarded.[64]

Denials of relief can be appealed to the Court of Appeal if permission is granted by either the Administrative Court or the Court of Appeal.[65] Where permission is denied by the Administrative Court, the applicant can apply directly to the Court of Appeal.[66] Decisions of the Court of Appeal may be appealed to the UK Supreme Court if the Supreme Court grants permission.[67]

Habeas corpus was traditionally the main method for obtaining release of individuals unlawfully detained in England and Wales.[68] In fact, Britain

[58] Nationality, Immigration and Asylum Act 2002, s 103A (but then it was s 101).

[59] See, eg Criminal Justice and Courts Act 2015, c 2, Pt 4, received Royal Assent on 12 February 2015; The First-tier Tribunal and Upper Tribunal (Chambers) (Amendment) Order SI No 2011/2342; The First-tier Tribunal and Upper Tribunal (Chambers) (Amendment No 2) Order SI No 2013/2068.

[60] Senior Courts Act 1981, c 54, s 31(3), received Royal Assent on 28 July 1981.

[61] See, eg *R (Akangbe) v SSHD* [2008] EWHC 2295 (Admin) 7; *R (CM (Somalia)) v SSHD* [2010] EWHC 640 (Admin).

[62] If permission is refused based on papers, the applicant can request reconsideration at an oral hearing. See Civil Procedure Rules, Practice Direction 54A, 8.5–8.6.

[63] See, eg *R (JM) v SSHD* [2014] EWHC 151 (Admin) 20; *R (Badah) v SSHD* [2014] EWHC 364 (Admin) 20; *R (Ismail) v SSHD* [2013] EWHC 3921 (Admin) 10.

[64] Human Rights Act 1998, c 42, s 8.

[65] Civil Procedure Rule 52.3(2), (5). Permission to appeal will be granted if the Court believes that there is a realistic prospect of success, or for some other compelling reason.

[66] Civil Procedure Rule 52.3(3).

[67] The Supreme Court Rules 2009, SI 1603 (L 17), s 11. See also Constitutional Reform Act 2005, c 4, s 40(2), received Royal Assent on 24 March 2005 granting jurisdiction to the Supreme Court over orders or judgments of the Court of Appeal in civil proceedings.

[68] Woolf et al (n 9) 17-007.

prided itself on the availability of the writ to all people in its territory, including non-nationals.[69] However, its use in recent years has diminished, in large part due to the development of judicial review. For example, habeas corpus used to be favoured because applications were treated with priority by the court, but in practice judicial review claims involving detention are now often treated with the same urgency.[70] Consequently, unlike in the USA, where habeas corpus is the only way for an immigration detainee to challenge detention, habeas corpus is rarely used in the UK. Habeas corpus does, however, remain a viable option in some cases.[71] Though habeas corpus was originally not intended to question the legality of the administrative acts leading to the detention, but rather the legality of the detention itself,[72] the modern approach seems to have abandoned this distinction.[73]

Applications for the writ are heard by the Administrative Court, and may be brought any time the person is in detention.[74] Permission is unnecessary.[75] Though a judge may consider an application initially on paper, it is equally possible to consider the application at a hearing.[76] The applicant bears an initial burden of demonstrating that he or she is being unlawfully detained, but once that burden is discharged, the respondent must justify the legality of detention. If the respondent can show that he or she was exercising a legitimate power, the applicant must then successfully argue that the power was exercised unlawfully and that detention is therefore illegal. If illegality is established, the court is obligated to grant relief.[77] The applicable standard of proof is that of the balance of probabilities, though, as the House of Lords has pointed out, the requisite degree of probability will be higher where liberty is at issue.[78] Appeals against refusals of the writ operate according to the same rules as appeals against refusals of judicial review relief.

[69] D Wilsher, *Immigration Detention: Law, History, Politics* (Cambridge University Press, 2012) 5. See also M Lobban, 'Habeas Corpus, Imperial Rendition, and the Rule of Law' (2015) 68 *Current Legal Problems* 27.

[70] J Farbey and RJ Sharpe (with S Atrill), *The Law of Habeas Corpus*, 3rd edn (Oxford University Press, 2011) 59.

[71] Denholm and Dunlop suggest it is most appropriately used in cases where the claim is that no authority to detain existed, or where the legality of detention is threatened based on a breach of the *Hardial Singh* principles or a material public law error: G Denholm and R Dunlop, *Detention under the Immigration Acts: Law and Practice* (Oxford University Press, 2015) 19.68.

[72] *R (Muboyayi) v SSHD* [1992] 1 QB 244; *R (Cheblak) v SSHD* [1991] 1 WLR 890. In both of these cases, the challenge to detention was collateral to challenges to underlying immigration decisions.

[73] Farbey and Sharpe (n 70) 56–64.

[74] Civil Procedure Rules, Pt 87, s II.

[75] Civil Procedure Rule 87.2.

[76] Civil Procedure Rules 87.3–87.5.

[77] The relief granted is typically release, but the Court is also empowered to adjourn the case for a further hearing, and make any other orders to resolve the application. See Civil Procedure Rule 87.5.

[78] *Khawaja v SSHD* [1983] UKHL 8, 13 (per Lord Fraser of Tullybelton).

B. Habeas Corpus in the USA

As in the UK, immigration detainees may apply for immigration bail (called bond) to obtain release, or petition for habeas corpus for release based on illegality. Bond must be set at no less than \$1500.[79] Obtaining release on bond does not imply that the individual was unlawfully detained. The assessment made with regard to an application for bond is centred on whether the applicant is a danger or a flight risk, but the legality of detention is presumed, and the person may be redetained at any time, even if he or she is released.[80]

In addition to bond applications, non-citizens detained under the mandatory provisions in section 236(c) of the INA may challenge their inclusion within that provision through a Joseph Hearing.[81] Joseph Hearings are important because they represent a non-citizen's only chance to secure release from mandatory detention. However, it is by no means a simple process.[82] The non-citizen has the burden of demonstrating that the state is 'substantially unlikely' to establish its mandatory detention charges at the removal hearing.[83] He or she essentially has only three arguments to make: (i) the crime is not one that falls within the mandatory detention framework; (ii) he or she was not convicted; or (iii) he or she is a citizen.[84] This can be problematic because of the difficulties of amassing relevant evidence and witnesses while in detention.[85] Succeeding at the Joseph Hearing does not mean that the non-citizen will be released; it only means that he or she was improperly included within the mandatory detention framework. Successful non-citizens must still have a bond hearing to establish whether release will pose a danger to the community or the presence of a flight risk.

Habeas corpus review in the federal district courts is the only route for due process challenges to detention that is independent of the immigration courts and the framework of the Executive Office for Immigration Review. Habeas corpus is a constitutional mechanism grounded in Article I, section 9, clause 2 of the USA Constitution, which reads: 'The Privilege of the Writ of Habeas Corpus shall not be suspended, unless when in Cases of Rebellion or Invasion

[79] INA, s 236(a)(2)(A).

[80] INA, ss 236(b), 241.4(l).

[81] *Matter of Joseph* (BIA 1999) 22 I&N Dec 799.

[82] For a clear explanation of exactly what a Joseph Hearing entails, see M Noferi, 'Cascading Constitutional Deprivation: The Right to Appointed Counsel for Mandatorily Detained Immigrants Pending Removal Proceedings' (2012) 18 *Michigan Journal of Race and Law* 63.

[83] *Matter of Joseph* (n 81).

[84] Noferi (n 82) 89.

[85] ibid 114–15. Bhargava has championed the need for procedural reform in connection with Joseph Hearings because it is the only chance for a non-citizen to challenge his or her detention under the mandatory scheme. See S Bhargava, 'Detaining Due Process: The Need for Procedural Reform in "*Joseph*" Hearings after *Demore v Kim*' (2006–2007) 31 *New York University Review of Law and Social Change* 51.

the public Safety may require it.' The Supreme Court has long been of the view that the writ is available to citizens and non-citizens alike.[86]

Following the introduction of the IIRIRA and AEDPA, the opportunities for immigration detainees to challenge the legality of their detention before an independent judiciary became drastically reduced. First, the new section 236(c) of the INA required certain non-citizens to be detained automatically without bond or the possibility of parole if they may be deported because of criminal or terrorism-related convictions or qualifying sentences. Secondly, the courts were precluded from judicially reviewing decisions by the Attorney General regarding the detention of non-citizens.[87] The question of whether habeas corpus remained available to challenge the lawfulness of detention was addressed during congressional debate concerning the Real ID Act of 2005,[88] where it was specifically noted that habeas challenges to detention independent of challenges to removal orders remained viable under the general habeas corpus statute in Title 28, section 2241 of the United States Code because habeas review 'does not cover discretionary determinations or factual issues that do not implicate constitutional due process'.[89] The US Supreme Court confirmed this by underscoring its availability for statutory and constitutional challenges to detention (as opposed to challenges to exercises of discretion, which were prohibited).[90] Section 2241 provides that 'writs of habeas corpus may be granted by the Supreme Court, any justice thereof, the district courts and any circuit judge within their respective jurisdictions'.[91] Though it provides some detail in relation to when it is appropriate to apply for habeas corpus (including that the person must be in custody at the time of his or her application), it does not

[86] In *Nishimura Ekiu v United States* (1892) 142 US 651, Mr Justice Grey stated that 'An alien immigrant ... is doubtless entitled to a writ of habeas corpus to ascertain whether the restraint is lawful' (660). Halliday explains that this logic is derived from an implied 'local allegiance' of non-citizens on the King's territory (including enemy aliens) who, though they could not own property, were entitled to the King's protection as long as they were not hostile. See PD Halliday, *Habeas Corpus* (Belknap Harvard, 2010) 201-08. Halliday notes that though some lawyers claimed that non-citizens were not entitled to habeas corpus, this issue was largely unacknowledged in the early days of the writ.

[87] INA, s 236(e) reads: 'No court may set aside any action or decision of the Attorney General under this section [s 236] regarding the detention or release of any alien or the grant, revocation, or denial of bond or parole.'

[88] Real ID Act 2005, Pub L 109-13, 119 Stat 302. The full title is 'An Act to establish and rapidly implement regulations for State driver's license and identification document security standards, to prevent terrorists from abusing the asylum laws of the United States, to unify terrorism-related grounds for inadmissibility and removal, and to ensure expeditious construction of the San Diego border fence'.

[89] House Report Vol 109 No 72, 109th Congress, 1st Session, 175. See also D Cole, 'Jurisdiction and Liberty: Habeas Corpus and Due Process as Limits on Congress's Control of Federal Jurisdiction' (1998) 86 *Georgetown Law Journal* 2481, 2497–98; GL Neuman, 'Habeas Corpus, Executive Detention, and the Removal of Aliens' (1998) 19 *Immigration and Nationality Law Review* 307.

[90] *Zadvydas v Davis* (2001) 533 US 678, 688; *Demore v Kim* (2003) 538 US 510, 517; See also *Louisaire v Muller* (SDNY 2010) 758 F Supp 2d 229, 234.

[91] 28 USC 2241(a).

specifically address the situation of immigration detainees, outside the context of non-citizens detained as enemy combatants, in which case there is no entitlement to habeas corpus relief.[92]

Habeas corpus review is aimed at determining whether there has been a violation of the Due Process Clause of the Fifth Amendment. Habeas petitions may be heard in the US Supreme Court or the federal district courts. In the context of immigration detention, the latter have jurisdiction at first instance. A hearing, where both parties are present, will typically be held if the facts are in dispute – which is nearly always the case in immigration habeas petitions.[93] A habeas review will consider whether the decision to detain was made in conformity with the due process requirements in the Constitution. The courts must ensure that any authority granted to the Executive was exercised according to the limits provided by law (including applicable procedures). Traditionally, this meant assessing whether the reasons for detention were sufficiently detailed and reasonable, and that detention was based on a statutory authority to detain,[94] but the scope for review has widened in light of the USSC case law discussed below in section V.B. It is also the role of the courts, according to 28 USC 2243, to 'summarily hear and determine the facts'.

If the petitioner succeeds in demonstrating illegality, some form of relief will be granted, such as an order for release (possibly under conditions) or an order to conduct a new hearing that complies with the district court's decision.[95] Denials of relief can be appealed to the Federal Courts of Appeal, and the Supreme Court if it grants a writ of certiorari. Morawetz suggests that, in some cases, the government places strategic limits where habeas corpus applications can be filed by detainees so as to ensure control over the litigation and, in some cases, move detainees into a 'law-free zone'.[96] It is not possible, however, to determine, by virtue of an examination of the judgments in this book, whether this has been the experience of the detainees in my case pool.

C. Preliminary References at the Court of Justice of the EU

As is the case in the UK and USA, EU Member State national courts determine the legality of detention under the Return Directive. However, it may be the case that the national courts need assistance in interpreting the Directive before they can arrive at a judgment. In such cases, the national courts may

[92] 28 USC 2241(e).

[93] RP Sokol, *Federal Habeas Corpus* (The Michie Company, 1969) §13.

[94] Halliday (n 86) 104.

[95] The law requires the court to 'dispose of the matter as law and justice require': 28 USC 2243.

[96] N Morawetz, 'Detention Decisions and Access to Habeas Corpus for Immigrants Facing Deportation' (2005) 25 *Boston College Third World Law Journal* 13, 17.

make a preliminary reference to the CJEU under Article 267 TFEU. National courts (at all levels) may make a reference to the CJEU for a ruling on the interpretation of the Treaties or of secondary legislation, such as the Return Directive. In most cases, the national courts have discretion to determine whether a reference is necessary, for example, because they cannot give judgment without the interpretation. However, national courts of last instance are required to make a preliminary reference where resolution of the issue is necessary to enable the national court to give judgment.[97] Such references are made while national proceedings are in process, though they will be suspended pending the CJEU ruling. The ruling is not a judgment in the classic sense; rather, it is a decision on interpretation of EU law essential to the national case, and it is returned to the national court to apply in its proceedings. National courts have discretion regarding how to apply the preliminary ruling, but they are bound to apply it, and the other Member States courts are also bound by it. In that way, preliminary references have a very wide impact. Lenz suggests that the preliminary reference procedure gives the CJEU a 'monopoly of interpretation' on questions of EU law that ensures the EU law is applied uniformly in the Member States.[98] This is especially important given the key role that Member States play in enforcing EU law at the national level. In that way, the Member States and the CJEU co-operate to ensure that EU law is being applied consistently and enforced uniformly across the 28 Member States.[99] The possibility for lower courts and tribunals to refer questions of interpretation to the CJEU is arguably the most important aspect of this process, as these courts handle the bulk of national legal disputes. On this, Tridimas has said that the preliminary ruling procedure has 'emancipat[ed] lower courts from the obligation, or at least the pressure, to follow the rulings of higher courts'.[100]

Sometimes the CJEU has to reformulate the questions referred by the national court because it 'has a duty to interpret all provisions of EU law which national courts need in order to decide the actions pending before them, even if those provisions are not expressly indicated in the questions referred'.[101] Ultimately, the national court retains control over the outcome of its case, but it is under a duty to apply the interpretation provided by the CJEU.[102]

[97] Art 267(3) TFEU.

[98] CO Lenz, 'The Role and Mechanism of the Preliminary Ruling Procedure' (1994) 18 *Fordham International Law Journal* 388, 389.

[99] ibid 390.

[100] T Tridimas, 'Knocking on Heaven's Door: Fragmentation, Efficiency and Defiance in the Preliminary Reference Procedure' (2003) 40 *Common Market Law Review* 9, 10–11.

[101] Case C-38/14 *Zaizoune* [ECR TBC] para 25.

[102] Case 69/85 *Wünsche Handelsgesellschaft GmbH & Co v Federal Republic of Germany* [1986] ECR 947.

IV. LEGAL REPRESENTATION AND ACCESS TO JUSTICE FOR DETAINEES

The impact of legal representation on case outcomes cannot be overstated, particularly when comparing UK and US case outcomes. The UK has a strong tradition of legal aid and pro bono advice. In the USA, though legal aid began its life as an initiative to assist non-citizens, it is no longer widely available to them. Indeed, in 2017, the US Department of Justice issued a cease and desist letter to an immigrants' rights organisation that provides free legal services to non-citizens.[103] Finally, the CJEU has a specific system for legal aid in relation to the preliminary ruling procedure.

In England and Wales, legal aid is available to immigration detainees through the UK's Legal Aid Agency, which is an executive agency sponsored by the UK Ministry of Justice.[104] The Legal Aid, Sentencing and Punishment of Offenders Act 2012 regulates the provision of free legal services. 'Legal services' is defined to include the provision of advice regarding: (i) the application of law in certain circumstances; (ii) legal proceedings; (iii) the prevention, settlement or other resolution of legal disputes; and (iv) the enforcement of decisions.[105] Advocacy is not included except in specific cases, including in proceedings before the High Court.[106] Legal services for civil cases are available as long as they are included in Schedule 1 of the Act and the individual qualifies for them.[107] Immigration detention and habeas corpus proceedings are each given specific attention, and are included within the scope of civil legal services.[108] The UK Ministry of Justice publishes quarterly statistics regarding the application for and grant of legal aid. Though it does not keep separate track of immigration detention cases, the statistics do include a category for immigration cases. In 2018, there were 1,511 applications for representation assistance in immigration and asylum matters, of which 1,131 were granted – a success rate of over 75 per cent.[109] In all of the Administrative Court cases considered in this book, the detainees were represented by an attorney, but it is unclear whether they were provided through legal aid. It bears repeating that the rate of success in these cases was 49.2 per cent.

[103] RB Tiven, 'The Airport Lawyers Who Stood Up to Trump Are Under Attack', *The Nation* (19 May 2017) www.thenation.com/article/the-airport-lawyers-who-stood-up-to-trump-are-under-attack/.

[104] See 'What We Do' www.gov.uk/government/organisations/legal-aid-agency.

[105] Legal Aid, Sentencing and Punishment of Offenders Act 2012, c 10, s 8(1), received Royal Assent on 1 May 2012 (LASPO).

[106] ibid pt 3, s 3.

[107] ibid s 9(1). LASPO, s 11 gives the Lord Chancellor the power to make regulations concerning qualification for legal aid. These regulations are The Civil Legal Aid (Merits Criteria) Regulations 2013 SI No 2013/104, which entered into force on 1 April 2013. See, in particular, ss 39, 60.

[108] Habeas corpus *ad subjiciendum*: Sch 1, Pt 1, s 20; immigration detention: Sch 1, Pt 1, s 25.

[109] Ministry of Justice and Legal Aid Agency, 'Legal Aid Statistics England and Wales October to December 2018' www.gov.uk/government/statistics/legal-aid-statistics-quarterly-october-to-december-2018.

In the USA, detainees applying for habeas corpus may apply for appointed counsel.[110] Heeren notes how publicly funded legal aid for immigrants is controversial and thus, not widely available, despite legal aid in the USA originating as a means of safeguarding immigrants' rights in the late nineteenth century.[111] This is especially true in the context of contesting deportation and removal.[112] Whether counsel is appointed is a discretionary matter for the court, which should consider 'the petitioner's likelihood of success on the merits, the complexity of the legal issues raised by the petition, and the petitioner's ability to investigate and present the case'.[113] The court must also consider whether an evidentiary hearing is required, in which case it should counsel in favour of appointing counsel.[114]

Of the 15 successful habeas petitions in this book (or 13.6 per cent of US cases), 10 detainees had legal representation, though it is unclear whether the legal representation was court-appointed or paid for by the detainee. In all, only 25 of the 110 detainees clearly had legal representation. In comparison to the UK, the results are striking and arguably reflect the fact that the detainees there had legal representation. Though undoubtedly the success rate in UK cases is owed partly to the nature of judicial review proceedings and the need to obtain permission to proceed, the fact that all of the detainees in the UK had legal representation cannot be ignored as a contributing success factor, especially when viewed in comparison to the US cases, where most unrepresented detainees were unsuccessful. Though the Second Circuit has held that the constitutional claims of pro se claimants should be 'liberally construed' by the courts,[115] there is no evidence from this pool of cases that this is occurring in practice.

The Statute of the CJEU requires that parties other than Member States and EU institutions be represented in proceedings before it,[116] but does not make reference to legal assistance. The Return Directive refers to legal aid and legal assistance in its preamble, and in the substantive articles. Paragraph 11 of the preamble states that legal aid should be made available for those who are in need of it, while Article 13 more strongly requires the Member States to 'ensure' that legal aid and/or representation is granted without charge where necessary under national law, although it permits the Member States to subject the grant of such assistance to certain conditions.[117] A 2009 information note specifies that

[110] See, eg *Coita v Leonardo* 1998 WL 187416 (NDNY) 1.

[111] G Heeren, 'Illegal Aid: Legal Assistance to Immigrants in the United States' (2011) 33 *Cardozo Law Review* 619, 621.

[112] IV Eagly and S Shafer, 'A National Study of Access to Counsel in Immigration Court' (2015) 164 *University of Pennsylvania Law Review* 1.

[113] *De Los Rios v United States* 1994 WL 502635 (SDNY) 6.

[114] *US ex rel Cadogan v LaVallee* (2d Cir 1974) 502 F 2d 824, 826.

[115] See, eg *Fleming v US* (2d Cir 1998) 146 F 3d 88, 90; *Williams v Kuhlman* (2d Cir 1983) 722 F 2d 1048, 1050 (citing *Haines v Kerner* (1972) 404 US 519, 520–21).

[116] Protocol (No 3) on the Statute of the Court of Justice of the European Union [2010] OJ C83/210, Art 19.

[117] In particular, those set out in Art 15(3)–(6) of the EU Asylum Procedures Directive 2005/85.

where a party has insufficient means to cover its costs, national courts may grant legal aid, including lawyers' fees, if the national law permits this.[118] However, the CJEU itself may also grant legal aid if the individual is not in receipt of aid under the national framework, or has received only partial legal aid. The judgments do not address the issue of, or indicate whether, the detainees were represented, either at their own cost or through legal assistance.

Commentators in the UK and USA have written about the difficulties that detainees face in accessing legal representation on a practical level. For example, a 2018 survey conducted by the not-for-profit organisation Bail for Immigration Detainees indicates that only 51 per cent of surveyed detainees have a legal representative, and just over half of those individuals had their representation funded through legal aid.[119] A number of barriers to accessing immigration legal advice in detention were identified, including substantial delays in obtaining an appointment in legal advice information sessions in detention centres; a lack of ongoing legal advice for individuals detained long-term; and the negative impact of detainee transfers between detention centres on the ability to retain a lawyer.[120] A study by two scholars in the USA expresses similar concerns, including a finding that only 14 per cent of detained immigrants acquired legal counsel between 2007 and 2012, compared to two-thirds of those not detained during the same period.[121]

It is also important to remember that the likelihood of having the legality of detention reviewed by the judiciary is low. The only chance to challenge the lawfulness of detention in the UK and USA is through an application for judicial review or habeas corpus. There is no automatic review of legality. The ability of a detainee to make such an application may depend on whether he or she is represented, which, in turn, often depends on the availability of legal aid. In the UK, there is the additional hurdle of having to pass the permission phase, which knocks out unmeritorious cases before proceeding to a full hearing. Though the process by which a detention case reaches the CJEU is not directly comparable, access may nonetheless prove difficult, especially where it is difficult to persuade a domestic court to make a request for a preliminary ruling. Otherwise, detainees must rely on the domestic courts' obligation to apply the Return Directive as interpreted by the CJEU.

[118] CJEU, 'Information Note on References from National Courts for a Preliminary Ruling' [2009] OJ C297/1, paras 27–28.

[119] 'Legal Advice Survey – Autumn 2018', 1 http://hubble-live-assets.s3.amazonaws.com/biduk/redactor2_assets/files/757/FINAL_Presentation_of_Results_AUTUMN_2018.pdf. The situation is exacerbated for detainees held in prisons, where only 7 of 40 detainees surveyed received independent legal advice (2).

[120] Bail for Immigration Detainee, 'Submission to the APPG on Refugees and APPG on Migration's Parliamentary Inquiry into the Use of Immigration Detention in the UK' (September 2014).

[121] Eagly and Shafer (n 112) 32.

V. MODERN JUDICIAL REVIEW OF DETENTION

Chapter two began to trace the historic development of judicial intervention into immigration by discussing how the courts in each of the three jurisdictions gave effect to the right to liberty in general and specifically in relation to immigration detainees. This section fast-forwards slightly and outlines modern cases that have influenced judicial review of prolonged immigration detention as conducted by the courts today.

A. United Kingdom

The conservative tide marked by *Azam* and *Hassan* began to change in the early 1980s, with the judgment of the House of Lords in *Khawaja* in 1983,[122] which changed the way in which judges consider the legality of continued detention. The two appellants before the House of Lords were determined by immigration officers to be 'illegal entrants' under the 1971 Act who should be detained pending their removal. The House of Lords was asked to consider two issues: the first was the meaning of 'illegal entrant' and the second was the standard of review for the courts when dealing with applications for judicial review in the context of immigration. In particular, the House of Lords considered whether their function was limited to determining whether the immigration officer's decision was reasonable, as concluded by the Court in an earlier case,[123] or whether it was broader and required that they decide whether the decision was justified in light of the evidence. The House of Lords concluded that the latter was the proper function of the Court, thereby establishing the role of the courts as primary decision maker.[124]

Khawaja also established the following principles. First, that the burden of proof lies with the Secretary of State if seeking detention or removal.[125] Secondly, that non-citizens are entitled to equal protection of the law.[126] Thirdly, that where the liberty of an individual is at stake, the court must 'regard with extreme jealously any claim by the Executive to imprison a citizen without trial'.[127] These three principles, and that above regarding the role of the courts, appear frequently in the case law examined in this book.[128]

[122] *Khawaja* (n 78). *Azam v Secretary of State* [1974] AC 1 and *R (Hassan) v Governor of Risley* [1976] 1 WLR 971 were discussed in ch 2 above.
[123] *Zamir v SSHD* [1980] UKHL 14.
[124] *Khawaja* (n 78) 39(3). See also chapter 7, s II.A below.
[125] ibid 39(2).
[126] ibid 67.
[127] ibid 106.
[128] See, eg *R (Abunasir) v SSHD* [2015] EWHC 2145 (Admin) 50; *R (Mhlanga) v SSHD* [2012] EWHC 1587 (Admin) 21; *R (Raki) v SSHD* [2011] EWHC 2421 (Admin) 16; *R (SK) v SSHD* [2008] EWHC 98 (Admin) 4; *R (Kumar) v SSHD* [2003] EWHC 846 (Admin) 15.

Later in the same year, the Queen's Bench established standards by which to adjudicate the legality of continued detention in its judgment in *Hardial Singh*.[129] Lord Woolf, in the High Court of England and Wales, set forth a number of principles aimed at determining the reasonableness of continued detention. Lord Woolf was asked to consider the habeas corpus application of Mr Singh, an Indian national who had been detained for six months. Concluding that the Home Office had not taken appropriate action to ensure that the removal of Mr Singh occurred within a reasonable period from the start of his detention, Lord Woolf elucidated the following four principles, now known as the *Hardial Singh* principles:

(1) The Secretary of State must intend to deport the person and can only use the power to detain for that purpose.
(2) The deportee may only be detained for a period that is reasonable in all the circumstances.
(3) If, before the expiry of the reasonable period, it becomes apparent that the Secretary of State will not be able to effect deportation within a reasonable period, she should not seek to exercise the power of detention.
(4) The Secretary of State should act with reasonable diligence and expedition to effect removal.[130]

In *R (I) v Secretary of State for the Home Department*, Lord Dyson of the Court of Appeal built upon the *Hardial Singh* principles by specifying a number of factors that should assist the courts in their determination of what is reasonable. These include:

(1) whether the detainee has co-operated with the deportation process;
(2) the likelihood of absconding or reoffending (if the person is a foreign national offender);
(3) the length of detention to date;
(4) the obstacles in the path of deportation and the way in which the Secretary of State addresses them;
(5) the conditions of detention; and
(6) the effect of detention on the detainee and his or her family.[131]

The *Hardial Singh* principles bear some resemblance to the principles elucidated by the ECtHR. For example, the Article 5 requirement that detention can only be maintained as long as deportation/removal proceedings are in progress[132] can be likened to *Hardial Singh* principle 3. Like principle 4, Article 5 requires that the state act with due diligence in seeking removal.[133] Article 5 does not

[129] *R (Hardial Singh) v Governor of Durham Prison* [1983] EWHC 1 (QB).
[130] This exact formulation was set forth by Lord Dyson in the Court of Appeal in *R (I) v SSHD* [2002] EWCA Civ 888, 46.
[131] ibid 46.
[132] *A and Others v UK* [2009] ECHR 301, para 164.
[133] ibid para 164; *Amie and Others v Bulgaria* [2013] ECHR 141, para 72.

explicitly require that detention be reasonable in all the circumstances like principle 2, but it does require that detention be maintained only as long as reasonably required for the purpose pursued.[134] Though the judgment in *Hardial Singh* was published prior to the earliest ECtHR cases discussing these issues,[135] the ECtHR has asserted that the *Hardial Singh* principles were modelled on the requirements of Article 5.[136]

The *Hardial Singh* principles have since been endorsed by the UK Supreme Court[137] and approved by the European Court of Human Rights.[138] They therefore remain the main method by which the Administrative Court assesses the lawfulness of continued detention. The inquiry is heavily fact-dependent, which has led the courts to emphasise that, unlike in most cases of judicial review, in the context of assessing the reasonableness of detention, the court acts as the primary decision maker.[139]

B. United States

(i) Zadvydas v Davis *and Indefinite Detention Pending Removal*

Plenary power doctrine strongly influenced jurisprudence in the USSC for many years, with few inroads made until 2001, when the legality of continued detention following a final removal order was evaluated by the Court in *Zadvydas v Davis*.[140] In that case, two individuals were placed in immigration detention prior to removal on national security-related grounds. The issue before the Court was whether the 90-day statutory removal period permitted indefinite detention. At the time, the INA provided for periodic review of the appropriateness of detention. However, this review could go on indefinitely in practice if removal could not be achieved. As a result, the two petitioners had been detained for approximately one year awaiting removal.

The Court interpreted the INA as including a reasonableness requirement,[141] and held that post-removal order detention is implicitly limited to the time reasonably necessary to achieve removal. To interpret the INA otherwise would permit indefinite detention, which would raise serious constitutional questions.[142] The majority also took umbrage with the limited procedural

[134] *Yoh-Ekale Mwanje v Belgium* [2011] ECHR 2421, paras 117–19.
[135] *Kolompar* and *Quinn v France* [1995] ECHR 9.
[136] *JN v UK* [2016] ECHR 434, para 98.
[137] *Lumba* (n 51), 22.
[138] *JN* (n 136).
[139] See, eg *R (SM) v SSHD* [2011] EWHC 338 (Admin) 60; *MA & TT v SSHD* [2010] EWHC 2350 (Admin) 10–12.
[140] *Zadvydas* (n 90).
[141] Now INA, s 241(a)(6).
[142] *Zadvydas* (n 90), 682.

protections available to these detainees, which were administrative in nature and which placed the burden of proof regarding dangerousness and flight on the detainee.[143] The Court set a presumptively reasonable period for detention at six months.[144] Where removal is unlikely upon the expiration of six months, the non-citizen should be released, perhaps under conditions.[145] The court did not, however, shift the burden of proof onto the government, despite its criticism.

This case is significant because, in theory, it should put an end to indefinite detention during the removal period. Though detention is obligatory during the 90-day removal period, there were clearly circumstances, such as Mr Zadvydas's, in which removal could not be effected. Indeed, many of the NY district court cases examined in this book provide examples of this scenario. One scholar has commented on the hope that it represented for thousands of detainees, and in fact, just two months later, the INS announced it had released 359 non-citizens who were deemed not to be dangerous.[146] Stumpf has hailed the decision as a positive move by the USA's highest court, which recognises the 'constitutionally troubling disconnect' between detention and removal.[147] However, the cases evaluated in this book suggest that *Zadvydas* is not the 'new hope'[148] that it was thought to be, in the main because the presumptively reasonable six-month period has become a default minimum period of detention.[149] This will be explored more in chapter six, section IV.B.

Following the decision, the government put in place regulations aimed at helping immigration officials determine whether removal is likely in the foreseeable future.[150] The rules now provide for release in some cases where detention has continued beyond the 90-day removal period. In order for those people to obtain release, they must prove that they do not pose a danger or a significant risk of flight.[151] In making the decision, the immigration officer will consider several factors, including formal issues such as whether travel documents are available, employment and criminal history, family ties or financial ability to

[143] ibid 692.
[144] ibid 701.
[145] ibid 699–700.
[146] M Peitzke, 'The Fate of "Unremovable" Aliens before and after September 11, 2001: The Supreme Court's Presumptive Six-Month Limit to Post-Removal-Period Detention' (2002) 30 *Pepperdine Law Review* 769, 803.
[147] JP Stumpf, 'Civil Detention and Other Oxymorons' (2014) 40 *Queens Law Journal* 55, 89–90.
[148] The author references here Episode IV of the Star Wars franchise, *A New Hope*.
[149] A few years later, the Supreme Court applied the holding in *Zadvydas* to *Clark v Martinez* ((2005) 543 US 371), which involved the detention of detainees who were paroled into the USA and therefore considered 'inadmissible' under immigration law. At the time of the *Zadvydas* decision, the Supreme Court maintained a distinction between inadmissible non-citizens and those already within the territory of the USA (the situation in *Zadvydas*). In *Clark v Martinez*, the USSC concluded that it did not make sense to apply INA, s 241 concerning continued detention beyond the 90-day removal period differently for each category of non-citizen. However, the distinction still remains for inadmissible non-citizens who have not yet been given a final removal order.
[150] 8 CFR 241.13.
[151] ibid 241.4(d)(1).

post bond.[152] These are all in aid of determining whether the criteria for release have been met, which focus largely on risks of danger or flight.[153]

The idea that detention must be limited to the period reasonably necessary to achieve removal has today evolved in the federal district courts to a consideration of whether, in light of the individual circumstances, removal is likely. In making this determination, courts will consider a number of factors, including the efforts made by the state to effect removal, the detainee's behaviour (including whether he or she has co-operated in effecting removal, or poses a flight risk or a danger to the public) and, sometimes, the time the person has spent in detention to date.

It is interesting to note that, whereas in the USA, the highest court in the nation developed the reasonableness standard, in the UK, it was the High Court, a lower court in comparison. In addition, the High Court arrived at this standard nearly 20 years earlier than the US Supreme Court, and applies it to all types of immigration detention, rather than restricting it to detention after a statutory removal period, as in the USA. This discrepancy may partly be due to differences in the judicial hierarchy in the two jurisdictions. The federal district courts are trial courts, primarily tasked with applying law to facts and rendering decisions in individual cases, rather than developing legal principles. In contrast, the High Court, though also subordinate to an appellate court and a supreme court, is a court of review, with responsibility for assessing the legality of executive action and developing legal principles to assist it in so doing.

(ii) Demore v Kim *and Mandatory Pre-removal Order Detention*

The constitutionality of mandatory pre-removal order detention under section 236(c) INA was unsuccessfully challenged in *Demore v Kim*.[154] Mr Kim was a citizen of South Korea and a US lawful permanent resident (LPR). In 1996, when he was 18 years old, he was convicted of two crimes that rendered him liable to deportation from the USA. He was therefore detained according to the mandatory detention rules, pending his removal hearing. Rather than challenge his removal and his inclusion within the framework for mandatory detention, he filed a petition for habeas corpus in the relevant district court to challenge the validity of the mandatory detention law itself.[155] He was successful at the district court level and released. The US Court of Appeals affirmed the decision, holding that the mandatory detention provision was unconstitutional because Kim was an LPR and LPRs 'constitute the most favored category of aliens admitted to the United States'.[156] The USSC reversed the decision, holding that Congress had

[152] ibid 241.4(f).
[153] ibid 241.4(e).
[154] *Demore* (n 90).
[155] He challenged INA, s 236(c) as codified in 8 USC 1226(c).
[156] *Kim v Ziglar* (9th Cir 2002) 276 F3d 523, 18.

identified certain classes of non-citizens as posing a particular threat in terms of both reoffending and flight risk. Congress had validly determined that such individuals could be detained briefly pending a decision on removal, whether or not they were LPRs, and without the need for an individual determination of suitability for release.[157] This decision has been roundly criticised.[158]

C. Early Cases under the EU Return Directive

Unlike the UK and USA key cases, the two cases that I have designated as key EU cases are included in the pool of cases and analysed in the remaining chapters. Therefore, this section will not go into detail regarding either case, but will instead focus on broader issues.

Kadzoev was the first case to reach the CJEU under the Return Directive concerning immigration detention.[159] Mr Kadzoev had been picked up without identification by the Bulgarian authorities, ordered to be deported and put into immigration detention until the correct documentation and funds could be obtained.[160] The Bulgarian authorities spent two years trying to return him to Russia, but were unsuccessful. The CJEU was asked by the Administrative Court in Sofia (Administrativen sad Sofia-grad) to interpret a number of provisions in the Directive concerning such issues as: (i) whether to include in the calculation of Kadzoev's detention period under Article 15(5) and (6) the time he was detained during his asylum appeal and the time during which removal was suspended because of a lack of identification documents; (ii) how to determine when removal is no longer reasonably possible; and (iii) whether release is permissible despite the fact that Kadzoev did not have identification documents, had displayed aggressive behaviour in the past and did not have the means to support himself. The Court's responses to these questions, which will be considered in detail in chapters five to seven, laid the groundwork for its future interpretation of the detention provisions in the Return Directive and, in particular, underscored the absolute nature of the statutory maximum.

[157] *Demore* (n 90), 518–28.

[158] Aleinikoff suggests that the Supreme Court had mistakenly equated Kim's admission of removability with an admission that he was an aggravated felon and therefore ineligible for relief: M Aleinikoff et al, *Immigration and Citizenship Process and Policy*, 7th edn (West, 2011) 1250. See also Stumpf (n 147) 83; T Silva, 'Toward a Constitutionalized Theory of Immigration Detention' (2013) 32 *Yale Law and Policy Review* 227; FR Anello, 'Due Process and Temporal Limits on Mandatory Immigration Detention' (2013) 65 *Hastings Law Journal* 363; W Chelgren, 'Preventive Detention Distorted: Why It Is Unconstitutional to Detain Immigrants without Procedural Protections' (2011) 44 *Loyola Los Angeles Law Review* 1477; BB Banias, 'A "Substantial Argument" Against Prolonged, Pre-removal Mandatory Detention' (2009) 11 *Rutgers Race and Law Review* 31; Bhargava (n 85); MH Taylor, '*Demore v Kim:* Judicial Deference to Congressional Folly' in DA Martin and PH Schuck, *Immigration Stories* (Foundation Press, 2005).

[159] Case C-357/09 PPU *Kadzoev* [2009] ECR I-11189.

[160] ibid paras 13–29.

The second case, *El Dridi*, was a case examining the criminalisation of migration in Italian law and considered the issue of whether the Member States could impose criminal penalties (in this case, imprisonment) on the sole basis of violating immigration law, prior to instigating removal under the Return Directive. The applicant was sentenced to one year's imprisonment for unlawful presence in Italy, and for the violation of a removal order previously entered against him.[161] The Court of Appeal in Trento, Italy requested the preliminary ruling. In holding that criminal imprisonment was contrary to the Directive, the CJEU focused on an outcome that would ensure the effective functioning of the Directive. It also considered that permitting criminal imprisonment in these circumstances would jeopardise the establishment in the Directive of a maximum period of detention. The judgment therefore represents the first in a line of cases under the Directive which focus on the effectiveness of the Directive, thus indirectly protecting the liberty of third-country nationals by preventing detention in addition to that which may be imposed under the Directive.

VI. CONCLUSION

Judicial review and habeas corpus are valuable forms of relief because they uphold the rule of law by bringing an element of independence to the decision-making process[162] and reinforcing the independence of the judiciary from the Executive by instilling it with the power to supervise the administration of the state and the distribution of powers between the different branches of government.[163] This review power represents the role of the courts as information providers to the public. Through their decisions, the courts provide the public with information regarding the way the government is exercising its powers, so that the people can take action if the government has exceeded its constitutional limits.[164] The extent to which this review power assists immigration detainees in practice will be considered during the case evaluation in the remaining chapters.

A small, but important takeaway from this chapter is the difference between bail/bond and judicial review or habeas corpus. The former methods of securing

[161] Case C-61/11 PPU *El Dridi* [2011] ECR I-3015.

[162] SH Legomsky, 'Fear and Loathing in Congress and the Courts: Immigration and Judicial Review' (2000) 78 *Texas Law Review* 1615, 1630–31.

[163] Halliday (n 86) 304; Guarnieri and Pederzoli (n 24) 10. See also Shetreet and Turenne (n 8) 19. Though there are disagreements concerning the content of 'rule of law', its overarching principles are universal. 'Rule of law' as used in this book means legal certainty, accessible and prospective laws that are equally enforced, and access to justice where rights may be asserted through fair trials before an independent judiciary. See also *R (Smith) v Ministry of Defence)* [1995] EWCA Civ 22, 338 (Sir Thomas Bingham MR, as he then was): the High Court has 'the constitutional role and duty of ensuring that the rights of citizens are not abused by the unlawful exercise of executive power'.

[164] DS Law, 'A Theory of Judicial Power and Judicial Review' (2009) 97 *Georgetown Law Journal* 723, 747–51. However, the ability of the people to apprehend the judgments is unclear (749).

release are not concerned with illegality or wrongdoing by the state in its decision to detain. They presume the legality of detention, but offer release in situations where the detainee is not dangerous or a flight risk. Redetention is possible at any time. When someone petitions for judicial review or habeas corpus, they are asserting that their detention is unlawful and that they are therefore entitled to release or, in some cases, a bond/bail hearing. The assessment is therefore not the same. A finding of unlawful detention sends a signal to the state that it has not conducted itself according to the law, and it forces the state to rectify its behaviour. This is an important tool for safeguarding liberty.

Another important lesson from this chapter is that having legal representation can mean the difference between release and continued detention, especially when comparing the UK, which offers a system of legal aid and has a higher success rate in the cases examined here, to the USA, where legal assistance in the context of immigration matters is rare and success rates are poor.

On a structural level, it is important to note that these judgments do not represent the final word in a case, as they may be appealed to superior courts in both the UK and the USA. Similarly, preliminary rulings by the CJEU must still be implemented by the referring national court, leaving some room for error. However, preliminary references arguably have more impact at the national level, especially because they can be issued in response to references from national courts at all levels of the judiciary. The CJEU therefore influences national case law in a way that judgments of the Administrative Court, and especially the federal district courts, do not.

Modern UK and US detention jurisprudence demonstrates an evolution away from rights-restricting stances to a more rights-protecting approach, though at different speeds. In the UK, this occurred most notably in the early 1980s, when *Khawaja* and *Hardial Singh* each had a lasting impact on the way detention is reviewed in the Administrative Court. Though nearly 20 years later, the US Supreme Court followed suit in *Zadvydas*, which changed the way the federal district courts assess detention today.

The CJEU's experience in reviewing detention is comparatively new, but has already reached the stage arrived at by the courts in the UK and USA, with the CJEU emphasising the rights-protecting purpose of the Return Directive in order to ensure that detention is limited and employed only where necessary and for only as long as removal is imminent. It has even gone so far as to extend the Directive to prohibit criminal detention prior to implementation of a return decision, thus indirectly proscribing the Member States' ability to deprive third-country nationals of their liberty in the context of removal.

Suffice it to say that there is a clear trend in the direction of protecting the fundamental rights of detainees and permitting them to challenge the legality of their detention based on standards of reasonableness. The way in which these landmark decisions have impacted practice today will be explored in detail in the following chapters.

5

Balancing Factors

I. INTRODUCTION

THIS BOOK HAS explored the development of the law relating to immigration detention and the way the right to liberty is guaranteed in the UK, USA and EU. Its principle aim thus far has been to explain why detention is used in these jurisdictions and when detention is permissible. It has also described the ways detainees can bring their detention outside the administrative context and into the judicial context so that the legality of their detention can be considered by independent decision makers. This and the following chapters move beyond principle to practice by examining how all of those factors impact judicial review. As explained in chapter one, the specific focus is on the lower judiciary, with the exception of the CJEU, which interprets the EU Return Directive for referring national courts at all levels.

Before getting into the substantive analysis of the 191 judgments, this introduction sets out some of the main features of the cases in each jurisdiction, including detainee characteristics and the circumstances surrounding the cases. This is to demonstrate the types of cases included in this book, and to assist the reader in understanding the typical circumstances encountered by the judges in their review of ongoing detention.

Legomsky has written about the impact that a criminal sentence has on whether an individual will be detained,[1] and notes the fact that, in many cases, non-citizen criminal defendants will be advised to plead guilty without being warned of the immigration consequences of a guilty plea in light of the mandatory deportation and detention provisions.[2] Most of the detainees in the 173 cases from the UK and USA have been convicted of either an immigration or a criminal offence, which has contributed in some way to the state's decision to detain them. These offences range from entry without permission to drug offences of all levels, and to more violent crimes, such as assault or manslaughter.[3] This is significant when

[1] SH Legomsky, 'The Alien Criminal Defendant' (1977) 15 *San Diego Law Review* 105.

[2] SH Legomsky, 'Transporting *Padilla* to Deportation Proceedings: A Due Process Right to Effective Assistance of Counsel' (2011) 31 *St Louis U Public Law Review* 43.

[3] See, eg *R (I) v SSHD* [2002] EWCA Civ 888, indecent assault on a minor; *R (Lumba) v SSHD* [2008] EWHC 2090 (Admin), grievous bodily harm; *R (Raki) v SSHD* [2011] EWHC 2421 (Admin), theft; *Charran v Philips* 2014 WL 296429 (WDNY), driving while intoxicated, petty larceny (among others); *Copes v McElroy* 2001 WL 830673 (SDNY), criminal possession of marijuana, cocaine.

one considers that, in the context of the EU Return Directive, Member States are permitted to exclude from the scope of the Directive third-country nationals who are subject to return because they have committed a qualifying crime under domestic law.[4] If the numbers in the UK and US cases are representative, it may be that many third-country nationals in the EU subject to return under domestic law could be without the protection of the Directive if the Member State chooses to implement this exception.

Deportation may also be the result of unsuccessful immigration applications, for example, for leave to remain or asylum, or because immigration laws have been breached. For example, in ten cases, the detainees had only committed immigration offences, such as entry by deception or applying for asylum using false information.[5] In six of the 173 cases, there was no mention of criminal history, but I am unable to state with confidence whether that is because the detainee had not been convicted of a crime or because the judgment simply left out that data.[6] However, it is important to stress that this high incidence of criminal history is not surprising, but nor is it representative of all migrants.[7] That is because the cases I have chosen to examine concern the legitimacy of ongoing detention, with the subjects still in detention at the point at which they seek judicial review. Criminal history is a key factor in the state's determination of whether detention is appropriate, often resulting in the conclusion during judicial review that continued detention is permissible. Therefore, people with past criminal convictions are more likely to be in detention than those without convictions. If an individual does not have a criminal history, they are less likely to be detained, and therefore would not be seeking judicial review of their detention and would consequently not be in my pool of cases.

In many cases, a determination that the individual poses a danger to the community or a risk of absconding, coupled with a difficulty in achieving removal, means that the detention of many of these detainees is prolonged. One judge in the Administrative Court remarked in a case that I observed that in 1971, when the Immigration Act entered into force, it was likely that no one imagined that it could be so difficult to remove people, especially those whose

[4] Directive 2008/115/EC of the European Parliament and of the Council on 16 December 2008 on common standards and procedures in Member States for returning illegally staying third-country nationals, Art 2(2)(b).

[5] See, eg *R (Qaderi) v SSHD* [2008] EWHC 1033 (Admin), applying for asylum using false documents; *R (Davies) v SSHD* [2010] EWHC 2656 (Admin), possession of false passport; *Azad v Interim District Director, NY ICE and Riley* 2009 WL 2569132 (SDNY), failure to depart after issuance of final removal order; *Islam v Philips* 2015 WL 1915106 (WDNY), attempted unlawful entry.

[6] See, eg *Greenland v INS/Ice Dep't of Homeland Sec* (2009 WDNY) 599 F Supp 2d 365; *Powell v Ashcroft* (2002 EDNY) 194 F Supp 2d 209; *Hwez v SSHD* [2002] EWHC 1597 (Admin); *R (Badjoko) v SSHD* [2003] EWHC 3034 (Admin).

[7] However, Bosworth and Kaufman have written about the over-representation of foreign national offenders in US prisons, including immigration detention centres. See M Bosworth and E Kaufman, 'Foreigners in a Carceral Age: Immigration and Imprisonment in the United States' (2011) 22 *Stanford Law and Policy Review* 429.

presence was considered not conducive to the public good.[8] Indeed, it is a real problem felt in both the UK and the USA, whether because the target state is not co-operating or because it is taking a long time to identify a person's true nationality.

In addition, because of the similarities in the tests for lawfulness in the UK and USA, arguments posed by the parties are often the same. For example, detainees will often argue that the state has not acted diligently in securing removal, or that, because the target state (ie the state to which the detainee would be removed) has been unresponsive to requests by the removing state to receive the detainee, removal in the foreseeable future is unlikely. Conversely, the state typically focuses on arguments that the detainee has been unco-operative, for example, in providing identification documents, or that it has been diligent in seeking removal and that removals to the target country in question have a history of success and will likely be successful in the individual case.

Success rates are easier to quantify with regard to the UK and US cases. 'Successful' in this book includes cases where the court orders release or a bond/bail hearing, issues a declaration of unlawfulness or gives the state a deadline to effect removal.[9] Of the 173 UK and US cases, 46 (26.58 per cent) resulted in a successful outcome. The following sections provide a breakdown by jurisdiction. However, the USA was the poorer performer on two counts, with lower rates of success and also with longer instances of detention. In terms of the length of detention, detainees in the USA were held for an average time of 2.4 years, versus 2.1 years in the UK. This is quite a long time to be detained without having committed any offence (and in most cases having already completed a prison term) in what Dow refers to as a 'gulag', at least in the context of American detention centres.[10] However, as noted in chapter one, the judgments considered here involve special cases of prolonged detention in which the detainees have not managed to secure release through administrative processes. Therefore, the statistics discussed above should be read within that context and should not be considered as representative of overall detention lengths in any of the jurisdictions evaluated.

The cases from the CJEU are different from the UK and US cases for two reasons. First, as will be explained below, not all of the CJEU cases strictly involve immigration detention, though most involve detention in some form. Secondly, although there is discussion regarding the circumstances of each case, particulars regarding criminal history are rarely included in the CJEU judgments. This is perhaps owing to the fact that the role of the CJEU is not to determine the facts of the case, but rather to interpret the Return Directive.

[8] *G v SSHD* [2016] EWHC 3232 (Admin). Hearing dates 15–16 November 2016.

[9] For example, in one US case, the government was given 60 days to remove the petitioner, otherwise habeas would issue and release would follow. See *Gumbs v Heron* 2009 WL 2958002 (WDNY).

[10] M Dow, *American Gulag: Inside US Immigration Prisons* (University of California Press, 2004).

This means that evidence relating to the detainee's personal characteristics would be confined to proceedings at the national level. However, the CJEU is a worthy comparator because the Return Directive employs essentially the same test as those used in the UK and the USA, and the way in which it interprets the test components may serve as a model for those jurisdictions. With regard to the arguments made by the parties, although the standard in the Directive mimics that which is seen in the UK and the USA, again, because the focus is on the interpretation of the Directive rather than the legitimacy of the facts at hand, parties' arguments focus on the way in which the CJEU should construe the relevant provisions of the Directive.

II. CASE BASICS

This book includes 63 cases from the Administrative Court of England and Wales. Most of the detainees were detained under either Schedule 2 or Schedule 3 of the 1971 Act. A small minority of people (seven) were detained under the mandatory provisions of the UK Borders Act 2007. When that is the case, the *Hardial Singh* principles may be applied slightly differently, depending on the issue in dispute (discussed below). The average length of detention in the UK cases was 2.1 years.[11] Out of the 63 cases, 31 judicial review applications (49.2 per cent) were successful.

The book also considers 110 federal district court cases from the Second Circuit in the USA. The majority (76) come from the Western District of New York (WDNY), followed by 28 from the Southern District of New York (SDNY) and six from the Eastern District (EDNY).[12] These cases roughly fall into two main categories: (1) '*Zadvydas*' cases (82 cases); and (2) mandatory detention cases under section 236(c) of the Immigration and Nationality Act 1952 (INA) (28 cases).[13] The successful cases under category (2) were successful not because they led to a finding that detention is unlawful (though many detainees argue legality), but because the courts concluded that the detainees were entitled to a bond hearing because their detention had become prolonged.

Of the 110 US cases examined in this book, 15 resulted in successful petitions – that is, 13.6 per cent of the cases. The average length of detention in the US cases

[11] Only one case did not include the requisite data to determine detention length. One case (*R (A) v SSHD* [2008] EWHC 142 (Admin)) involved four detainees, so the average duration was calculated using the number 65 to account for the 63 cases, minus the case with no data but plus an additional three detention periods in *R (A) v SSHD*.

[12] Three petitioners have two petitions each in this batch of cases, making 102 individual detainees.

[13] Category (1) includes cases both before and after the USSC decision in *Zadvydas*, which consider whether the individual has been detained for an unlawful period and should be released, and which also engage in analysis of whether the individual would be a flight risk or a danger to society, should he or she be released.

was 2.4 years.[14] This can be broken down further into cases involving prolonged detention under section 236(c) of the INA (ie mandatory detention cases), where the average duration of detention was 1.9 years, and detention under section 241(a) (ie *Zadvydas* cases), with an average length of 2.8 years.

Finally, this book considers 17 cases under the Return Directive that were sent to the CJEU for a preliminary reference, including those where immigration detention is not the focus of the case, or even the main issue. This is because, in comparison to the UK and USA, there are far fewer decisions under the Return Directive on immigration detention – in fact, just six. By expanding the scope of the EU comparison to include non-detention cases, this book can more accurately draw conclusions regarding the comparative themes examined here and in chapters six and seven because many of the substantive themes found in the tests employed in the three jurisdictions are present in judgments interpreting the Return Directive outside the context of Article 15. Therefore, in light of the small number of detention cases, this broadened look at the Return Directive provides a more complete picture of judicial practice at the CJEU level and allows for a fuller comparison to the UK and USA.

For purposes of analysis, I have divided the CJEU cases into three categories. In Category A are six cases specifically focused on immigration detention and the interpretation of Chapter IV of the Directive.[15] Category B comprises eight cases concerning the criminalisation of migration by the Member States, and focuses primarily on the question of whether imposing criminal sanctions for violations of immigration law at the national level is permitted under the Return Directive.[16] In several of these cases, the Directive's detention provisions take centre stage because the CJEU is asked to consider whether the Directive permits criminal detention prior to initiating return. Finally, in Category C are three cases that concern issues purely to do with return, rather than detention of any kind.[17] This includes two cases on the right to be heard prior to being issued with a return decision and one on the meaning of risk in relation to granting a period of voluntary departure. The discussion in this and the next chapter will focus primarily on the first two categories. However, cases in Category C are illustrative of the CJEU's style of legal reasoning and demonstrate how the CJEU makes its decisions. They will therefore be referenced as appropriate during the comparative analysis.

[14] Seven cases lacked the requisite data to determine detention length.

[15] Case C-357/09 PPU *Kadzoev* [2009] ECR I-11189; Case C-534/11 *Arslan* [ECR TBC]; Case C-383/13 PPU *G and R* [ECR TBC]; Joined Cases C-473/13 and C-514/13 *Bero and Bouzalmate* [ECR TBC]; Case C-474/13 *Pham* [ECR TBC]; Case C-146/14 PPU *Mahdi* [ECR TBC].

[16] Case C-61/11 PPU *El Dridi* [2011] ECR I-3015; Case C-329/11 *Achughbabian* [2009] ECR I-12695; Case C-430/11 *Md Sagor* [ECR TBC]; Case C-522/11 *Mbaye* [ECR TBC]; Case C-297/12 *Filev and Osmani* [ECR TBC]; *Zaizoune*; Case C-290/14 *Celaj* [ECR TBC]; Case C-47/15 *Affum* [ECR TBC].

[17] Case C-166/13 *Mukarubega* [ECR TBC]; Case C-249/13 *Boudjilda* [ECR TBC]; Case C-554/13 *Zh and O* [ECR TBC].

Having set out some basic features of the cases considered in this book, the following sections will delve into the cases beyond statistics to look at how the machinery of judicial review operates in practice. In the main, they consider common components of the tests employed to determine the legality of detention and the way in which they are applied by judges. In doing so, they will take a detail-oriented approach to consider the mechanics of the judgments themselves, examining issues relating to the application of tests of legality, such as risk assessment and the impact of detainee non-co-operation in return or removal.

III. THE LEGALITY TESTS

The origin of the three jurisdictions' tests was explained in chapter four. That discussion demonstrated that the UK and US tests were developed by the courts partly in response to the indeterminate state of the statutory law on detention. In contrast, the test in the EU is statutory and very detailed after intense negotiations among the Member States during the legislative process. Any remaining gaps in coverage or questions about interpretation are for the CJEU to determine, much in the same way that the USSC addressed indefinite detention in *Zadvydas* and the Administrative Court developed the *Hardial Singh* principles. Despite being developed years apart and on different continents, these tests share characteristics, and are built upon the basic tenet that detention must be reasonable in all the circumstances. Thus, in the UK, the *Hardial Singh* principles require removal to take place within a reasonable period;[18] in the USA, *Zadvydas* requires that removal must be likely in the reasonably foreseeable future;[19] and under the EU Return Directive, there must be a reasonable prospect of removal.[20]

In such a fact-dependent inquiry, the application of the tests largely becomes a proportionality analysis where the judges have to weigh facts in evidence and balance competing interests. As described in chapter one, proportionality acts as a key safeguard on fundamental rights, limiting the state's right to exercise sovereign control over its borders. Each jurisdiction evaluated here considers a number of factors in its determinations of whether detention is proportionate and therefore lawful, some of which overlap. In the UK and USA, this includes an evaluation of whether the detainee poses a risk of flight or danger to the community, or whether the detainee has co-operated with the state. The UK goes beyond this to include consideration of the effect of detention on the

[18] *R (Hardial Singh) v Governor of Durham Prison* [1983] EWHC 1 (QB).
[19] *Zadvydas v Davis* (2001) 533 US 678.
[20] EU Return Directive 2008/115/EC, Art 15(4).

detainee and his or her family, and the conditions of detention.[21] The EU Return Directive refers to some of these elements when it specifies that detention is only permissible where there is a risk of absconding, or where an individual is avoiding or interfering with the return process. In some cases, particularly in the USA, a detainee's pursuit of remedies against removal or deportation will be factored into the court's review of whether detention is justifiable.

The evaluation is not one-sided. The state must work actively to secure removal. In the UK and EU, this is expressed as 'diligence', whereas in the USA, diligence is implied in evaluations of state efforts to remove. Detention may be considered unreasonable if the state is making no effort to remove the individual in question, for example, by failing to regularly communicate with the relevant foreign embassy or consulate to obtain identity documents. Detention under the Return Directive can only be maintained for as long as removal arrangements are in progress and are executed diligently.

Assessing reasonableness may also include an evaluation of the length of detention to date. The UK has no maximum, nor is any indicative period of reasonableness contemplated by the Administrative Court. The USA is essentially the same, except the Supreme Court has set a presumptively reasonable period for post-removal order detention of six months. However, the NY district courts do not often factor into their analysis the duration of detention at the time of the hearing. Finally, the Return Directive explicitly limits detention to six months, extendable by 12 months only where the detainee is not co-operating or where there are delays in obtaining the requisite documents from the target country – either of which must be causally linked to a delay in effecting return. The Directive also stresses that detention must be as short as possible and necessary.

Application of the legality tests in the context of mandatory detention under the UK Borders Act 2007 differs slightly. One judgment in particular identified a need to alter the *Hardial Singh* principles to take into account cases where individuals have been detained under the mandatory detention provisions of section 36 of the UK Borders Act 2007. In *Hussein*, Nicol J modified principles (i) and (iv) as follows:

> (i) The Secretary of State must intend to deport the person unless one of the exceptions in s.33 applies and can only use this power to detain for the purpose of examining whether they do.
>
> (iv) The Secretary of State should act with reasonable diligence and expedition to determine whether any of the exceptions in s.33 is applicable.[22]

[21] See, eg *R (Asekun) v SSHD* [2009] EWHC 1707 (Admin); *R (Mjemer) v SSHD* [2011] EWHC 1514 (Admin); *R (Rashid) v SSHD* [2011] EWHC 3352 (Admin); *R (JM) v SSHD* [2014] EWHC 151 (Admin), where the individual had been 'detained in a strict prison regime, locked alone in a cell for over 20 hours a day with limited use of a pay phone', but release was not ordered because of a significant risk of reoffending (91).

[22] *Hussein v SSHD* [2009] EWHC 2492 (Admin) 43.

The Court further specified that principle (iii) ('if, before the expiry of the reasonable period, it becomes apparent that the Secretary of State will not be able to effect deportation within a reasonable period, she should not seek to exercise the power of detention') would be violated in the context of mandatory detention when it becomes clear that *either* deportation would not be possible within a reasonable time *or* if the question whether any exceptions under section 33 to automatic deportation are applicable cannot be resolved within a reasonable period.[23] Because detention under section 36 is rare among the pool of cases examined in this book, there has not been much occasion to consider how this works in practice. However, it is interesting to note that the diligence requirement has been incorporated into the test in such a way as to try to ensure that time spent detained under mandatory provisions is kept to a minimum.

More broadly, this illustrates an important willingness to consider that mandatory detention requires different standards, arguably because of the potential for injustice inherent in the tests as they have been traditionally applied. The Administrative Court decision in *Hussein* represents a concern that the requirement of diligence should apply to the Secretary of State not only in seeking removal, but also in determining whether the mandatory provisions apply, because if they do not, people may be detained unlawfully for lengthy periods of time. However, the impact of the *Hussein* judgment on other judgments in the book pool seems thus far to be limited to that case, as subsequent cases of mandatory detention do not refer back to Nicol's formulation.[24] Though one case specified that the Secretary of State should be afforded a 'reasonable time' to determine whether the mandatory detention provisions apply,[25] no other case on mandatory detention in the case pool considered that the *Hardial Singh* principles might apply differently. This is most likely because most cases reached the Administrative Court after the Secretary of State made the decision that section 36 detention is appropriate. Upon such a determination, the *Hardial Singh* principles would presumably apply as normal – this appears to be the case, according to the judgments in this pool. However, Nicol's formulation has been cited and applied by the Court of Appeal and by Administrative Court cases excluded from the pool.[26]

Thus, though there are differences between the three jurisdictions, they each broadly review the legality of detention using the same criteria. However, the weight given to and evaluation of each factor differs, producing varied case outcomes. What follows is an examination of these test components in practice in

[23] ibid 44.

[24] See, eg *Mohammed v SSHD* [2010] EWHC 3323 (Admin); *R (AK) v SSHD* [2010] EWHC 3083 (Admin); *R (Ismail) v SSHD* [2013] EWHC 3921 (Admin).

[25] *Ismail* (ibid) 17.

[26] *R (Saleh (Sudan)) v SSHD* [2013] EWCA Civ 1378, 15; *Saleh v SSHD* [2013] EWHC 61 (Admin) 26–29; *R (Rahman) v SSHD* [2014] EWHC 1640 (Admin) 48; *R (Botan) v SSHD* [2017] EWHC 550 (Admin) 28.

the judgments collected for this book. Despite these similarities, the difference in case outcomes across jurisdictions (especially the UK and USA, where release can actually be ordered by the courts) demonstrates the subjective nature of this exercise.

IV. LIKELIHOOD OF REMOVAL AND DUE DILIGENCE

Each of the three jurisdictions considers the likelihood that removal will occur within a reasonable time. Coupled with this assessment is an evaluation of whether the state has acted conscientiously in seeking removal. Key to the assessment, especially in the UK and USA, is the placement of the burden of proof. This undoubtedly sets the tone for judicial review and impacts whether detainees will succeed in their applications. For example, where the state must make a case to continue detention, as is the situation in the UK, the Court is perhaps more sympathetic to detainee arguments. This is reflected in more rights-protecting outcomes in the UK. Conversely, though the US Supreme Court had the opportunity to rule on the constitutionality of placing the burden of proof on the detainee in *Zadvydas*, it opted not to do so. Thus, detainees in the USA begin judicial review at a procedural disadvantage. Indeed, US case outcomes are the poorest of the three jurisdictions evaluated. Though the CJEU has not had much occasion to consider this issue, it is clear that there must be a real prospect that removal is likely to occur and that the diligence of the state, on its own, will not justify continued detention.

A. United Kingdom

In UK judicial review proceedings, the burden of proof rests with the state, which has to demonstrate that detention is lawful and that removal is likely.[27] 'That principle is so well established in … law that citation of authority is hardly necessary for it.'[28] The Administrative Court has remarked that 'shifting the burden of proof to the detained person … is tantamount to overturning the rule of Article 5' ECHR.[29] The Secretary of State must prove on the balance of probabilities that removal within a reasonable period is likely.[30] In addition, some Administrative Court decisions demonstrate that, where gaps in evidence create doubt or uncertainty regarding specific facts, the court is permitted to draw adverse inferences in favour of the claimant.[31]

[27] See, eg *R (C) v SSHD* [2010] EWHC 1089 (Admin) 36; *R (Boukhalfa) v SSHD* [2003] EWHC 991 (Admin) 18.

[28] *R (Kumar) v SSHD* [2003] EWHC 846 (Admin) 15.

[29] *JM* (n 21) 20.

[30] *R (HY) v SSHD* [2010] EWHC 1678 (Admin) 10.

[31] *MA & TT v SSHD* [2010] EWHC 2350 (Admin) 31; *R (Azaroal) v SSHD* [2013] EWHC 1248 (Admin) 42.

Recall that the UK case rate of success is just under 50 per cent. The reason for this in most cases is because of the court's assessment that removal will not take place within a reasonable period. Whether removal will take place within a reasonable period is assessed in view of the state's efforts to seek removal, the behaviour of the relevant foreign consulate/embassy and, in certain target countries, the political climate. This means that there must be 'some prospect' beyond a 'mere hope' that the state will be able to carry out deportation within a reasonable time.[32] Moreover, even if a reasonable period of time in detention has not yet passed, if it becomes clear that the person cannot be deported within a reasonable period, detention will become unlawful.[33] For example, in a number of cases where the detainees were to be removed to Somalia, the court had to take into consideration the fact that there were difficulties removing anyone to Somalia, and that the ECtHR was due to render judgment on whether such removals were permissible.[34] In view of those problems, in one case, the court remarked that it was likely to be at least 18 months before a position could be reached regarding the possibility of effecting removal to Somalia.[35] In another, the court highlighted the state's inability to specify with any precision when it would be able to deport the detainee, and upon what evidence that expectation was based.[36] In the judge's view, the state had 'an uncertain expectation as opposed to a reasonable expectation' that deportation would be possible, and he ordered release.[37] In another case, detention was held to be

[32] *R (M) v SSHD* [2009] EWHC 629 (Admin) 21; See also *R (Babbage) v SSHD* [2016] EWHC 148 (Admin) 90: 'the acid test is always whether there is a realistic prospect of effecting a return'; *R (Belfken) v SSHD* [2013] EWHC 4658 (Admin) 21; *R (SM) v SSHD* [2011] EWHC 338 (Admin) 89, citing Richards LJ in *R (MH) v SSHD* [2010] EWCA Civ 1112, [65]: 'there can be a realistic prospect of removal without it being possible to specify or predict the date by which, or period within which, removal can reasonably be expected to occur and without any certainty that removal will occur at all', and that, while the extent of certainty or uncertainty will affect the balancing exercise, what is necessary is that 'there must be a sufficient prospect of removal to warrant continual detention when account is taken of all other relevant factors'. However, he also stated ([68(v)]) that as the situation drags on, so certainty becomes a factor of considerable and increasing importance and a greater degree of certainty and proximity of removal will be required to justify continued detention.

[33] *R (Hussein) v SSHD* [2010] EWHC 2651 (Admin) (ordering release where the detainee had been detained for about six months).

[34] See, eg *R (Daq) v SSHD* [2009] EWHC 1655 (Admin); *R (MM (Somalia)) v SSHD* [2009] EWHC 2353 (Admin).

[35] *MM (Somalia)* (ibid) 34. See also *R (Abdi) v SSHD* [2009] EWHC 1324 (Admin); *Daq* (ibid); *R (Egal) v SSHD* [2009] EWHC 2939 (Admin); *R (A) v SSHD* [2006] EWHC 3331 (Admin); *R (Aziz) v SSHD* [2011] EWHC 554 (Admin). Similar issues arose regarding returns to Iraq in *R (A (Iraq)) v SSHD* [2010] EWHC 625 (Admin).

[36] *R (IO) v SSHD* [2008] EWHC 2596 (Admin).

[37] ibid 48. See also C (n 27) 36–37: 'The Secretary of State has not pointed to any further information which might be forthcoming from the claimant or any other source which might create any realistic prospect of persuading X to accept the removal of the claimant there … Moreover … there was no evidence of any assessment of what further information might persuade the authorities of X to take a different view of the claimant and no attempt to explain how such information might be expected to be forthcoming.'

unlawful because it was not possible to issue removal directions and therefore removal within a reasonable period was not possible.[38]

Sometimes, though the court acknowledges that certain factors may counsel in favour of a finding that detention has become unreasonable, it will conclude otherwise. This can be, for example, because of assurances from the state that travel documentation will be forthcoming in the near future. Though in the case of *Badjoko*, the court specifically noted that, absent strong assurances regarding the timing of deportation, the court 'would not have been prepared to countenance an open-ended prospect of ill-defined certainty'.[39] In one case in particular, when evaluating the state's activity in effecting removal, the court recognised that 'the pressure under which officials work' must be balanced against 'individuals whose rights must be recognised and given effect to'.[40] The balance in that case fell in favour of the detainee, who was granted a declaration of illegality.

In some cases, the court permits continued detention, but acknowledges that the situation may need to be re-evaluated in the future under certain circumstances. For example, in *Chen*, there was evidence from China that it would take one to two months to acquire the evidence it needed to be able to accept the return of the detainee.[41] In view of that, and of concerns regarding risk of absconding, the court felt that it was not yet time to say that removal within a reasonable time is unlikely.[42] However, it also held that the state of relations with the Chinese Embassy must be kept under 'constant review'.[43] A similar conclusion was reached in *Lubana*, where the court stated that

> there is at least a real possibility that the time will come when the Secretary of State will have to face up to the difficulties raised by the Indian authorities and give serious consideration as to whether he is going to be able to remove the applicant within a reasonable time.[44]

In that case, rather than come to a judgment, the court adjourned the case and retained supervision over it.[45]

[38] *Hwez* (n 6).
[39] *Badjoko* (n 6) 22.
[40] *R (Abdullah) v SSHD* [2010] EWHC 259 (Admin) 64.
[41] *Chen v SSHD* [2002] EWHC 2797 (Admin).
[42] ibid 32.
[43] ibid 34.
[44] *R (Lubana) v SSHD* [2003] EWHC 410 (Admin) 13. See also *R (Giwa) v SSHD* [2013] EWHC 3189 (Admin) 82; *R (Mohamed) v SSHD* [2010] EWHC 1244 (Admin) 41: 'Having considered all of those factors and balanced them together, the Secretary of State has satisfied me that despite the length of time of the claimant's detention he, the Secretary of State, has a reasonable prospect of deporting the claimant within a reasonable time. Of course, I can only make that decision on the basis of matters as they stand today, and on the evidence that I have seen. The claimant has been in detention for a long time, and, if the Secretary of State does not keep up his endeavours and/or if the Somali authorities show a disinclination to accept his return and reasonably promptly, the balance may change. It will then be open to the claimant to make a further application on the basis of the new circumstances, no doubt by way of application to the tribunal for bail in the first instance.'
[45] See also *Kumar* (n 28) 30–31.

With the UK cases, the most important thing to stress in relation to the discussion of whether removal is likely is that a conclusion whether it is or not is not the only dispositive factor. As will become evident in subsequent sections, the Administrative Court will generally balance a finding that removal in the reasonable future is not likely against detainee criminal history and risk of absconding. The extent to which there is certainty regarding when removal will occur will obviously impact the balancing exercise.[46] This, of course, occurs in the US cases as well, but with two main differences. First, the balance almost always comes out in favour of a finding that removal is likely, which trumps all other considerations; and secondly, the balancing exercise itself is not scaled or weighted the way it is in the Administrative Court. For example, the Administrative Court in *Qaderi* considered that there was evidence of a lack of due diligence in seeking removal, but, viewed in consideration of other 'significant factors which point[ed] the opposite way', including 'stubborn' non-co-operation in effecting removal and a criminal conviction for using false documents in an asylum application, the court concluded that, on balance, the state's poor diligence should be given less weight.[47] Similar reasoning was used in *Chahboub*, where, though it was uncertain when the necessary documents would be issued, a view that the detainee would almost 'inevitabl[y]' abscond led the court to conclude that it was legitimate to keep the individual in detention.[48] More detail regarding risk assessment follows. However, at this point, I would stress that the Administrative Court explicitly engages in a balancing of factors to determine whether, in an individual case, detention is proportionate. It engages with the parties' evidence of likelihood and diligence, and assigns weight. I would argue that in most cases, this is done fairly because of the Court's overall awareness that multiple factors are at play.

However, it is interesting to juxtapose the findings in these cases with statistics published jointly by the All Party Parliamentary Groups on Refugees and Migration. The report notes specifically that at least one-third of detainees are released due to an inability to remove them.[49] This suggests that, at the administrative level, periodic reviews of detention may not be conducted as robustly as they are at the Administrative Court.

B. United States

Administrative Court practice contrasts sharply with US practice, where the balance seems to fall in favour of the state, especially regarding an assessment

[46] *R (Momoh) v SSHD* [2012] EWHC 3740 (Admin) 105.

[47] *Qaderi* (n 5) 35, 37–40.

[48] *R (Chahboub) v SSHD* [2009] EWHC 1989 (Admin) 33. See also *R (Said) v SSHD* [2010] EWHC 365 (Admin); *Mohamed* (n 44).

[49] Joint Inquiry by the All Party Parliamentary Group on Refugees & the All Party Parliamentary Group on Migration, 'The Report of the Inquiry into the Use of Immigration Detention in the United Kingdom', (March 2015) 17.

of whether it has acted diligently. To succeed on a *Zadvydas* claim, the *detainee* must demonstrate that removal in the reasonably foreseeable future is unlikely.[50] In doing so, the Supreme Court has held that non-citizens bear the burden of providing 'good reason to believe' that removal in the reasonably foreseeable future is unlikely, and that, if they sustain that burden, the government must provide 'sufficient evidence' to rebut it.[51] The immigration regulations require the detainee to submit evidence demonstrating 'that there is no *significant* likelihood of removal in the reasonably foreseeable future'.[52] This is a stricter standard than permitted by the Supreme Court. If the detainee manages to succeed in sustaining the burden of proof, it then passes to the government to rebut. Writing two years after the judgment in *Zadvydas*, Peitzke evaluated the reactions to the judgment in the Ninth and Fifth Circuits, and found that courts were applying the reasoning of the Supreme Court and 'closely analyzing the intent of Congress'.[53] The cases in this book do not suggest that this approach is still (if it ever was) taken by the NY district courts. In fact, these courts take a less nuanced approach to identifying what is reasonable. As a result, the discussion seems more black and white.

For example, the fact that the burden of proof is on the detainee can significantly impact results. In considering whether the petitioners have satisfied the burden of proof, the emphasis is on whether there are any 'institutional barriers to removal'.[54] This is established by demonstrating that the government has been communicating regularly with the consulate or embassy,[55] that there have been prior successful repatriations to the state at issue[56] or that travel documents had been previously issued to the petitioner.[57] Placing the burden of proof on the detainee is incongruous when compared to federal pre-trial detention and federal habeas corpus in the context of the war on terror, where the government bears the burden of proving that detention is justified by 'clear and convincing evidence'[58] and a 'preponderance of the evidence',[59] respectively. Kimball points out that, in fact, 'All other forms of civil commitment have a variety of more

[50] *Zadvydas* (n 19) 701.

[51] ibid.

[52] 8 CFR 241.13(d) (emphasis added).

[53] M Peitzke, 'The Fate of "Unremovable" Aliens before and after September 11, 2001: The Supreme Court's Presumptive Six-Month Limit to Post-Removal-Period Detention' (2002) 30 *Pepperdine Law Review* 769, 797.

[54] *Rahel v Tryon* 2013 WL 1878914 (WDNY) 6.

[55] See, eg *Dookhan v Holder* 2013 WL 1945950 (WDNY); *Mohamed v Holder* 2013 WL 2468738 (WDNY); *Juma v Mukasey* 2009 WL 2191247 (SDNY).

[56] See, eg *Alzubi v Tryon* 2015 WL 860792 (WDNY); *Campbell v Tryon* 2014 WL 3809747 (WDNY); *Ahmed v Holder* 2013 WL 2468732 (WDNY), *Tejeda-Estrella v Holder* 2013 WL 1570141 (WDNY).

[57] See, eg *Andreenko v Holder* 2012 WL 4210286 (WDNY); *Ricketts v Mule* 2009 WL 102953 (WDNY).

[58] Bail Reform Act 1984, Pub L No 98-473, 98 Stat 1976-87; see also, eg *US v Arena* (NDNY 1995) 894 F Supp 580.

[59] See MC Waxman, 'Guantánamo, Habeas Corpus, and Standards of Proof: Viewing the Law through Multiple Lenses' (2009) 42 *Case Western Journal of International Law* 245, 247. The burden

robust procedures not available to indefinitely detained non-citizens, including the right to have the government carry the burden of proof'.[60] Holper discusses burden of proof in the immigration bond hearing context, and the placement by the USSC in *Zadvydas* of the burden of proof on the detainee.[61] She argues that, though it appears that the burden is on the detainee to demonstrate that removal is unlikely, in fact, the government bears the ultimate burden of persuasion.[62] This would be significant if detainees had a genuine chance of sustaining their burden of proof, but the cases examined in this book demonstrate that this is highly unlikely and that therefore any burden of persuasion that the government might carry is meaningless in practice.[63] Indeed, it appears that US detainees are being held to the stricter standard of proof set out in the immigration regulations, which require a showing of significant evidence that removal will not occur soon. This has an impact on success rates.

The judgments demonstrate a clear link between legal representation and successful habeas petitions in the context of 'likelihood' arguments.[64] Though some thoughtful arguments were put forth by pro se applicants,[65] in most cases their arguments were rudimentary. For example, detainees often argued that removal was not likely in the reasonably foreseeable future without supplying any evidence as to why this was the case, or failing to demonstrate that he or she did not pose a flight risk or a danger to the community.[66] Some would go a step further by arguing that removal was not likely because travel documents had not been issued by the relevant consulate or embassy, and there was no certainty as to when they might be issued in the future – but in these cases the government was typically able to rebut the argument simply by showing that they were

also rests with the state in the context of civil mental health detention. See *Foucha v Louisiana* (1992) 540 US 71.

[60] KJ Kimball, 'A Right to be Heard: Non-citizens' Due Process Right to In-Person Hearings to Justify their Detentions prior to Removal' (2009) 5 *Stanford Journal of Civil Rights and Civil Liberties* 159, 186, fn 167.

[61] M Holper, 'The Beast of Burden in Immigration Bond Hearings' (2016) 67 *Case Western Reserve Law Review* 75.

[62] ibid 105.

[63] Moreover, McGinty Borg writes about the injustice of the fact that even in administrative immigration proceedings, the detainee 'incorrectly' bears the burden of proving that he or she is not dangerous. See M McGinty Borg, 'Freedom from the Deprivation of Liberty: The Supreme Court Imposes Limitations on Indefinite Detention of Criminal Aliens – *Zadvydas v Davis*' (2003) *William Mitchell Law Review* 951, 964, fn 96.

[64] See, eg *Minto v Decker* (2015 SDNY) 108 F Supp 3d 189; *Bugianishvili v McConnell* 2015 WL 3903460 (SDNY); *Monestime v Reilly* (2010 SDNY) 704 F Supp 2d 453; *Farez-Espinoza v Chertoff* (2009 SDNY) 600 F Supp 2d 488.

[65] See, eg *Worrell v Ashcroft* (2002 WDNY) 207 F Supp 2d 61; *Pan v Ashcroft* 2005 WL 1398601 (WDNY).

[66] *Dogra v Immigration Customs Enforcement* 2009 WL 2878459 (WDNY); *Adams v Holder* 2012 WL 1999488 (WDNY); *Toure v Holder* 2013 WL 1352288 (WDNY); *Adegbite v Holder* 2013 WL 1945734 (WDNY); *Haidara v Mule* 2008 WL 2483281 (WDNY); *Singh v Holmes* 2004 WL 2280366 (WDNY); *Powell* (n 6).

actively attempting to obtain the documents.[67] In one case, a detainee argued that removal was unlikely because, at the time, the DHS had temporarily halted removals to Haiti (the destination state for the petitioner) for some time, and had only recently resumed the removal of certain non-citizens (of which the petitioner was not one).[68] Despite the government arguing only that it anticipated removal in the foreseeable future following this resumption, the court held that the petitioner had not shown 'good reason to believe' that removal was not imminent.[69]

In rare cases, the court finds that the government has not acted diligently. For example, in *Scarlett*, the WDNY court remarked that removal of the detained individual had been delayed due to the state's attempts to 'forum shop' the underlying immigration proceedings in which the detainee was challenging his removal.[70] In most cases, regular communications with foreign consulates or embassies, coupled with previous successful removals, resulted in a finding that the state acted diligently and that removal in the foreseeable future is likely.[71] These cases indicate that the quality of response time by foreign consulates is not as important as state efforts to communicate with them in securing travel documents. However, in one case, the court remarked that 'the Government cannot exploit another nation's timetables to justify an indefinite detention'.[72]

In some cases, the courts indicated that as the period of detention under section 241(a) INA increases, what is considered as the reasonably foreseeable future will decrease in time. Judges making this statement relied on the part of *Zadvydas*, which stated that:

> After [the reasonable period of six months], once the alien provides good reason to believe that there is no significant likelihood of removal in the reasonably foreseeable future, the Government must respond with evidence sufficient to rebut that showing. And for detention to remain reasonable, as the period of prior post-removal confinement grows, what counts as the 'reasonably foreseeable future' conversely would have to shrink.[73]

This was the case in *Ramos*,[74] where the detainee had been detained for nearly two years at the time of the hearing, and in *Dogra*,[75] where detention had lasted

[67] See, eg *Tejeda-Estrella* (n 56); *Gonther v Napolitano* 2013 WL 1569311 (WDNY).

[68] *Gabriel v Cleary* 2009 WL 2413674 (WDNY) 2.

[69] ibid 4. This case was actually premature in terms of a *Zadvydas* claim, but the court considered it anyway.

[70] *Scarlett v US Department of Homeland Security Bureau of ICE* (2009 WDNY) 632 F Supp 2d 214, 223.

[71] See, eg *Toure* (n 66) 5; *Williams v Holder* 2013 WL 1352306 (WDNY) 5; *Jones v Holder* 2013 WL 2898069 (WDNY) 4; *McKoy v Holder* 2013 WL 5211500 (WDNY) 5; *Juma* (n 55) 4.

[72] *Muhury v Tryon* 2011 WL 6016606 (WDNY) 3.

[73] *Zadvydas* (n 19) 701.

[74] *Ramos v Chertoff* 2009 WL 1563894 (WDNY) 6.

[75] *Dogra* (n 66) 4. See also *Jama v Napolitano* 2013 WL 5503965 (WDNY) 4.

1.3 years. However, the detainees were not released in either of those cases, largely due to the court concluding that their behaviour warranted their continued detention, despite its length to date.

With regard to travel documents, the case law is rife with negative statements by the court to the effect that, at the time of the hearing, the embassy or consulate had not yet indicated that travel documents were not forthcoming.[76] For example, in one case, the court held that the detainee had failed to sustain his burden of proof because 'Antigua has not refused to issue petitioner travel documents, or has ambiguously answered when it would produce such documents, or failed to respond to ICE [US Immigration and Customs Enforcement] inquiries'.[77] This effectively requires the petitioner to prove a negative in order to sustain the burden of proof. The inappropriateness of this is not completely lost on the courts. In *Gumbs*[78] and *Azad*,[79] both petitioners were granted some form of relief due in part to the courts' recognition that

> the negative statement that the Consulate has not given ICE any reason to believe that a travel document *will not* issue is not equivalent to a statement that the Consulate has given ICE reason to believe that a travel document *will issue*.[80]

In Mr Gumbs's case, the court gave the government 60 days to try to remove him, after which release under supervision must follow. Mr Azad was ordered to be released within 14 days. In one case, the court hailed the fact that travel documents would be forthcoming after the detainee's challenge to removal was resolved as being 'critical to the analysis of reasonably foreseeable removal'.[81] That, coupled with the fact that the court deemed it likely that the detainee's removal challenge would fail and that his detention was not at risk of becoming indefinite, apparently justified a conclusion that his detention was lawful, despite his having been detained for a year and a half by the time of the habeas hearing.

C. European Union

In contrast to the UK and USA, where the likelihood of removal forms a substantial part of the case law, this aspect of the Return Directive has only been considered in one case before the CJEU. Article 15(1) and (5) of the Return Directive permit detention only 'as long as removal arrangements are in progress and executed with due diligence'. Article 15(4) also requires release where it

[76] See, eg *Duarte-Ceri v Napolitano* 2009 WL 1806694 (WDNY); *Ramos* (n 74).
[77] *Roberts v Bureau of Immigration and Customs Enforcement* 2007 WL 781925 (WDNY) 2. See also *Haidara* (n 66) 3.
[78] *Gumbs* (n 9).
[79] *Azad* (n 5).
[80] ibid 3 (emphasis in original); *Gumbs* (n 9), citing *Azad* (n 5) 3.
[81] *Dover v Holder* 2011 WL 4054952 (WDNY) 4. See also *Adams* (n 66) 4.

appears that there is no reasonable prospect of removal. As discussed in chapter four, in *Kadzoev*, the Bulgarian authorities had been trying for two years to return Mr Kadzoev to Russia. Faced with the circumstances of the case, the CJEU clarified that it must be apparent to the detaining authorities that a 'real prospect exists that the removal can be carried out successfully' in light of the duration of detention to date.[82] It went on further to hold that such a prospect does not exist where it is apparent that it is unlikely that the detainee will be successfully admitted to a third country.[83]

Thus, for the CJEU, the diligence of the state in seeking removal did not impact its decision about the unreasonable prospect of removal. This means that diligent state action will not, in itself, justify detention if the target third country is not going to admit the individual, even where the maximum period has not yet expired. In addition, the CJEU specified that: 'where the maximum duration of detention … has been reached, the question whether there is no longer a "reasonable prospect of removal" … does not arise. In such a case the person concerned must in any event be released immediately.'[84]

V. ASSESSING RISK

Part of a state's decision whether to detain inevitably involves a qualitative or quantitative assessment of risk. This risk comes in two forms: risk to the public through, for example, the commission of crime; and a risk of flight – that is, the concern that the state will be unable to remove non-nationals considered as undesirable from the territory because they cannot be located. The assessment may be confined to determining whether the individual has sufficient ties to the community to reduce the risk or flight, or it may consist of an evaluation of whether their criminal history would make them a danger to the community if they were to be granted bail or bond. In the UK and USA, we see both considerations in the cases, while the Return Directive, remarkably, does not include criminal history as a factor justifying detention.

Risk of flight and risk of dangerousness are often considered together by scholars and sometimes even within the relevant statutory provisions setting out what factors are suitable for consideration in determinations of either risk.[85] Though there may be some overlap in indicators, evaluation of flight risk should be separated from evaluation of whether an individual would pose a danger to the community if he or she is released.[86] The literature seems to be more

[82] *Kadzoev* (n 15) para 65.
[83] ibid para 66.
[84] ibid para 60.
[85] LP Gouldin, 'Disentangling Flight Risk from Dangerousness' (2016) *Brigham Young University Law Review* 837, 865.
[86] ibid 837.

preoccupied with dangerousness, and the case law from both the USA and the UK demonstrates that judicial review is focused more on dangerousness as well. Thus, the ensuing discussion will focus on dangerousness. However, it is important to note, on the subject of risk of flight, that scholars have argued that modern technological advances, such as electronic tagging, have rendered detention based on flight risk alone largely unnecessary.[87] Moreover, Noferi argues that risk of flight, at least in the USA, has never been as high as it has been made out to be and that the issue is rather that the public has a low tolerance for crimes committed following flight from authorities.[88]

Much scholarship laments the pitfalls of attempting to accurately predict risk of criminal behaviour.[89] For example, there is general debate surrounding the question whether the methods used to determine if a person is dangerous are reliable. There are three main categories of indicators of future dangerousness: past conduct of the individual (including past criminal behaviour); past conduct of other individuals in similar circumstances; and an evaluation based on experts.[90] Some additionally consider that certain immutable characteristics, such as age, gender and race, should be used as indicators.[91] Slobogin argues that race is an illegitimate basis for prediction.[92] This should perhaps be expanded to apply to nationality – another fairly immutable characteristic that is relevant to determinations of dangerousness in immigration detention. One scholar argues, in view of the risk of bias associated with immutable characteristics, that the only reliable indicator of future dangerousness is past criminal behaviour.[93] Indeed, this seems to play a large role in the UK, and even more so in the US courts under review here. However, this is not a view held by all, especially when the past criminal behaviour resulted in a minor conviction.[94] More broadly, it has been suggested that immigration detention is 'all about prediction' and that, because no one can actually predict the future, decision makers either fall back

[87] M Noferi, 'Mandatory Immigration Detention for US Crimes: The Noncitizen Presumption of Dangerousness' in MJ Guia et al, *Immigration Detention, Risk and Human Rights* (Springer, 2016) 227 et seq; LP Gouldin, 'Defining Flight Risk' (2018) 85 *University of Chicago Law Review* 677, 727.

[88] Noferi (ibid) 228.

[89] See, eg LI Appleman, 'Justice in the Shadowlands: Pretrial Detention, Punishment, & the Sixth Amendment' (2012) 69 *Washington and Lee Law Review* 1297, 1336–49; K Auerhahn, 'Selective Incapacitation and the Problem of Prediction' (1999) 27 *Criminology* 703; DJ Baker, 'Punishment without a Crime: Is Preventive Detention Reconcilable with Justice?' (2009) 34 *Australian Journal of Legal Philosophy* 120; A Das, 'Immigration Detention: Information Gaps and Barriers to Reform' (2013) 80 *University of Chicago Law Review* 137; LS Pershan, 'Selective Incapacitation and the Justifications for Imprisonment' (1984) 12 *New York University Review of Law and Social Change* 385.

[90] S Dimock, 'Criminalizing Dangerousness: How to Preventively Detain Dangerous Offenders' (2015) 9 *Criminal Law and Philosophy* 537, 556.

[91] J Freeman and C Slobogin, *Proving the Unprovable: The Role of Law, Science, and Speculation in Adjudicating Culpability and Dangerousness* (Oxford University Press, 2006) 112.

[92] ibid.

[93] J Monahan, 'A Jurisprudence of Risk Assessment: Forecasting Harm among Prisoners, Predators and Patients' (2006) 92 *Virginia Law Review* 391, 428.

[94] Noferi (n 87) 233.

on stereotypes or they err on the side of caution to avoid public condemnation in the event that the released individual commits a crime.[95]

Exacerbating the disagreement over which indicators are reliable and how dangerousness is best measured is the confusion surrounding what is meant by 'dangerous'. Parry argues that, over time, the definition of 'dangerousness' has become increasingly inclusive so that there are no straightforward boundaries.[96] As a result, 'dangerousness' includes such a long list of antisocial or criminal acts that its meaning has become arbitrary.[97] In this vein, it has been suggested that this has resulted in a situation where the state has too much power.[98] In addition, the meaning of dangerousness changes depending on the context. For example, in relation to capital punishment in the USA, dangerousness indicates 'propensity to commit serious bodily injury to another', while in civil detention, such as mental health detention, it can refer to whether the person is 'likely to do substantial physical or emotional injury on another'.[99]

Another problematic point is a lack of clarity regarding whether the decision maker is assessing an individual's *present* danger or whether *future* danger is being evaluated. Dimock argues that preventive detention (which includes immigration detention) can only be ordered where an individual poses a present risk of danger.[100] She suggests that this is necessary because it is only possible to accurately predict future dangerousness based on an assessment of their present circumstances.[101] This has profound implications for the case law evaluated in this chapter, especially for cases in the NY federal courts, where it appears that judges are using past criminal behaviour as evidence of future risk, regardless of severity or when the conduct occurred.

A final complicating factor is disagreement over what standard of proof is required to demonstrate dangerousness. Within the legal context generally, different standards of proof may be applicable depending on the type of liberty deprivation at issue.[102] Slobogin suggests that the unreliability of predicting future dangerousness means that no one's liberty should be deprived 'unless there is a high degree of certainty that the person will offend in the near future'[103] and that the standard of proof should be heightened as the length of the liberty deprivation increases.[104] He also argues that any civil commitment

[95] ibid 233, citing D Cole, 'Out of the Shadows: Preventive Detention, Suspected Terrorists and War' (2009) *California Law Review* 693, 696.

[96] JW Parry, *Mental Disability, Violence, and Future Dangerousness: Myths Behind the Presumption of Guilt* (Rowman & Littlefield, 2013) 98.

[97] ibid 98.

[98] C Slobogin, 'A Jurisprudence of Dangerousness' (2003) 98 *Northwestern University Law Review* 1, 18.

[99] Freeman and Slobogin (n 91) 100 and fns 6–7.

[100] Dimock (n 90) 544.

[101] ibid 544.

[102] Slobogin (n 98) 50.

[103] ibid 6, suggesting further that it is impossible to achieve this standard.

[104] ibid.

must involve a proportionality evaluation that includes three components. The first is that the length of detention must be reasonably related to the harm it is aimed at preventing. The second is that the type of detention employed must be reasonably related to the harm feared. Finally, there must be a periodic review of detention if it is ordered.[105]

Excluding the EU, which does not include future dangerousness as a justification for detention under the Return Directive, we see that the standards and proportionality analysis suggested above are rarely a part of detention review in the NY courts, though they feature in some form in the Administrative Court. Judgments from the latter suggest that, though the language may not be exactly the same as above, for the most part, the judges are considering the nature and timing of the detainees' past criminal behaviour in their assessment of whether detention is appropriate.

Regardless of whether you agree that risk of future behaviour, criminal or otherwise, is a proper justification for detention, it is clear that the courts in each of the three jurisdictions under examination consider risk in one form or another. Broadly, the determination of whether a detainee poses a risk of absconding or a danger to the community (eg through reoffending) centres on issues such as criminal history, family ties and identity documentation. The UK and US courts engage in a balancing test, though, on the whole, the Administrative Court considers the circumstances surrounding previous convictions or attempts to flee, rather than making a judgment based on the presence or absence of a criminal history or past flight, which is usually the case in the USA. The CJEU's exposure to these issues relates more to defining what risk means and how it can be legitimately evaluated by the Member States. Risk is specifically connected to whether or not detention can be extended beyond the initial six-month period under Article 15(6) of the Return Directive.

A. United Kingdom

Chapter three illustrated the way in which a computer algorithm is used in the USA to predict risk of future criminality at the point of the initial decision to detain. Interestingly, the UK analyses risk using a similar method, the Offender Assessment System (OASys), but in contrast to the USA, OASys is only used in connection with criminal offenders and is not meant to function as the main risk assessment tool for immigration authorities. The role of OASys reports in assessing risk in the context of immigration detention was addressed by the Administrative Court in *JM*, where the Court stated that:

> [the Secretary of State] has to have careful regard to the OASys assessments, in accordance with her policy. Nonetheless she was required to bring her own judgment

[105] ibid 13–15.

> to bear upon the facts in any particular case. The OASys is an assessment tool, designed for use by the decision maker, along with other information. It is necessarily mechanistic. It is *not a substitute for an exercise of judgment by the decision maker*, whether that is a sentencing judge or an immigration official.[106]

A High Court judge confirmed this perspective when I asked him about the role that such reports play in assessing risk. He noted that they are one factor among many others, including whether and to what extent completing a criminal sentence may have positively affected the individual in question, and that individual's feelings about his or her experience in prison.[107] He also indicated that the weight of an OASys report will decrease the older it is.[108]

Chapter 55 of the EIG, discussed in chapter three above, states that 'public protection is a key consideration underpinning … detention policy'.[109] It requires initial detention decision makers (ie immigration officials) to consider whether the presumption in favour of bail outweighs the risk of harm to the public and instructs them to look at all relevant factors. It also stipulates that convictions for serious offences are 'strongly indicative of the greatest risk of harm to the public and a risk of absconding', and that therefore the 'high risk of public harm carries particularly substantial weight when assessing if continuing detention is reasonably necessary and proportionate'.[110]

While this may be going on at the administrative level, there is no explicit evidence that the Administrative Court is undertaking the same review. However, there is evidence that the Court considers any risk of reoffending or dangerousness in light of 'the breach of the principle of liberty', and in doing so considers a range of relevant factors.[111] Indeed, I observed arguments at the Administrative Court where the judge lamented the failure of the Immigration Act to properly account for the potential of an individual's risk level to change over time, and admonished the Secretary of State for basing its risk assessment on a nine-year-old determination by another decision maker that the individual presented a danger.[112] Beyond that, the case law provides several examples of the judges balancing the severity of the offence with when it occurred. In doing so, they remind the parties that no single factor operates as a 'trump card'.[113] In the case of *H*, the Court discussed the likelihood of absconding. It felt that, if the state managed to prove the existence of such a

[106] *JM* (n 21) 101 (emphasis added).
[107] Anonymous Interview, August 2017.
[108] ibid.
[109] UK Visas and Immigration, 'Enforcement Instructions and Guidance', ch 55, s 55.3.A.
[110] ibid.
[111] *R (Polanco) v SSHD* [2009] EWHC 826 (Admin) 20.
[112] *G* (n 8). Note that the person was not detained, but was instead placed under house arrest (despite being wheelchair bound).
[113] *R (Egal) v SSHD* [2009] EWHC 2939 (Admin) 43.

risk, it 'should not be overstated' because 'it could become a trump card that could

> carr[y] the day for the Secretary of State in every case where such a risk was made out regardless of all other considerations, not least the length of the period of detention. That would be a wholly unacceptable outcome where human liberty is at stake.[114]

Therefore, a delicate balance must be struck between whether removal is likely and whether a risk is present. This balance must be based on objective facts, rather than speculation.[115] Many of the judgments cite the Court of Appeal in the case of *A* in support of this balancing exercise, where Toulson LJ held that:

> Be that as it may, a pertinent question in this case is whether, and to what extent, a risk of the individual absconding and a risk of him reoffending may be taken into account in considering what may be a reasonable time for attempting to bring about his removal or departure. The way I would put it is that there must be a sufficient prospect of the Home Secretary being able to achieve that purpose to warrant the detention or the continued detention of the individual, having regard to all the circumstances including the risk of absconding and the risk of danger to the public if he were at liberty.[116]

Indeed, in *HY*, the Court considered Toulson's judgment and concluded that:

> as regards the risk of offending if released, it is noteworthy that the court is enjoined always to consider the strength of its relevance by reference to [the] nature of the offences the claimant is likely to commit and the likelihood of the risk materialising. The more serious the type of offence the greater will be its relevance.[117]

In *Chahboub*, the court acknowledged that the claimant's risk of reoffending was so high as to be almost 'inevitable'.[118] However, the court went on to say that:

> It is true that the scale of offending … does not involve serious offences of violence to the person, nor does it involve, for example, sexual offences against women or children. Although the type of offending is not serious, there is a large amount of offending, and it is both the extent and the seriousness of offending which needs [*sic*] to be considered.[119]

However, the court tipped the balance in favour of continued detention, after determining that both risks were too high at the time of the hearing.[120]

The determination of whether a risk of absconding is present in a given case is undertaken in a similar manner. For example, in *Boukhalfa*, though the individual was an illegal entrant and had previously evaded the authorities, the

[114] *R (H) v SSHD* [2005] EWHC 1702 (Admin) 21, citing Dyson LJ in *I* (n 3) 53.
[115] *Kumar* (n 28) 20.
[116] *R (A) v SSHD* [2007] EWCA Civ 804, 45, cited by, eg *R (YG) v SSHD* [2008] EWHC 1735 (Admin) 14; *Asekun* (n 21) 14; *Abdi* (n 35) 41.
[117] *HY* (n 30) 24.
[118] *Chahboub* (n 48) 33.
[119] ibid.
[120] ibid. See also *MM (Somalia)* (n 34) 46.

court said the risk that he would abscond in the near future was diluted because he had been granted bail after he was arrested and did not abscond, and because he very much wanted to return to Algeria.[121] In the case of *A*, the court ordered release because removal was not likely within a reasonable time, but it noted that, had there been evidence that removal was likely, the individual's serious criminal offence and risk of absconding would have tipped the balance in favour of continued detention.[122] In *Qaderi*, the court first acknowledged evidence of a lack of due diligence by the state, but then considered that the detainee's conviction for using false documents in an application for asylum indicated that he would present a risk of absconding. Ultimately, the claimant was unsuccessful.[123] In contrast, in the case of *N*, the Court determined that the claimant presented a risk to public property because of prior convictions for theft and burglary, among other offences against property, but felt that the risk could be minimised with appropriate bail conditions.[124] This decision is interesting in light of the fact that the claimant had previously been released on criminal bail and had returned to crime immediately.[125]

The Administrative Court has determined that a refusal to return voluntarily presents a risk of absconding sufficient to justify continued detention, such as in *MMH*.[126] Similarly, bail conditions were deemed inadequate in the case of *A*, where the Court stated that

> The claimant evinced then and evinces now a single objective, namely to stay in this country by hook or by crook. If granted bail I am confident that he will make every effort to remain here, including, if he believes it necessary to achieve that objective, absconding, and removing or disabling any electronic device designed to assist in locating him.[127]

Finally, it is important to note that, in examining risk, the Administrative Court considers evidence anew, rather than limiting itself to determining whether the state acted reasonably in continuing to detain individuals. This is consistent with what the cases reveal about the role of the Administrative Court in judicial review, which will be discussed in chapter seven.

B. United States

In the Supreme Court's discussion of flight risk and danger in *Zadvydas*, Justice Breyer incorporated, by reference to judgments in the pre-trial detention

[121] *Boukhalfa* (n 27) 24.
[122] *R (A) v SSHD* [2008] EWHC 142 (Admin) 17.
[123] *Qaderi* (n 5) 37.
[124] *R (N) v SSHD* [2014] EWHC 1593 (Admin) 46.
[125] ibid 17.
[126] *R (MMH) v SSHD* [2007] EWHC 2134 (Admin) 40.
[127] *A* (n 35) 41.

context, a number of standards in the Court's habeas corpus review of the Fifth Circuit's decision to authorise Mr Zadvydas's continued detention. The cases referred to required a showing by the detaining authority of a 'sufficiently strong special justification' to permit indefinite civil detention.[128] The Court considered the government's stated purpose of immigration detention – to ensure the appearance of individuals at immigration proceedings and to prevent danger to the community – and concluded that, where removal is a 'remote possibility at best', flight risk as a justification is 'weak or non-existent'.[129] Preventive detention justified by dangerousness, on the other hand, is only traditionally permitted in circumstances where the individual is 'specially dangerous' and where strong procedural protections apply.[130] The Court cited three criminal law cases concerning preventive detention which reinforced this notion, including one which required 'proof of dangerousness by clear and convincing evidence', and another requiring a special circumstance, such as mental illness, in addition to the dangerousness claim.[131] The immigration regulations adopted in order to implement the decision in *Zadvydas* state that once a non-citizen demonstrates that there is no significant likelihood of removal in the reasonably foreseeable future, and there are no special circumstances justifying continued detention, release must follow.[132] The term 'special circumstances' is not defined, and it is unclear whether this represents an assessment of danger or flight risk.

Some clarity on the types of risk of concern to the state can be found within the immigration regulations pertaining to initial decisions to detain. They state that the immigration officer can order release if he is satisfied that 'such release would not pose a danger to property or persons and that the alien is likely to appear for any future proceeding'.[133] Confusingly, however, the equivalent standard in relation to bond hearings before an immigration judge requires that detainees 'demonstrate, by clear and convincing evidence, that release would not pose a danger to the safety of other persons or of property'.[134] Absconding does not appear to be a concern.

Looking at what has happened to these standards in practice in the district courts, one sees quite quickly that the more strict USSC approach to risk has not been respected. In fact, the issue of risk is seldom addressed because, especially in the WDNY, petitioners usually fail to sustain their burden of proving that removal in the foreseeable future is unlikely.[135] Moreover, whether the petitioner

[128] *Zadvydas* (n 19) 690.
[129] ibid.
[130] ibid 691.
[131] ibid, citing *Hendricks, Salerno* and *Foucha*.
[132] 8 CFR 241.13.
[133] ibid 1236.1(c)(8).
[134] ibid 1236.1(c)(3).
[135] An example of where this burden was satisfied is *Rajigah v Conway* (EDNY 2003) 268 F Supp 2d 159, 166.

is a flight risk is often not considered because they have already been deemed a danger.

Recall that ICE uses an automated risk assessment tool to initially determine whether detention is permissible.[136] Problems identified by scholars indicate that the algorithm disproportionately results in the detention of individuals.[137] This is important because in habeas corpus proceedings the courts seemingly rely on determinations of risk by the immigration authorities, especially where the detainee is unrepresented and fails to present opposing evidence. Perhaps it is because of their reliance on this method of risk calculation that the courts generally do not look at the evidence in a nuanced manner.[138] Though they may occasionally indicate that a crime was 'violent' or 'aggravated', or that there has been a prior flight, there is generally no consideration of whether circumstances may have changed with time or, indeed, of the circumstances surrounding the crime at the time. One scholar has argued that, to avoid a due process violation, the right to liberty can only be limited through an individualised assessment of need.[139] Though it is arguable that the district courts are technically doing this in assessing risk with reference to detainees' criminal records, the failure to engage fully with the relevant facts, such as the severity of the crime and its temporality, would suggest that their analysis falls short of satisfying due process.[140] Moreover, though the district courts weigh risk against likelihood of removal, in most cases where risk is assessed, the court agrees with the state's determination that there is a risk that the person would flee or pose a danger to the community if released. The very fact of a criminal history plays a large role, though there is often not a lot of discussion. Usually, a finding of risk is based on whether the detainee committed an aggravated felony or has fled previously in the criminal or immigration context.[141]

For example, in *Pan*, after determining that the detainee failed to sustain his burden of proof, the WDNY court went on to hold that the state was nevertheless correct in detaining him because of the 'nature and seriousness of

[136] See ch 3, s V.B above.

[137] R Koulish, 'Immigration Detention in the Risk Classification Assessment Era' (2016) 16 *Connecticut Public Interest Law Journal* 1, 19: 'a second factor that likely contributed to high detention rates in the Baltimore sample is that the RCA assessed the vast majority of these discretionary cases as being medium or high for at least one risk factor – while RCA did not recommend release if either risk factor was medium or high'.

[138] An important caveat here is that, given how few cases considered risk in the USA, my conclusions cannot be said to be representative of overall practice.

[139] Anonymous, 'Making Outcasts Out of Outlaws: The Unconstitutionality of Sex Offender Registration and Criminal Alien Detention' (2004) 17 *Harvard Law Review* 2731, 2739.

[140] Senate Bill 36, the 'Keep Our Communities Safe Act of 2017', 115th Congress (2017–2018), was introduced by Republican Senator James Inhofe in January 2017. Among other relevant provisions, it seeks in s 4(2) to ensure that non-citizens who qualified for automatic detention under INA, s 236(c) are detained beyond the 90-day removal period under s 241 without possibility for release, even where detention is prolonged. It is unclear whether this Bill will pass, but, in any case, this seems to be occurring in practice simply as a result of a prior criminal record.

[141] *Dover* (n 81) 4.

[his] federal criminal convictions for racketeering and extortion'.[142] However, there was no real discussion of the circumstances of these crimes or the risk, and the detainee appeared not to offer any evidence to the contrary. This is a common occurrence. The state need only demonstrate that it acted reasonably in detaining based on risk.[143] In *Dover*, the court listed several factors justifying continued detention, including the fact that the individual had fled before and is an aggravated felon.[144]

In *Fofana*, the court did not believe that the detainee presented a risk of absconding, but concluded that the state was reasonable to determine that he posed a danger to the community because of a previous sex offence.[145] Again, no exploration of the severity of the offence or consideration of whether it occurred sufficiently long ago to indicate that risk might be low was undertaken by the court. In *Miller*, a lack of family ties was enough to consider the detainee a flight risk,[146] and in *Adler*, the very fact that the detainee was liable to deportation seemed to be enough to convince the court that he presented a risk of absconding.[147]

On the more positive side of the scale, in *Azad*, the court ordered release after finding that the detainee posed no risk of danger because he did not have a criminal record, nor was he deemed a risk of absconding because he had never attempted to conceal his identity or address upon being released from prison.[148] The *D'Alessandro* case indicates that, though it does not seem to occur very often, the federal district courts are willing to review the government's determination that continued detention is justified because of a risk of flight or dangerousness.[149] In that case, the WDNY judge concluded that such a finding was 'patently unreasonably in light of the evidence in the record'[150] and that the Supreme Court has traditionally required 'the dangerousness rationale be accompanied by some other special circumstance, such as mental illness, that helps to create the danger'.[151] This is the only case that based a finding of non-dangerousness on this rationale.

Some legal theory suggests that when judges are trying to choose between two possible rulings, they consider what consequences each would have and how acceptable those consequences are in light of considerations such as common sense, public policy, convenience and expediency.[152] In the immigration context,

[142] *Pan* (n 65) 6.

[143] See, eg *St Louis v Heron* 2011 WL 2746787 (WDNY) 3; *Fofana v Holder* (2013 WDNY) 947 F Supp 2d 329, 334.

[144] *Dover* (n 81) 3.

[145] *Fofana* (n 143) 334. See also *Iturralde-Manosalva v Reno* 2001 WL 1398689 (SDNY) 4.

[146] *Miller v Shanahan* 2010 WL 481002 (SDNY) 4.

[147] *Adler v US Department of Homeland Security* 2009 WL 3029328 (SDNY) 2.

[148] *Azad* (n 5) 3.

[149] *D'Alessandro v Mukasey* (WDNY 2009) 628 F Supp 2d 368.

[150] ibid 377.

[151] ibid 380, citing *Zadvydas* (n 19) 690–91.

[152] N MacCormick, *Legal Reasoning and Legal Theory* (Oxford University Press, 1994) 101–19 and ch 6.

one former judge expressly remarked that 'a judge must have the common sense and humility … to consider the rights of the next victim of a violent thug pleading his human rights'.[153] This approach may explain the way in which the Administrative Court considers risk in degrees, by reference to the nature and timing of the incident or crime. That is, the more severe a prior conviction, the more drastic the potential consequences. Consequences framed in terms of convenience and expediency may, in contrast, over-inform the conclusions of the US district courts, which seem to assess risk quickly and overwhelmingly in favour of state determinations with a view towards ensuring that removal occurs.

C. European Union

With regard to the CJEU, the judgment in *Mahdi* addresses the relationship between a lack of identification documents and the risk of absconding. The referring court in Bulgaria asked the CJEU whether the Directive precludes national law permitting an extension of detention beyond the initial six months solely based on the fact that the detainee lacks identification documents, and is therefore considered to present a risk of absconding.

Though an initial decision to detain can be based on a risk of absconding according to Article 15(1) of the Return Directive, the CJEU emphasised that, when it comes to extending detention beyond the initial six-month period, Article 15(6) contemplates only two circumstances: (i) where the detainee is not co-operating; and (ii) where there are delays in obtaining requisite documents from the third country to where the detainee will be removed.[154] Article 15(6) does not permit a lack of identification documents on its own to serve as a basis for extending detention, nor does it repeat the language in Article 15(1) regarding absconding as a justification for detention. However, the Court held that Article 15(6) must be read alongside Article 15(4), which requires the cessation of detention when there is no longer a reasonable prospect of removal or where the conditions in Article 15(1) no longer exist.[155] This means that any decision to extend detention beyond six months must include a re-examination of the initial reasons for detention, including whether the person poses a risk of absconding.

The Directive defines 'risk of absconding' in Article 3(7), which makes it clear that the determination of risk must be based on an individual, objective assessment of the facts.[156] While it is permissible to consider a lack of identity documents as one factor in the determination of whether there is a risk of

[153] J Hanratty RD, *The Making of an Immigration Judge* (Quartet, 2016) 159.
[154] *Mahdi* (n 15) para 68.
[155] ibid para 59.
[156] ibid para 70.

absconding, a lack of documents on its own cannot serve as a basis for extending detention.[157] However, in *Md Sagor*, the Court held that a risk of absconding can justify a Member State's decision not to grant a period of voluntary departure under Article 7(4) of the Directive.[158]

This is an interesting outcome because Article 15(6) does not, on its face, require Member States to re-evaluate the circumstances of detention under Article 15(1) when deciding whether to extend detention beyond the initial six-month period. It refers only to two specific grounds: lack of co-operation and delays in obtaining documentation. This means, as Mitsilegas explains, that Member States cannot extend detention automatically because of a presumption of risk[159] or a prior determination of risk. It seems that the CJEU has gone beyond the requirements of the Directive to require a fuller examination of whether an extension is appropriate. This is consequently a more rights-protecting approach by the Court.

In *Kadzoev*, the CJEU considered whether the maximum detention period could be exceeded in cases where the detainee is aggressive or where he or she does not have identification documents and may therefore flee. This is discussed more fully in chapter six below, in relation to the impact of a maximum detention period. For the purposes of this section, it is important to stress that, rather than attempt to define these terms, the CJEU reiterated that the maximum period of detention is absolute and cannot be exceeded even where the detainee may pose a risk of fleeing. In so doing, the CJEU has limited the circumstances under which a Member State can detain third-country nationals based on risk of absconding.[160]

The Court addresses the impact of criminal activity only in relation to a Category C case on voluntary return and the concept of risk to public policy. *Zh and O* considers whether the fact that a third-country national is suspected of committing, rather than has been convicted of, a criminal offence can be considered a risk to public policy in the context of determining whether to grant a period of voluntary return (and for how long) under Article 7(4) of the Directive.[161] The Court emphasised that voluntary return should only be withheld in limited circumstances because the aim of Article 7 is to ensure that the fundamental rights of third-country nationals subject to return are protected. Any derogations from rights-protecting provisions must be interpreted strictly.[162] The Member State must be able to prove, in an individual case, that the third-country national actually poses a risk.[163] This means that the

[157] ibid paras 72–73.
[158] *Md Sagor* (n 16) para 41.
[159] V Mitsilegas, *The Criminalisation of Migration in Europe: Challenges for Human Rights and the Rule of Law* (Springer, 2015) 102.
[160] ibid 99.
[161] *Zh and O* (n 17).
[162] ibid paras 42, 47.
[163] ibid para 46.

relevant authorities must 'properly [take] into account the national's personal conduct and the risk that that conduct poses to public policy', having regard to the principle of proportionality.[164] Therefore, the fact that a third-country national is suspected, *or has been convicted*, of a criminal offence, on its own, is not enough to justify withholding return.[165] However, suspicion of a criminal offence may serve as a basis for a determination that the individual poses a risk to public policy alongside other relevant factors.[166] This is because, ultimately, it is for the states to determine the meaning of 'public policy' for the purpose of Article 7. Despite this statement, the CJEU goes on to discuss the meaning of 'risk' in the context of Article 7, which it says is to be distinguished from the concept of 'risk of absconding' and must be interpreted as requiring a 'genuine, present and sufficiently serious threat affecting one of the fundamental interests of society'.[167] This makes sense in light of the Court's holding that findings of risk must be based on individual determinations. However, the Court appears to consider 'risk' in relation to public policy to require a heightened evidence base. Though this may seem strange within the context of the Return Directive, this standard is employed in the context of the EU Citizenship Directive, which addresses the validity of Member State decisions to restrict the free movement of EU nationals or expel them.[168]

The CJEU recently decided a detention case in the context of asylum seekers in the Dublin III Regulation,[169] which might impact the Court's future case law dealing with the risk of absconding.[170] The Dublin III Regulation defines 'risk of absconding' in the same way as the Return Directive.[171] In *Al Chodor*,[172] the Court held that Member States' domestic laws must include objective criteria to assist in determinations of whether there is a risk of absconding, and that such law must be a provision of general application in order to ensure that detention is not arbitrary.[173] Thus, Poli argues that the same should be true within the

[164] ibid para 50.

[165] ibid.

[166] ibid para 52.

[167] ibid paras 56, 60.

[168] Directive 2004/38/EC of the European Parliament and of the Council of 29 April 2004 on the right of citizens of the Union and their family members to move and reside freely within the territory of the Member States [2005] OJ L158/77, Art 27(2) and related case law.

[169] Regulation 604/2013/EU of the European Parliament and of the Council of 26 June 2013 establishing the criteria and mechanisms for determining the Member State responsible for examining an application for international protection lodged in one of the Member States by a third-country national or a stateless person (recast) [2013] OJ L180/31.

[170] T Poli, 'Immigration Detention and the Rule of Law: The ECJ's First Ruling on Detaining Asylum-Seekers in the Dublin System', *EU Law Analysis* (5 May 2017) http://eulawanalysis.blogspot.co.uk/2017/05/immigration-detention-and-rule-of-law.html.

[171] EU Dublin III Regulation 604/2013 (n 169) Art 2(n).

[172] Case C-528/15 *Policie ČR, Krajské ředitelství policie Ústeckého kraje, odbor cizinecké policie v Salah Al Chodor and Others* [ECR TBC].

[173] ibid paras 39–46.

context of the Return Directive, which also requires the Member States to base their determinations on objective criteria.[174]

Perhaps the most important thing to take away from the CJEU judgments on risk is the absence of risk of dangerousness from the assessment of whether detention is permitted. The Return Directive does not, in any provision, draw upon criminal history or risk of dangerousness as a justification for detention either at the initial part of the return process, or in relation to decisions to extend detention beyond the initial six-month period. This is remarkable especially considering how prominent a role criminal risk and dangerousness play in the US cases.

VI. DETAINEE NON CO-OPERATION

An individual's behaviour during the removal process will impact the length of his or her detention. Behaviour becomes relevant in particular where detainees do not engage in voluntary return procedures, or where they do not communicate with relevant consulates or embassies in an attempt to obtain identity or travel documents. This evaluation is often part of, or in direct proximity to, the discussion of risk. Again, three outlooks can be observed. In the UK, the Administrative Court's assessment of the impact of non-co-operation on the detainee's judicial review application is part of an overall balance of factors much in the same way that it considers risk. Non-co-operation alone cannot act as a trump card which guarantees the legality of continued detention. In the USA, non-co-operation is a statutory basis for extending the 90-day removal period in section 241 INA. Thus, many cases reject detainees' habeas applications based on non-co-operation. Finally, in the EU, the CJEU has interpreted the Return Directive as requiring a causal relationship between the detainee's non-co-operation and any delays in effecting return.

A. United Kingdom

As with a risk of absconding, detainees' non-co-operation in the UK is considered one factor among many to be balanced in assessing whether detention is reasonable, though extensive non-co-operation will counsel against release.[175] As the court stated in *Mahfoud*: 'Any relevant factor may affect the length of time of detention that might be regarded as reasonable. Whilst in a specific case one or more factors may have especial weight, no factor is necessarily determinative. There is no "trump card"',[176] not even a refusal to take part in

[174] EU Return Directive 2008/115/EC, Art 3(7).

[175] *R (Yegorov) v SSHD* [2011] EWHC 3358 (Admin) 31; *R (Noureddine) v SSHD* [2012] EWHC 1707 (Admin) 85.

[176] *R (Mahfoud) v SSHD* [2010] EWHC 2057 (Admin) 14.

voluntary return.[177] A number of standards used by the Administrative Court were derived from the Court of Appeal and the Supreme Court.[178] The Supreme Court in *Lumba* provided three of the four standards relevant to this discussion. First, detainees who do not comply with the documentary process associated with removal, or who behave badly in detention and can be considered to be 'doing everything [they] can to hinder the deportation process, may reasonably be regarded as likely to abscond'.[179] Secondly, a refusal to participate in voluntary return cannot result in an automatic inference that the person poses a risk of absconding.[180] Thirdly, there must be a causal link between non-co-operation in return and the fact that removal is not possible.[181] In addition, in the case of *I*, Lord Dyson held in the Court of Appeal that non-co-operation alone cannot make a period of unreasonable detention reasonable.[182]

It is interesting to see how these principles have been applied and interpreted by the Administrative Court. In particular, the need for a causal link between non-co-operation and failure to effect removal runs through many of the cases. For example, in *Davies*, the Administrative Court looked to the Court of Appeal decision in *WL Congo*[183] for its conclusion that 'Non-co-operation has the greatest relevance to the legality of detention when it has a material bearing on removability'.[184] Though non-co-operation may not have a direct relationship to non-removability, it should still be considered a factor that can impact whether the person presents an abscond risk. However, the Court noted that under Article 5 ECHR, detention to compel co-operation is impermissible.[185] Therefore, the degree to which non-co-operation operates as a factor in determining the legality of detention will vary depending on the individual circumstances of the case. Still, 'the legal policy is clear: a person cannot complain about the legality of immigration detention if … it is a product of his own making'.[186] To give no weight to co-operation would permit situations where detainees could avoid removal simply by refusing to take any part in the removal process. This, said the court, 'would frustrate the Parliamentary intention behind the removal provisions'.[187] However, in this particular case, the detainee was considered to be 'uncooperative in every sense' and no relief was awarded. Likewise, in *Smith*, the detainee's non-co-operation was given

[177] *Mjemer* (n 21) 23.
[178] See *Momoh* (n 46) for a list of these standards, beginning para 105.
[179] *Lumba (WL) v SSHD* [2011] UKSC 12, 123; this was also noted in *MH* (n 32) 68(iii).
[180] *Lumba* (ibid) 123.
[181] ibid 127.
[182] *I* (n 3) 51, as cited by *Chen* (n 41) 18.
[183] Prior to reaching the Supreme Court, as cited as *Lumba* (n 179), the Court of Appeal case was cited as *WL (Congo) v SSHD* [2010] EWCA Civ 111.
[184] *Davies* (n 5) 17.
[185] ibid 18.
[186] ibid 19.
[187] ibid.

'considerable weight' because it was, in the court's view, aimed at manipulating the immigration system to frustrate removal.[188]

In *Said*, the Administrative Court refused relief on the basis that the detainee's lengthy detention was substantially his own making and that, had he co-operated, it is likely that removal would have been effected.[189] In one of the more egregious examples of non-co-operation, the Court in *Noureddine* refused relief because the case was not simply one in which

> The claimant had told lies about his history or even claimed one or two false identities; rather, he provided detailed information about, for example, the identity of his employers in Algiers and their telephone numbers and addresses, and had provided a false birth certificate, all the time knowing that the information that he provided was untrue. He knew perfectly well that the UK Border Agency officials would act upon this false information and try unavailingly and over a long period to persuade the authorities of Algeria to accept it. Even now, the claimant continues to refuse to provide necessary true information about himself.[190]

The Court went on to hold that 'A detained person who has conducted himself as this Claimant has, must accept most, if not all, of the blame for the delay in removing him which results from the false information provided by him'.[191] This non-co-operation, coupled with a risk of absconding, persuaded the court that further detention was reasonable.[192]

In *Lamrani*, the detainee's refusal to co-operate in obtaining travel documents was not counted against him by the Court because removal would not have been possible regardless, owing to the fact that he was in the process of appealing his removal at all times and could not, therefore, be removed legally.[193]

On the other end of the scale, the detainee in *Abdullah* was granted relief because the court did not consider that the evidence demonstrated that he was 'heavily obstructive'.[194] Rather, the court felt that, at most, he could be considered 'grumpy and reluctant about engagement with the Sudanese Embassy'.[195]

B. United States

The INA mandates an extension of the 90-day removal period if the detainee fails to co-operate in effecting removal:

> The removal period shall be extended beyond a period of 90 days and the alien may remain in detention during such extended period if the alien fails or refuses to make

[188] *R (Smith) v SSHD* [2010] EWHC 2774 (Admin) 22.
[189] *Said* (n 48) 43.
[190] *Noureddine* (n 175) 85.
[191] ibid 89.
[192] ibid 90–91.
[193] *R (Lamrani) v SSHD* [2011] EWHC 3059 (Admin) 54.
[194] *Abdullah* (n 40) 29.
[195] ibid.

> timely application in good faith for travel or other documents necessary to the alien's departure or conspires or acts to prevent the alien's removal subject to an order of removal.[196]

Thus, in most cases where the court makes a determination that the petitioner has failed to co-operate, continued detention will be justified as a matter of law. This can be seen, for example, in *Alzubi*, where the court cited 'a consistent pattern of deliberate conduct on the part of petitioner aimed at frustrating the removal process, triggering suspension of the removal period' when it refused relief.[197] Similarly, in *Powell*, the court noted that the petitioner had 'repeatedly provided the INS with inconsistent information regarding his identity, and these inconsistencies have demonstrably hampered the INS in carrying out his removal' when it rejected the habeas application.[198] In *Diallo*, the court dismissed the habeas petition, stating that the 'petitioner would not be in confinement had he co-operated with Respondent's attempt to effectuate his removal [on two occasions]' and that 'the only reason he continues to remain in detention is because he refuses to leave the country'.[199] In *Ramos*, a finding that the immigration authorities failed to conduct a custody review prior to the expiry of the 90-day removal period did not excuse the detainee's withholding of identity information and provision of false information.[200]

In the rare positive cases, such as *Farez-Espinoza*, the courts have noted that a failure to appear for removal proceedings on its own does not trigger extension of the 90-day removal period.[201] The judgment in *Leslie* relied on *Farez-Espinoza* to arrive at the same conclusion.[202] In *Farez-Espinoza*, the petitioner was granted release, while in *Leslie* the court withheld its decision for lack of adequate information regarding the diligence of the state. However, the overwhelming majority of cases evaluated as non-co-operation resulted in an extension of detention. This is likely due in part to the fact that the INA includes non-co-operation as an express ground for extending detention beyond the 90-day removal period. Because the language is obligatory, the courts may feel that they have no choice but to allow continued detention.

[196] INA, s 241(a)(1)(C).

[197] *Alzubi* (n 56) 6. See also *Dogra* (n 66) 2 ('petitioner has consistently thwarted the attempts of DHS to effectuate his removal').

[198] *Powell* (n 6) 210. See also *Ricketts* (n 57) 6, where the petitioner 'repeatedly failed to cooperate with Respondent's requests to assist in obtaining travel documents and continues to reference fraudulent documents in support of his claim to United States citizenship'; *Ncube v INS* 1998 WL 842349 (SDNY) 16; *Jiang v Holder* 2015 WL 3649739 (WDNY) 3–4.

[199] *Diallo v Immigration and Customs Enforcement* 2010 WL 3769506 (WDNY) 5.

[200] *Ramos* (n 74) 6. Indeed, the immigration regulations explicitly state this. See 8 CFR 241.4(g)(5)(iv).

[201] *Farez-Espinoza* (n 64) 501.

[202] *Leslie v Heron* 2010 WL 4226561 (WDNY) 4.

C. European Union

In great contrast to the USA, the CJEU has held that non-co-operation must bear a causal relationship to the delay in effecting removal. In *Mahdi*, the CJEU was asked whether a lack of identity documents can be considered a 'lack of cooperation' for purposes of Article 15(6)(a), and thus a permissible reason to extend detention beyond the initial six months. In Mahdi's case, the Embassy of the Republic of Sudan had refused to provide him with an identity document, thus making removal impossible. The question for the CJEU was whether it was possible to attribute that refusal to Mahdi, who refused to return voluntarily to Sudan.[203] The CJEU considered that a determination that there was a lack of co-operation under Article 15(6) requires the national court to examine the detainee's conduct during his or her initial period of detention to ascertain whether he or she has failed to co-operate in removal.[204] However, the national court must also consider the likelihood that removal has been or will be delayed owing to the person's conduct.[205] If not, 'no causal link may be established … and therefore no lack of cooperation on his part can be established'.[206] In addition, before determining whether there is a failure to co-operate, the decision-making authority must be able to show that removal is lasting longer than anticipated, 'despite all reasonable efforts', including continuing efforts by the state to obtain the requisite documents.[207] This means that the detainee's non-co-operation must be directly linked to any delay in removal, and that the state must continue to act with due diligence in effecting removal, before detention can be extended under Article 15(6)(a).

Moreover, given the Court's decision discussed above regarding extending detention beyond the initial six-month period under Article 15(6) and its conclusion that, prior to any decision to extend, the decision maker must re-examine the initial reasons for detention, it is arguable that non-co-operation itself cannot justify an extension beyond the six months without a re-evaluation of all the evidence in favour of detention initially.

VII. PURSUIT OF LEGAL REMEDIES AGAINST REMOVAL OR DEPORTATION

Courts in each of the three jurisdictions address the impact that a detainee's pursuit of legal remedies against deportation or removal has on the lawfulness of his or her detention. The approaches take two main forms. The UK

[203] *Mahdi* (n 15) para 77.
[204] ibid para 82.
[205] ibid.
[206] ibid.
[207] ibid para 83.

and the EU each consider that legitimate attempts to seek relief should not be held against detainees. In the UK, this means that such judicial review is one of many factors to consider in determining whether detention is reasonable; in the EU, it means that the time spent pursuing legitimate review of return cannot be excluded from the calculation of the maximum detention period because to do so would lead to varied detention lengths across the Member States and the maximum period would effectively be rendered optional. The USA presents a completely opposing picture, where pursuit of legal remedies, in general, is counted against detainees. For the most part, any delay due to review of removal is attributed to the detainee and not viewed as unreasonable. Though some judgments reflect on the idea that merit should play a role in this determination, for the most part it does not.

A. United Kingdom

In the UK, the pursuit of legal remedies against removal generally functions as 'simply a factor to be taken into account rather than a factor which is to be discounted in assessing the period, for the purpose of *Hardial Singh* principles for which it is reasonable for him to be detained'.[208] Similarly, it was stressed by the Court in *Aziz* that 'Generally, a deportee's legal challenges cannot, without regard to other factors, be a trump card in the hands of the Secretary of State'.[209] Somewhat allaying the concerns expressed by members of the House of Lords that a maximum period of detention would be exploited through disingenuous applications for judicial review of removal/deportation,[210] the Administrative Court has held that more weight will be given to appeals that have merit. For example, in *Saleh*, though the Administrative Court felt that the claimant was dishonest and presented a risk of reoffending, the court stated:

> He cannot be criticised for using legal procedures to challenge the decisions which are adverse to him but the overall picture which emerges is that the Claimant has used and will use all available avenues in order to delay matters.[211]

Some judgments have held that the claimant cannot 'complain' of prolonged detention when it is due to his or her pursuit of legal remedies.[212] Others state that, for purposes of determining the length of detention, the clock will not

[208] *AK* (n 24) 28. See also *Abdi* (n 35) 29; *Giwa* (n 44) 73.
[209] *Aziz* (n 35) 25.
[210] See ch 3, s II.A above.
[211] *R (Saleh) v SSHD* [2009] EWHC 2395 (Admin) 54.
[212] *A (Iraq)* (EWHC 2010) 20; *R (Bashir) v SSHD* [2007] EWHC 3017 (Admin) 12, citing *A* (n 116) 55 (per Toulson LJ).

begin to run until after all appeal rights are exhausted.[213] This is just a small minority of cases, however.[214]

B. United States

The most surprising treatment of this issue comes from the US federal district courts, which apply what I refer to as the 'attribution principle'. In 41 cases, the court denied relief in part (sometimes in the main) based on the fact that the detention was prolonged due to the individual's pursuit of judicial remedies.[215] The delay is therefore attributed to the detainee making use of available judicial processes, and detention is permitted to continue. The language used by the courts is couched in blame. For example, in *Miller*, the WDNY court stated that the 'petitioner's own actions', including applying for citizenship, resulted in delays justifying his lengthy detention.[216]

Some courts reasoned that, where the detainee was pursuing judicial or administrative remedies against removal, and there were no other obstacles to removal, there was consequently no Fifth Amendment Due Process violation because the end of litigation marked the end of detention – hence it was not indefinite.[217] The attribution principle was most remarkably found in the *Reyes-Cardenas* case, where the petitioner had been detained for over seven years at the time of the hearing, and was kept in detention because of his pending proceedings.[218]

The court refused to apply the attribution principle in only three cases. In *Rajigah*, where the petitioner was granted immediate release, the court said that the petitioner had not 'in any way acted in bad faith' but was 'simply avail[ing] himself of judicial process'.[219] Similarly, in *Bugianishvili*, the court held that

[213] *AK* (n 24) 25; *Asekun* (n 21) 24.

[214] Moreover, one case indicates that the Nationality, Immigration and Asylum Act 2002 prohibits removal while appeals against certain immigration decisions are pending. See *AK* (n 24) 31. A second case notes that the claimant could not have been removed during a specific period while his asylum and deportation appeals were pending, but does not indicate the legal basis for such suspension. See *A* (n 35) 45. These are the only two cases that mention such practice. Because this issue is beyond the scope of this book, I have not examined whether there are other statutory bases for suspending removal. Certainly, none of the other cases indicated that it is a common occurrence. However, it is clear from s 94 of the same Act that claims for asylum or human rights that are 'clearly unfounded' do not have a suspensive effect.

[215] See, eg *Dover* (n 81); *Guang v INS* 2005 WL 465436 (EDNY).

[216] *Miller v Tryon* 2013 WL 5592484 (WDNY) 6. See also *Morales v Holder* 2014 WL 1117827 (WDNY) 6; *Campbell v Tryon* 2014 WL 3809747 (WDNY) 6.

[217] See, eg *Newell v Holder* (2013 WDNY) 983 F Supp 2d 241, 247: 'Accordingly, because the detention challenged by the habeas petition in this action has been prolonged by petitioner's own pursuit of judicial review of the final order of removal, the duration of his detention cannot be found to constitute a violation of his rights under the due process clause of the Fifth Amendment'; *Neil v Holder* 2015 WL 3937280 (WDNY) 5; *Johnson v Phillips* 2010 WL 6512350 (WDNY) 7; *Reyes-Cardenas v Gonzales* 2007 WL 1290141 (SDNY) 7; *Abassi v Secretary, Department of Homeland Security* 2010 WL 199700 (SDNY) 4.

[218] *Reyes-Cardenas* (ibid). See also, eg *Abassi* (ibid); *Andreenko* (n 57).

[219] *Rajigah* (n 135) 166.

'the mere fact that a non-citizen opposes his removal, without distinguishing between bona fide and frivolous arguments in opposition, is insufficient to defeat a finding of unreasonably prolonged detention'.[220] However, in that case, the court also made it clear that detainees 'may not rely on the extra time resulting [from pursuit of legal remedies] to claim that [their] prolonged detention violates substantive due process'.[221] It went on to order that a bond hearing be held within seven days.

The attribution principle is a product of the case law, rather than any statute. MacCormick suggests that pressure due to society and the nature of the judicial role means that it is highly likely that the course chosen in a judgment will be reasonable or correct.[222] However, the decision by most district judges to penalise detainees for pursuing relief against removal seems unreasonable, given that the lesson from these cases seems to be that prolonged detention, even beyond the presumptively reasonable six months pronounced in *Zadvydas*, is permissible as long as the delay cannot be imputed to the government, even where the delay results simply from the detainee making use of available judicial processes. It may be possible to suggest that if the district court judges felt any societal pressure, it would be to ensure that people liable to removal remain in detention; so, in that sense, perhaps this behaviour could be viewed as correct. It cannot, in my view, be seen as reasonable, however. Apart from the discussion in *Rajigah*, the issue of the detainees' good or bad faith was not addressed by the district courts in their determination that detention is lawful owing to pursuit of a legal remedy. To conclude, then, that the petitioner effectively deserves to be detained on this basis seems arbitrary. In some cases, however, additional factors, such as detainee non-co-operation or risk, contribute to a finding of legality.

In addition to the attribution principle, the Second Circuit has an informal agreement with the DHS that the DHS will not remove people who have sought a stay of removal in addition to a petition for review of the removal order.[223] This 'forbearance' policy operates as the 'equivalent of a court-ordered stay of removal',[224] effectively justifying prolonged detention in several cases, many of which are 'cookie-cutter' judgments emanating from the WDNY.[225] Forbearance policy, coupled with the attribution principle, means that virtually all applicants' detention will be considered lawful while review is pending. Holding an individual's pursuit of available legal remedies against him or her in a determination of whether detention should continue seems like an arbitrary exercise of the power to detain, which effectively functions as a punishment unwarranted by the INA.

[220] *Bugianishvili* (n 64). See also *D'Alessandro* (n 149) 386.

[221] *Bugianishvili* (n 64) 7.

[222] MacCormick (n 152) 34.

[223] *Khaleque v Department of Homeland Security* 2009 WL 81318 (WDNY) 3.

[224] *Luna-Aponte v Holder* (2010 WDNY) 743 F Supp 2d 189, 197. See also *Khan v Herron* 2011 WL 4899994 (WDNY) 1–2; *Mathews v Philips* 2013 WL 5288166 (WDNY) 3.

[225] See, eg *Tejeda-Estrella* (n 56) 5; *Rahel v Tryon* 2013 WL 1878914 (WDNY) 5; *Haley v Holder* 2013 WL 1945704 (WDNY) 6.

C. European Union

In the EU, this discussion has taken place in two contexts: judicial review of a removal order and applications for asylum. The former was addressed in *Kadzoev*, where one of the questions was whether a detainee's time spent disputing return in judicial review proceedings should count towards the maximum detention period in the Return Directive. The CJEU considered that the maximum period of detention in Article 15(6) of the Directive is aimed at limiting deprivations of liberty and ensuring that detention periods are consistent across the EU; to hold otherwise would risk varied detention lengths, depending upon the length of judicial review.[226] In addition, the Directive also requires Member States to afford third-country nationals subject to return procedures an effective remedy to appeal or seek review of a removal decision.[227] These conclusions, together with the fact that Article 15 does not explicitly permit the Member States to use pursuit of legal remedies against return (therefore suspending the return process) as a ground for extending detention, led the Court to conclude that the Directive requires that Member States take into account time detained whilst appealing removal, even if removal is not possible owing to such an appeal.[228]

The latter instance in which the impact of pursuing remedies against removal has arisen in the EU context is with regard to the interaction between the framework of the Return Directive and that of the EU CEAS,[229] but for now it is important to note that the CJEU concluded that where an application for asylum is made during the course of the removal process, the CEAS framework is triggered. This means that detention under the Return Directive is paused and the detention framework in the CEAS governs. Ultimately, this means that the total length of detention could potentially exceed the 18-month maximum in the Return Directive.

VIII. CONCLUSION

This chapter was intended to illustrate that, though the three jurisdictions use roughly the same tests for legality, the way they are applied during judicial review leads to different interpretations of the test components and different case outcomes. Indeed, one can see patterns emerging, particularly when comparing the UK to the USA. The dominant theme in the UK cases is that the circumstances of the case must be balanced against each other. The balance is not

[226] *Kadzoev* (n 15) paras 54, 56.
[227] ibid para 50.
[228] ibid paras 52, 57.
[229] See ch 6, s IV.C below, discussing the *Arslan* judgment in the context of detention time limits.

inferred, but, rather, explicitly undertaken in the judgments, especially in those discussing the notion of a 'trump card'. The UK decisions generally exhibit a more grounded approach, where, for example, the likelihood of removal must be more than just a mere hope, or where a person's past criminal activity must be viewed in light of its severity and when it occurred. This should be distinguished from the USA, where risk and non-co-operation play key roles in the decision-making processes of the NY district courts – effectively amounting to the very trump card that the Administrative Court admonishes. The CJEU case law most closely resembles that of the Administrative Court, but because of the nature of the questions asked by the referring national courts, it is difficult to directly compare the CJEU judgments to those of the other jurisdictions. Like the Administrative Court, the CJEU has emphasised that removal must be a realistic prospect and that the diligence of the state on its own is not enough to warrant continued detention under the Directive. Though it is not possible to conclude whether the Court balances risk factors like the Administrative Court, it is interesting to note that the Return Directive does not include past criminal behaviour as a basis for detention. Thus, this discussion is not present in any of the judgments – a glaring absence in view of the prominence this discussion has in the NY judgments.

In summary, what is evident thus far from the judgments is that they roughly fall into three categories. The first is the USA, with its quicker and less-nuanced balancing of whether detention is reasonable in all circumstances, often settling on the side of the state. The second is the EU, with a more high-level discussion of concepts aimed at fulfilling the aim of the Return Directive to limit detention. The third is the UK, which seems to be a bit of both in the sense that it engages in a balancing of reasonableness in a more detail-oriented way, where even the items it balances are themselves scaled and weighted. This is seen most prominently with regard to consideration of risk. At the same time, it is working to give meaning to core concepts by reference to judgments of the Court of Appeal and Supreme Court. The next chapter will explore the impact of additional interpretive principles on the application of the legality tests and, consequently, judicial review outcomes.

6

Using the Law

I. INTRODUCTION

CHAPTER FIVE FOCUSED on the detail of the legality tests in each jurisdiction and how judges balance their various components or assign meaning to concepts like 'diligence' or 'likelihood'. This chapter takes a step back and looks at the bigger picture by examining the way in which the courts use broader legal principles to evaluate the legality of detention. In particular, four issues are explored: first, the role that adherence to precedent plays in decision-making; secondly, the extent to which judges make reference to fundamental rights principles, such as the right to a fair trial and, of course, the right to liberty; thirdly, whether the presence or absence of a maximum period of detention helps or hinders the judges' assessment; and finally, how the quality of the law on detention in each jurisdiction plays a role in whether case outcomes are positive or negative, as well as how it impacts the way in which judges exercise judicial review.

II. THE DOCTRINE OF PRECEDENT

Reference to precedent is an essential tool of legal reasoning, especially in common law jurisdictions like the UK and USA. It ensures consistency of the legal system and enhances legal certainty.[1] Engaging with prior detention judgments demonstrates to judges how the legality tests have been applied, which issues have traditionally been considered by judges and how much weight those issues should be given in a specific case. This section demonstrates two approaches to precedent in the cases under examination. The CJEU and the Administrative Court engage with precedent in a meaningful manner. Precedent is not merely referred to in a citation that makes a statement of principle without analysis; rather, both courts spend a great deal of time examining the circumstances of prior cases to understand how conclusions were made. The CJEU goes one step further by anticipating facts likely to arise in subsequent cases. By contrast, the NY federal district courts spend very little time considering the facts and distinguishing cases from one another. As a result, judgments

[1] N MacCormick, *Legal Reasoning and Legal Theory* (Oxford University Press, 1994) 213–24.

are typically short and often appear to have been drafted according to a standardised template. This presents problems in relation to the effectiveness of the right to appeal district court decisions and arguably implies that the NY district courts are less concerned with ensuring that the law on the legality of detention is applied consistently. Both of these approaches are discussed below.

A. United Kingdom

Looking first at the UK, it is clear that the Administrative Court is bound by its own judgments.[2] This is borne out in the case law, which demonstrates that, almost without failure, the judges at the Administrative Court carefully and thoughtfully consider precedent. Their judgments consider their own prior efforts, and the efforts of the Court of Appeals and House of Lords/Supreme Court to interpret the *Hardial Singh* principles. Generally, evaluation of some or all of the same seven cases is conducted.[3] The judges trace the foregoing judges' application of law to the facts in those cases and then attempt to distil principles and apply them to the facts at hand – including seeking clarification of the facts in previous cases from the lawyers in order to distinguish or liken the case at hand.[4] They actively work through the reasoning in prior cases to determine whether the same reasoning can be applied to the cases before them. For the most part, this is done coherently among judges who settle on what I consider to be logical resolutions of the matters. For example, discussions of risk and detainee non-co-operation draw heavily on case law from the Court of Appeal and the UK Supreme Court to understand the weight to be attributed to these factors in a given case. However, one judge remarked that

> when the court is being invited to exercise a defined and established principle, a detailed reference to earlier exercises of the discretion inherent in that principle and comparison between the detail of the respective cases is not necessarily a helpful exercise. To my mind, that is a point of general impact, because it will often involve unnecessary mental gymnastics in the comparisons, when what in each case is being done is to exercise the relevant principle with the benefit of the guidance that has been given.[5]

These 'mental gymnastics' are visible in the judgments. For example, in *Momoh*, the Administrative Court began its analysis by listing ten principles to guide its judgment, derived from the Court of Appeal and the Supreme Court.[6] It then

[2] K Malleson, *The Legal System*, 3rd edn (Oxford University Press, 2007) 7.12.

[3] *Lam v Superintendent of Tai A Chau Detention Centre* [1996] UKPC 5; *R (I) v SSHD* [2002] EWCA Civ 888; *R (A) v SSHD* [2007] EWCA Civ 804; *R (MH) v SSHD* [2010] EWCA Civ 1112; *Lumba (WL) v SSHD* [2011] UKSC 12; *Khawaja v SSHD* [1983] UKHL 8; *R (Khadir) v SSHD* [2005] UKHL 39.

[4] Author observations in Administrative Court on 15–16 November 2016.

[5] *R (MM (Somalia)) v SSHD* [2009] EWHC 2353 (Admin) 27.

[6] *R (Momoh) v SSHD* [2012] EWHC 3740 (Admin) 105.

considered each of these principles in light of the facts of the case, assigning weight depending on, for example, the nature of the detainee's past criminal history and when it occurred, or the exact steps taken by the state to effect removal. This is not a criticism; when reading these decisions, one can see that the judges generally engage in a true evaluation of what has gone before them and how they might apply it to the facts at hand. As noted above, in one judgment, the Court even altered the *Hardial Singh* principles to take into account the fact that the claimant was detained under the UK Borders Act 2007 provisions on automatic deportation and detention, and was awaiting a decision by the Home Secretary as to whether he was properly detained based on those provisions.[7]

B. United States

In the USA, it is disputed whether the federal district courts follow precedent. Mead argues that their practice is varied, and that, increasingly, the district courts are becoming less deferential.[8] However, it is clear from the NY federal district court cases examined in this book that, in practice, the courts treat prior decisions from district courts in their circuit as binding, or at least as highly persuasive. This is confirmed by Weinstein.[9]

In the cases under examination, where there is a prior case on point, the district courts will refer to it, but mainly by stating the principle from the case and adding the case citation. Otherwise, the lack of binding precedent demonstrates a sort of need to reinvent the wheel, especially in cases where the courts are split as to how to deal with prolonged mandatory detention (see section IV below). In such cases, a split in approach between district courts results in an inconsistent application of the law and consequently an inability for detainees to anticipate likely outcomes.

A number of US cases demonstrate a real lack of engagement with the facts or circumstances of the precedent, or attempts to apply the precedent to the

[7] *Hussein v SSHD* [2009] EWHC 2492 (Admin). The principles as applied in the case of automatic detention are as follows: '(i) The Secretary of State must intend to deport the person unless one of the exceptions in s.33 [of the UK Borders Act 2007] applies and can only use this power to detain for the purpose of examining whether they do … (ii) The detainee may only be detained for a period that is reasonable in all the circumstances … (iii) If, before the expiry of the reasonable period it becomes apparent that the Secretary of State will not be able to effect deportation within that reasonable period he should not seek to exercise the power of detention … (iv) The Secretary of State should act with reasonable diligence and expedition to determine whether any of the exceptions in s.33 is applicable' (44).

[8] JW Mead, 'Stare Decisis in the Inferior Courts of the United States' (2012) 12 *Nevada Law Journal* 787, 800.

[9] JB Weinstein, 'The Roles of a Federal District Court Judge' (2011) 76 *Brook Law Review* 439, 451: 'A direct precedent on point is binding unless clearly undermined or eroded.'

situation at hand. This is especially true in a number of cases on post-removal order detention (ie the *Zadvydas* line of cases) coming from the WDNY, which I have designated 'cookie-cutter' cases. Since 2013, there have been nearly 40 cases in which virtually the same text is employed for analysis by the court.[10] Once it is determined that section 241(a) of the INA applies and that the six months under *Zadvydas* have been reached, a standard formula follows, typically using standard wording. First, the court will go through the basic principles of the *Zadvydas* case, referring to Due Process under the Fifth Amendment, the six-month reasonable period and the fact that the Attorney General promulgated regulations regarding custody reviews in order to comply with the ruling in *Zadvydas*. The court will then consider whether the detainee has demonstrated that removal is not likely in the foreseeable future. In those cases, this is never achieved by the detainee, and habeas relief is consequently not granted. In rare cases, the court will continue the analysis, despite the detainee's failure to show that removal is not likely, by assessing whether the detainee is a flight risk or a danger. However, because this evaluation is based on criminal history, the result is usually an automatic determination of risk, no matter what type of crime is at issue.[11]

The US cookie-cutter judgments arguably represent an extreme example of following precedent, whereby not only is prior case law cited, but actual text in the body of the opinions is repeated. This raises the question of how using standard text impacts the judges' decision-making process. Where one is simply repeating standard words and phrases, and subbing in names and places to deal with the particular situation at hand, there is a risk that the judicial decision-making process becomes something more akin to a rubber-stamping exercise. Perhaps there is an advantage to using boilerplate language. For example, one could argue that it promotes legal certainty for detainees, especially where they are unrepresented. In response is a comment by a judge in the SDNY regarding use of form letters in relation to denials of parole: 'The uniformity in these letters suggests that the INS is affording alien parole applicants considerably less than the individualized consideration that due process requires.'[12] This suggests that the courts should be required to actively demonstrate that they are engaging with the issues and facts, especially in light of the fact that the subject at issue is the serious one of individual liberty.

[10] This includes cases where the court determined that INA, s 241(a) applies if in dispute by the parties, and cases where the claim under *Zadvydas v Davis* (2001) 533 US 678 was determined to be premature, but the court nevertheless considers the detainee's chances of success under *Zadvydas*. See, eg *Neil v Holder* 2015 WL 3937280 (WDNY); *Campbell v Tryon* 2014 WL 3809747 (WDNY); *Hunt v Holder* 2015 WL 860778 (WDNY).

[11] Although not a s 241 case, it is worth mentioning that a decision in the EDNY included a finding that the then INS was correct to determine that the petitioner posed a danger to the community partly because he is HIV positive. *Lovell v INS* 2003 WL 22282176 (EDNY) 5.

[12] *Cruz-Taveras v McElroy* 1996 WL 455012 (SDNY) 4.

One may also question whether the cookie-cutter approach is a problem in view of the fact that these cases can be appealed and any errors of law can be adjusted by subsequent litigation. I argue that it is a problem for two main reasons. First, these cases turn on the facts rather than the law, and it is difficult to argue that the cases in my pool exhibit any errors of the law. For the most part, the judges apply the language of the *Zadvydas* judgment faithfully. There are some arguable errors of law, which will be discussed below, but such errors are the result of a lack of clear standards in the applicable test. Secondly, nearly all of the US detainees are unrepresented, and it is unlikely that they will be able to secure legal representation for an appeal. This is exhibited in the many judgments concluding with a refusal to give leave the detainees to appeal as a poor person.[13] In such circumstances, it is important to judge as accurately as possible at first instance.

Finally, it is interesting that, when viewing the UK and US judgments together, we see positive outcomes in terms of liberty in the former and negative ones in the latter. Though both jurisdictions technically follow precedent, it is only where there is rich engagement with prior case law that positive outcomes occur.

C. European Union

Somewhat of an outlier in this respect, the CJEU is not technically bound by its precedent. This means that national courts may still refer questions to the Court that have been previously addressed. Because there is no formally binding system of precedent, everything stated by the Court in its judgments can have equal force in terms of binding future courts.[14] In practice, however, the Court rarely departs from it.[15] Arnull suggests that adherence to the doctrine of precedent developed as a means of effectively handling the Court's large caseload, and also to ensure respect for the rule of law requirement of legal certainty.[16] Beck suggests that the Court refers to its own case law more than any other tool of interpretation.[17]

One of the most useful examples of how the CJEU engages with precedent is in its reasoning surrounding when it is permissible to criminalise immigration through the use of imprisonment under the Return Directive in *Achughbabian* and *Celaj*. Building on the judgment in *El Dridi*, which prohibited criminal imprisonment as a consequence of illegal stay on the territory prior to initiating return proceedings, the Court in *Achughbabian* had to consider the best

[13] See, eg *Dover v Holder* 2011 WL 4054952 (WDNY) 4; *St Louis v Heron* 2011 WL 2746787 (WDNY) 4; *Leslie v Heron* 2010 WL 4226561 (WDNY) 4.

[14] A Arnull, *The European Union and its Court of Justice*, 2nd edn (Oxford University Press, 2006) 631.

[15] ibid 632–33.

[16] ibid 622.

[17] G Beck, *The Legal Reasoning of the Court of Justice of the EU* (Hart Publishing, 2012) 239.

way to address situations where an individual to whom the return process had previously been applied in full refused to comply with the obligation to return.[18] The *El Dridi* judgment had contemplated a situation such as this, though in that case, the time had not yet come where return procedures had been applied but failed to take effect.[19] Citing *El Dridi*, the CJEU concluded that criminal imprisonment would be permissible where 'coercive measures [under the Return Directive] have not made it possible for the removal of an illegally staying third-country national to be effected'.[20]

Approximately four years later, the CJEU was faced with another variation in the fact pattern in *Celaj*. However, in the circumstances of that case, Italy had imprisoned a third-country national who had previously been removed under the Directive, but then re-entered Italy unlawfully. This time, the Court considered both *El Dridi* and *Achughbabian*, and determined that they were 'clearly distinct' because in those cases, the third-country nationals had been subjected to return procedures for a first instance.[21] By contrast, the individual at issue in *Celaj* had gone through the entire process, was returned, but then came back to Italy, only to be subject to return for a second time. The CJEU specifically returned to *Achughbabian*, reasoning that, in that case, the Court had clearly held that the Member States could criminalise third-country nationals to whom the Directive had already been applied, but yet remained unlawfully.[22] Therefore, concluded the Court, criminal imprisonment was even more appropriate in a situation such as that in *Celaj*, where the individual was illegally present not once, but twice.[23]

Finally, in *Affum*, the CJEU went beyond the situations in *El Dridi*, *Achughbabian* and *Celaj* to consider whether and how the Directive applies to third-country nationals in transit through a Member State. Ms Affum was travelling from Belgium to the UK, when she was stopped at the Channel Tunnel in France for an identity check. At that point, she was identified as being an illegal entrant, and was taken into criminal custody by the French police in preparation for her return to Belgium. She argued that she should not have been subject to criminal custody in light of the Court's case law on imprisonment prior to return under the Directive. After concluding that the Directive applied to the facts at hand,[24] the Court went on to consider how the holdings in *El Dridi* and *Achughbabian* might apply. Because the Court considered Ms Affum to be illegally staying in France, it had no choice but to conclude that she could not be subject to criminal imprisonment prior to initiating return procedures because of the judgment in *El Dridi* reiterating that such individuals must be subject to

[18] Case C-329/11 *Achughbabian* [2009] ECR I-12695.
[19] Case C-61/11 PPU *El Dridi* [2011] ECR I-3015, paras 52, 60.
[20] *Achughbabian* (n 18) para 46.
[21] Case C-290/14 *Celaj* [ECR TBC] para 28.
[22] ibid para 29.
[23] ibid para 30.
[24] Case C-47/15 *Affum* [ECR TBC] para 49.

the common standards and procedures in the Directive. *Achughbabian* counselled in favour of the same conclusion, because, even though the individual in that case had been subject to a return procedure that failed, the return process had not yet been completed (because Achughbabian had not yet been subjected to immigration detention under Article 15). Therefore, because Ms Affum was subject to return procedures for the first time, and they were still in progress, it was unlawful for her to be imprisoned as a consequence of her illegal presence.

The way the CJEU worked its way through these three cases demonstrates its attention to detail and its awareness that different fact patterns require different approaches. Its detailed examination of the facts marks an awareness of the value of precedent in the application of the law to specific circumstances. This has resulted in a situation of legal consistency that provides clarity to the national authorities responsible for the implementation of the Directive and to judges having to grapple with these issues in the future. Consequently, CJEU judgments on the Return Directive are well-reasoned and tend to result in rights-protecting outcomes.

III. FUNDAMENTAL RIGHTS

This section considers the extent to which the right to liberty and other fundamental rights play a part in judicial review and what impact they have on case outcomes. In particular, it evaluates the way the courts manage fundamental rights in light of certain practical issues that routinely arise across the three jurisdictions.

As discussed in chapter two, each jurisdiction upholds the right to liberty and prohibits arbitrary detention in its constitution. This, of course, means that certain rights are afforded to detainees to ensure that their detention is judicially reviewed at an appropriate standard. Griffith claims that judges are not 'natural defenders of liberty', but rather are preoccupied with maintaining order.[25] This statement cannot be applied sweepingly to all the judges rendering the decisions considered in this book, as they each consider liberty in different ways. For many Administrative Court judges, liberty is largely their guiding principle. It sets the tone in many judgments, and even provides a legal justification for taking on a more active role in safeguarding liberty. The extent to which this occurs will be discussed in more depth below, in chapter seven. Suffice it to say at this stage that the fundamental nature of the right to liberty has led the Administrative Court to assign itself a heightened standard of review of immigration detention that differs from typical judicial review of administrative action.

In the USA, liberty does not seem to be the driver of judgments in the district courts, where the focus is less about detainees' rights and more about national

[25] JAG Griffith, *The Politics of the Judiciary*, 5th edn (Fontana Press, 1997) 342.

security. Consequently, reasoning is focused on whether detainees have demonstrated that removal is unlikely or whether the state has actively pursued its obligation to remove. The difference in approaches is reflected in the rates of relief in the two jurisdictions, with only 13.6 per cent of habeas applicants being granted some form of relief in the USA, compared to 49.2 per cent of applicants in the UK.

The EU judgments demonstrate a third approach to liberty. Though liberty underpins the Return Directive and provides the basis for the maximum period of detention and the legality test in Article 15, what largely motivates the CJEU judgments is a desire to ensure that the Directive is applied uniformly in the Member States. Therefore, when a Member State asks, for example, whether detention can be extended based on a ground not explicitly set forth in the Directive, or if it can imprison third-country nationals for illegally staying on the territory prior to initiating return procedures, the CJEU will answer in the negative because such activity would hamper the correct functioning of the Directive and the procedures therein. This results in an indirect protection of the right to liberty, but liberty itself is not the explicit motivation of these judgments. Nevertheless, it seems clear, as Crosby has suggested, that the CJEU is employing principles it typically turns to in its decision-making to protect third-country nationals from unnecessary detention.[26]

In addition to the right to liberty, two of the three jurisdictions touch on fair hearing principles – specifically, the right to be heard and the right to reasons for detention. However, the way that fair hearing principles arise in the cases under examination differs quite substantially because the factual and legal contexts are diverse. In the USA, several judges struggled with the question whether the Due Process Clause of the Fifth Amendment requires a bond hearing for those in prolonged detention under the mandatory provisions. In the EU, the CJEU grappled with establishing the impact that a breach of the right to reasons and the right to be heard has on a decision to extend detention beyond the initial period. In each of these cases, the courts have been somewhat reserved in their decision-making.

A. United Kingdom

The right to liberty is safeguarded in the UK by virtue of the Human Rights Act 1998 and the common law.[27] Regard to the right to liberty is often present in the UK judgments, whether it is mentioned explicitly or impliedly, often in relation to a discussion of the role of the Administrative Court. After all, 'The liberty of

[26] A Crosby, 'The Political Potential of the Return Directive' (2014) 3 *Laws* 117, 123.
[27] See ch 2, s II above.

the subject is a fundamental principle in a democratic and pluralist society'.[28] In some cases, the judges remark that 'English law regards with jealous care the deprivation of any person's liberty, particularly where what is under examination is administrative detention',[29] and even where they are 'illegal entrants'.[30] In *Lamrani*, 'the starting point in [the] judgment is the liberty of the individual'.[31] Because of this, the Court held in *Boukhalfa* and *Saleh* that any deprivations of liberty must be 'narrowly construed'[32] or considered with anxious scrutiny,[33] and any risk of absconding or reoffending must be balanced against 'the breach of the principle of liberty'[34] and not become a trump card, which would 'be a wholly unacceptable outcome where human liberty is at stake'.[35] Indeed, Lord Dyson has commented that when it comes to the rights guaranteed by the Human Rights Act, the role of the court is to act as guardian.[36] Judges in the pool case have also remarked on several occasions that the fact that liberty is involved warrants their playing the role of primary decision maker in reviewing detention. This will be examined in great detail in chapter seven, but for now it is important to emphasise the point that, because the liberty of the individual is at stake, judicial review in the Administrative Court takes on a special form and permits Administrative Court judges to engage in *de novo* review rather than limiting them to a review of whether the Executive has acted unreasonably.

In addition, the Administrative Court refers to the ECHR or case law of the ECtHR in about one-third of its judgments. However, it is unclear from the cases whether this is done on the Court's own initiative, or in response to the claimant's pleadings.[37] In some cases, it is obvious that the claimant has raised an argument that his or her detention violates Article 5 ECHR.[38] In others, it seems the Court discusses Article 5 because of its obvious relevance.[39] In a third category of cases, the Court refers to Article 5, but then makes the observation that the common law offers equal protection and that therefore the common law will be the focal point of the judgment, or that there is no need to entertain the

[28] *R (Abunasir) v SSHD* [2015] EWHC 2145 (Admin) 117.

[29] *R (Badah) v SSHD* [2014] EWHC 364 (Admin) 20. See also *R (Kumar) v SSHD* [2003] EWHC 846 (Admin) 16; *R (Mhlanga) v SSHD* [2012] EWHC 1587 (Admin) 21.

[30] *Kumar* (ibid) 16.

[31] *R (Lamrani) v SSHD* [2011] EWHC 3059 (Admin) 26.

[32] *R (Boukhalfa) v SSHD* [2003] EWHC 991 (Admin) 19.

[33] *R (Saleh) v SSHD* [2009] EWHC 2395 (Admin) 49.

[34] *R (Polanco) v SSHD* [2009] EWHC 826 (Admin) 20.

[35] *R (H) v SSHD* [2005] EWHC 1702 (Admin) 21, citing Dyson LJ in *I* (n 3) 53 (also discussed above in relation to calculating risk).

[36] Lord Justice Dyson, 'Some Thoughts on Judicial Deference' (2006) 11 *Judicial Review* 103, 18, citing *International Transport Roth GmbH v Secretary of State for the Home Department* [2002] EWCA Civ 158 [2003] QB 72, 27 (Simon Brown LJ).

[37] J Bengoetxea, *The Legal Reasoning of the European Court of Justice: Towards a European Jurisprudence* (Clarendon Press, 1993) 145.

[38] *R (I) v SSHD* [2002] EWHC 750 (Admin); *R (Mohamed) v SSHD* [2010] EWHC 1244 (Admin).

[39] *R (Abdullah) v SSHD* [2010] EWHC 259 (Admin) 39; *R (Davies) v SSHD* [2010] EWHC 2656 (Admin) 18.

Article 5 claim.[40] This apparent lack of reference to fundamental rights instruments should not be viewed negatively, as it does not appear to have any direct impact on the Court's understanding of the great value of liberty and the magnitude of the role they play in reviewing detention.

B. United States

The situation is markedly different on the other side of the Atlantic, despite the protections of the Due Process Clause in the Constitution, which safeguards liberty. Many judgments dispose of the habeas petition by reference to the holdings in *Zadvydas* or *Demore*, and therefore indirectly engage with the importance of the right to liberty, simply because they are quoting language from the Supreme Court's discussion of fundamental rights and constitutional due process. The standard text is: 'In *Zadvydas*, the Supreme Court was presented with the challenge of reconciling this apparent authorisation of indefinite detention with the Fifth Amendment's prohibition against depriving a person of their liberty without due process.'[41] Outside of such reference, the term 'liberty', or equivalent phrases like 'arbitrary detention' and 'freedom from detention', are rarely used. Where liberty is discussed, it is often in the context of the Fifth Amendment, which safeguards the right to freedom from arbitrary deprivations of liberty.

One of the main exceptions to this discussion is the judgment in *D'Alessandro*.[42] Though the WDNY court referred to liberty in citing the Supreme Court in *Zadvydas*, it discussed in detail the importance of the right to liberty stemming from other judgments concerning confinement and procedural due process. For example, the court cited another district court's judgment in *Bonitto*, for the proposition that the post-order custody review process 'contemplated by the regulations is a meaningful individualized review, as the interest involved is the "most elemental of liberty interests – the interest in being free from physical detention"'.[43] The court referred to that case in depth to discuss the concern it had regarding US Immigration and Customs Enforcement (ICE)'s failure to conduct custody reviews, as well as to emphasise the importance of procedural rights for detainees and determinations of whether detainees presented a risk of danger.[44] In contrast to most of the other federal district

[40] *R (Mjemer) v SSHD* [2011] EWHC 1514 (Admin) 28; *R (Akram) v SSHD* [2012] EWHC 1432 (Admin) 9; *R (Raki) v SSHD* [2011] EWHC 2421 (Admin) 47.

[41] See, eg *Scarlett v US Department of Homeland Security Bureau of ICE* (2009 WDNY) 632 F Supp 2d 214; *Toure v Holder* 2013 WL 1352288 (WDNY).

[42] *D'Alessandro v Mukasey* (WDNY 2009) 628 F Supp 2d 368.

[43] ibid 402, citing *Bonitto v Bureau of Immigration and Customs Enforcement* 547 F Supp 2d 747, 758 (quoting *Foucha* at 80).

[44] *D'Alessandro* (n 42) 395–98.

court judgments, the court in *D'Alessandro* took the time to consider the facts in *Bonitto* and compare them to the facts before it.

Moving away from liberty to fair hearing principles, some headway was temporarily made regarding whether individuals in mandatory detention should be entitled to a hearing. Of the 15 successful cases across each district court, 10 were cases of mandatory detention where the courts determined that a bond hearing was appropriate.

In the USA, the INA rules out any prospect of a hearing on the lawfulness of detention where it has been ordered under section 236(c). However, a number of federal district judges in the Second Circuit have nonetheless elected to undertake an examination of whether a bond hearing should be held, especially where detention has become prolonged in light of the US Supreme Court statement in *Demore* that pre-removal order detention typically lasts 'a month and a half'.[45] Indeed, Justice Kennedy's dissenting opinion discussed the possibility that mandatory detention under section 236(c) could become unreasonable if prolonged, and suggested that in such cases it might be necessary to give the detainee a bond hearing.[46] This opinion has taken root in a number of federal circuits that have held that a bond hearing is required after six months. Within the pool of cases considered in this book, this occurred six times.[47]

In these cases, the main issue for the courts was whether the length of time that the petitioners had spent in mandatory detention had rendered the detention unlawful so as to require a bond hearing. Ultimately, the courts willing to consider that mandatory detention has become unreasonable seem to evaluate the same factors used by the courts when making a determination in *Zadvydas*-based cases.[48] There are both good and bad outcomes. Good case outcomes include *Bugianishvili*, where the petitioner's 18-month detention was found to be unreasonable and unjustifiable by the government.[49] The court admonished the government for attempting to place the blame for the delay in removal proceedings on the petitioner because he was opposing removal. In *Monestime*, the focus was on the fact that it had been eight years since the petitioner had been convicted of his crimes (which were misdemeanours) and that the then-temporary halting of removals to Haiti meant that the petitioner was likely to face indefinite detention. These facts together raised 'serious constitutional concerns' for the court, which ordered a bond hearing.[50] Finally, in *Araujo-Cortes*, the court concluded that the petitioner, who had been in mandatory

[45] *Demore v Kim* (2003) 538 US 510, 530.

[46] ibid 531–32, citing the reasoning of the Court's holding in *Zadvydas* (n 10).

[47] See, eg *Adler v US Department of Homeland Security* 2009 WL 3029328 (SDNY); *Miller v Shanahan* 2010 WL 481002 (SDNY); *Andreenko v Holder* 2012 WL 4210286 (WDNY); *Johnson v Phillips* 2010 WL 6512350 (WDNY).

[48] See, eg *Gordon v Shanahan* (2015 SDNY) 2015 WL 1176706.

[49] *Bugianishvili v McConnell* 2015 WL 3903460 (SDNY) 6–9.

[50] *Monestime v Reilly* (2010 SDNY) 704 F Supp 2d 458.

detention for just over six months, was entitled to a bond hearing because his continuing detention had 'become unreasonable'.[51] This was because the court felt it had a duty to consider the legality of the petitioner's detention in all the circumstances and 'considering factors such as which party bears responsibility for the prolonged detention, whether the continued duration of the detention is finite or near conclusion, and the interests served by continued detention'.[52]

Cases with poor outcomes included *Adler*, where, after acknowledging that the Sixth and Ninth Circuits have interpreted section 236(c) as containing an implicit limitation on the duration of detention, the court maintained detention because it felt that the fact that Mr Adler was subject to deportation on its own meant that he was a flight risk, despite having already been detained for 15 months at the time he filed for relief.[53] In *Johnson*, the court determined that the petitioner's 17-month detention was attributable to the judicial review of his removal order rather than state delays, so the lack of a bond hearing was permissible.[54] A similar analysis was made in *Vaskovska*, where the petitioner had been detained for nearly two years.[55] In *Luna-Aponte*, the petitioner had been detained for over three years and was denied a bond hearing because the court felt that *Demore* completely closed out this possibility.[56]

In *Lora v Shanahan*, the Second Circuit Court of Appeal joined the Ninth Circuit in holding that those detained under section 236(c) INA must have a bond hearing before an immigration judge within six months.[57] At the bond hearing, the government must demonstrate by clear and convincing evidence that a person poses a risk of flight or a danger to the community.[58] If it fails to do this, the person must be released.[59] Considering that all individuals detained under section 236(c) will necessarily have a criminal record, it is imperative that the state demonstrate an 'identifiable and articulable threat to an individual or

[51] *Araujo-Cortes v Shanahan* (2014 SDNY) 35 F Supp 3d 533, 549.

[52] ibid 549, citing *Johnson v Orsino* (2013 SDNY) 942 F Supp 2d 396, 409.

[53] *Adler* (n 47) 2.

[54] *Johnson* (n 47).

[55] *Vaskovska v Holder* 2014 WL 4659316 (WDNY). See also *Lucien v Tryon* 2012 WL 5373455 (WDNY) (detained for three years, 311 days).

[56] *Luna-Aponte v Holder* (2010 WDNY) 743 F Supp 2d 189.

[57] *Lora v Shanahan* (2d Cir 2015) 804 F 3d 601. The Ninth Circuit case is *Rodriguez v Robbins* (9th Cir 2013) 715 F 3d 1127, *cert granted* 20 June 2016 as *Jennings v Rodriguez* (2018) 583 US ___; 138 S Ct 830. The Third and Fifth Circuits, by contrast, have taken a case-by-case approach. See M Firmacion, 'Protecting Immigrants from Prolonged Pre-removal Detention: When 'It Depends' Is No Longer Reasonable' (2014) 42 *Hastings Constitutional Law Quarterly* 601. The US Supreme Court judgment in *Jennings* is discussed below.

[58] This is the standard applied in cases where removal is not foreseeable under 8 CFR 241.14, and also the standard used to determine whether bail is appropriate in the context of pre-trial detention under s 3142(f) of the Bail Reform Act 1984 (implemented as 18 USC 3143).

[59] Senate Bill 36, the 'Keep Our Communities Safe Act of 2017', discussed above in ch 6, s VI, provides in ss 3(f) and (h) that 'an alien may be detained under [s 236(c)] for any period, without limitation' except if he or she successfully demonstrates by clear and convincing evidence that there is no flight risk or danger.

the community' rather than relying on a criminal record alone.[60] It is interesting, in light of the discussion on risk above, to see that the standard of proof to be applied in the bond hearing context is higher than in habeas hearings. It is unlikely that the district courts' treatment of prior convictions in the pool judgments would stand up to this heightened scrutiny. It is not clear why two different approaches should be taken. Only two cases in the pool considered this issue after *Lora*. In one, the court adopted the clear and convincing evidence standard;[61] in the other, it was not mentioned, though *Lora* was cited as the appropriate precedent;[62] and in neither was relief granted. The feasibility and necessity of the Second and the Ninth Circuits' approach to prolonged mandatory detention has been questioned by Firmacion, who argues that the six-month rule is not adequate in terms of safeguarding liberty and may be unfairly resource-intensive for the government.[63] Given the poor outcomes in *Zadvydas* (ie non-mandatory detention cases), this is not surprising. However, in light of the six-month period established by the US Supreme Court in *Zadvydas*, it is also not surprising that these circuits would choose the same time period in assessing what they think to be reasonable in the context of section 236(c) INA.[64] In November 2018, this issue was put to rest by the US Supreme Court in *Jennings v Rodriguez*, when it held that individuals in prolonged detention under section 236(c) were not entitled to a bond hearing at any point during their detention.[65]

The positive outcomes in mandatory detention cases demonstrate an acknowledgement that prolonged deprivations of liberty should not be permitted to continue without a hearing as to whether continued detention is appropriate.

[60] See *US v Salerno* (1987) 481 US 739, 751. See also *Singh v Holder* (9th Cir 2011) 638 F 3d 1196, 1205.

[61] *Chen v Decker* (2015 SDNY) 148 F Supp 3d 325, 2.

[62] *Raju v Shanahan* 2015 WL 7567455 (SDNY) 1.

[63] Firmacion (n 57).

[64] A distinct set of mandatory detention cases involve a dispute as to whether s 236(c) applies, based on differing interpretations of the INA after an application of the *Chevron* doctrine. INA, s 236(c)(1)(D) gives ICE the authority to detain certain 'criminal aliens' 'when the alien is released' from a custodial sentence and is on parole, supervised release or probation. The disagreement was as to whether ICE apprehension under 236(c)(1)(D) must occur immediately following release (ie whether the statute should be given a time-based interpretation) or whether apprehension could occur at any time following release (ie a duty-based interpretation). In practical terms, some non-citizens liable to deportation were released following completion of their custodial sentence, but then not apprehended by ICE until months, or sometimes years, later. See, eg *Johnson* (n 52) 402; *Young v Aviles* (2015 SDNY) 99 F Supp 3d 443, 448; *Reynoso v Aviles* (2015 SDNY) 87 F Supp 3d 549; *Araujo-Cortes* (n 51). This split was initially resolved by the Second Circuit Court of Appeal's decision in *Lora v Shanahan* (n 57). Not only did the court settle the issue of mandatory detainees' entitlement to a bond hearing, it also concluded under *Chevron v Natural Resources Defense Council* (1984) 467 US 837 that the provision was unambiguous, choosing to interpret INA, s 236(c)(1)(D) as being unequivocally duty-based (ibid 609). The *Chevron* decision is discussed in ch 7, s III.B below. In March 2019, the USSC weighed in and agreed with that interpretation in *Nielsen v Preap* (2019) 586 US ___; 139 SCt 954.

[65] *Jennings v Rodriguez* (2018) 583 US ___; 138 S Ct 830.

This may be an indication that, as MacCormick suggests, judicial values in relation to mandatory detention are changing over time, thus resulting in judgments that distinguish from precedent.[66] The judges willing to consider that mandatory detention without a hearing is unlawful have distinguished prior holdings confirming the strict application of *Demore*. The behaviour of these judges would also support the argument by Bhargarva that *Demore* was an interruption in a line of Supreme Court case law that had been on a more rights-protecting trajectory, especially where lawful permanent residents were at issue.[67]

C. European Union

The CJEU refers to liberty most often with respect to the pure detention cases in Category A, but chooses to rely instead on the principle of effectiveness in cases falling under Categories B and C.[68] The resultant case law thus far has been largely rights-protecting despite the Court's failure to rely explicitly on fundamental rights as the basis for its reasoning.

Recall from chapter two that the Charter of Fundamental Rights and the general principles of EU law established by the CJEU work together in protecting the right to liberty for all individuals where EU law is at issue. Indeed, liberty underpins the decisions in each of the three case categories, though it may not always be explicitly referenced or discussed at length. For example, in *Kadzoev*, the CJEU makes it clear that the 18-month maximum is absolute and that any time spent detained in the context of a return must be counted towards the maximum, so as to ensure that the objective of the Directive – to limit the deprivation of liberty – is given effect.[69] In *Pham*, the Court reminds the parties that the obligation to house returnees in specialised facilities gives effect to one of the aims of the Directive, which is to ensure full respect for the fundamental rights and dignity of third-country nationals.[70] This language, which is contained in Recitals 2 and 17, is repeatedly drawn upon by the Court.[71] In other cases, the Court engages in more in-depth consideration of fundamental rights in relation to the application of the Directive. In *Mukarubega* and *G and R*, cases which

[66] MacCormick (n 1) 223.

[67] S Bhargava, 'Detaining Due Process: The Need for Procedural Reform in "*Joseph*" Hearings after *Demore v Kim*' (2006–2007) 31 *New York University Review of Law and Social Change* 51.

[68] By way of reminder, Category A cases specifically focus on immigration detention and the interpretation of Ch IV of the Directive. Category B cases concern the criminalisation of migration by the Member States, and focus primarily on the question of whether national law that imposes criminal sanctions for violations of immigration law is permitted under the Return Directive. Finally, Category C cases concern issues purely to do with return, rather than detention of any kind. See ch 5, s II, above for more detail.

[69] Case C-357/09 PPU *Kadzoev* [2009] ECR I-11189, para 56.

[70] Case C-474/13 *Pham* [ECR TBC] para 20.

[71] See, eg Case C-383/13 PPU *G and R* [ECR TBC] para 42; *El Dridi* (n 19) para 31.

both focus on the scope of the right to be heard under the Returns Directive, the Court engages in a discussion of the constitutional status of the right to be heard and its place within broader defence rights, respect for which is a general principle of EU law, which can be traced to the rights conferred in the ECHR.[72] Finally, in *Mahdi*, the Court interpreted the Directive as requiring the state authorities to reissue written reasons when a decision to extend detention beyond the initial period is made because, according to the Court, a decision to extend detention is just as much a deprivation of liberty as the initial decision to detain.[73]

What is perhaps more interesting about cases under the Return Directive is the way in which the CJEU has adapted the traditional concept of effectiveness, or *effet utile*.[74] Effectiveness plays perhaps a larger role in Category B cases, on criminalisation of immigration, and in fact originated in this line of cases. In one judgment, it is made clear that effectiveness and the duty of loyal co-operation, which is rooted in Article 4(3) of the Treaty on European Union, work together to require Member States to give effect to EU law.[75] In every Category B case, the CJEU held that the obligation to give effect to EU law (in this case, the Return Directive) means that they cannot impose criminal sanctions that will hinder the effective implementation of the provisions in the Return Directive. For example, in *El Dridi*, the CJEU held that Member States could not imprison people under criminal law as a consequence of illegal stay because it would delay the return process, especially in relation to Article 6(1), which requires Member States to issue a return decision once they have determined that a third-country national is illegally staying on their territory.[76] From that point, the machinery of return must be put in motion and cannot be interrupted by imprisonment or any carceral punishment that cannot be terminated once return is possible.[77] Conversely, the CJEU permitted national law penalising illegal stay with a fine or an order for immediate expulsion in *Md Sagor* because neither would prevent a return decision from being made and implemented.[78] However, imposition of a fine instead of a removal order was not permitted in a subsequent case because a fine which would allow them to remain in the Member State would not give effect to the Directive's objective of returning illegally staying third-country nationals.[79] As discussed above in the context of judicial use of precedent, there are only two exceptions to this general rule. In *Achughbabian*, the CJEU permitted imprisonment for illegal stay where the removal process had previously been applied to an illegally staying third-country

[72] *G and R* (ibid) para 32; Case C-166/13 *Mukarubega* [ECR TBC] paras 42–52.
[73] Case C-146/14 PPU *Mahdi* [ECR TBC] paras 37–52.
[74] See ch 2.
[75] *Achughbabian* (n 18) para 45.
[76] *El Dridi* (n 19).
[77] Case C-430/11 *Md Sagor* [ECR TBC].
[78] ibid.
[79] Case C-38/14 *Zaizoune* [ECR TBC].

national who did not comply with the obligation to return.[80] In *Celaj*, the CJEU held that criminal imprisonment was permissible where a previously removed third-country national re-entered illegally.[81] But otherwise, effectiveness in the context of return of third-country nationals has operated so as to limit Member State competence in criminal law, especially in relation to the criminalisation of immigration.[82] This has ultimately safeguarded the liberty of detainees held within the scope of the Directive.

The detention cases in Category A do not employ effectiveness as a device for justifying conclusions as much, perhaps because the heart of the matter is the legality of detention under Article 15 of the Directive, which directly implicates the right to liberty and therefore perhaps cannot be avoided. However, in *G and R*, the CJEU confirmed that the right to be heard applies in the context of a decision to extend the initial period of detention, but it cannot be exercised in such a way as to undermine the effectiveness of the Directive.[83] The Court did not agree with the Advocate General's assessment that any breach of the right to be heard must result in the nullity of detention because no such breach could be considered minor in circumstances where the right to liberty is at stake.[84] Instead, the CJEU felt that nullifying detention in all cases of a breach of the right to be heard would impede the effective operation of the return procedures under the Directive, which sometimes requires detention to ensure removal occurs. As such, effectiveness was applied here in a less liberty-protecting way.

The CJEU has applied the principle of effectiveness in Category C cases addressing miscellaneous issues related to the return process. For example, in *Mukarubega*, the CJEU discussed the right to be heard prior to issuing a return decision. Following the reasoning in *G and R*, the Court began by reiterating that respect for defence rights is a general principle of EU law that must be respected in all proceedings.[85] Defence rights can be restricted if the restriction is proportionate and respects the principles of equivalence (individuals in comparable situations treated similarly) and effectiveness (in its traditional sense, it means that the limitations cannot make it impossible in practice or excessively difficult to exercise a right conferred by EU law).[86] However, the CJEU agreed with the Advocate General, who stated that the right to be heard 'cannot be used in order to re-open indefinitely the administrative procedure', the implication being that to do so would undermine the effective implementation of the

[80] *Achughbabian* (n 18).
[81] *Celaj* (n 21).
[82] V Mitsilegas, 'The Changing Landscape of the Criminalisation of Migration in Europe' in M João et al (eds), *Social Control and Justice: Crimmigration in the Age of Fear* (Eleven International Publishing, 2013) 98–110.
[83] *G and R* (n 71) para 36.
[84] Ibid, view of Advocate General Wathelet, para 55.
[85] *Mukarubega* (n 72) para 45.
[86] ibid para 51.

Return Directive.[87] The Court found similarly in *Boudjilda* with respect to the right to legal representation.[88]

Though the CJEU references fundamental rights in its consideration of the questions before it, it is clear that effectiveness is most often relied upon as the main justificatory device for its decision-making under the Directive. Until now, that has largely resulted in rights-protecting outcomes.[89] The use of effectiveness as a device to interpret the Return Directive has been criticised as 'giving tacit support to the criminalisation tendencies of Member States', especially in cases where return is not possible.[90] Though this cannot be said with regard to the use of criminal imprisonment in light of *El Dridi* and subsequent case law, one does wonder whether a better approach would be for the CJEU to speak explicitly in terms of fundamental rights in a manner similar to the Advocates General, who tend to rely more explicitly on fundamental rights to justify their opinions.[91]

Scholars have particularly criticised the Court's failure to consider Article 5(1)(f) ECHR in *G and R* on the right to be heard in the context of detention proceedings, especially in light of the Advocate General's opinion, which explicitly acknowledged the importance of the ECHR.[92] Such an obligation, it is argued, is derived from Article 1 of the Directive, which requires the Directive to be applied 'in accordance with fundamental rights as general principles of Community law as well as international law, including … human rights obligations'. The Court was clearly mindful of the potential impact on the effectiveness of the Directive were it to hold that all violations of the right to be heard should result in the annulment of detention.[93] Though it is understandable that the CJEU does not wish to risk compromising returns by forcing Member States

[87] ibid para 71.

[88] Case C-249/13 *Boudjilda* [ECR TBC] para 65.

[89] This arguably did not occur in *G and R* (n 71), where the CJEU held that fundamental rights principles must be balanced against the competing interest of ensuring the effectiveness of the Directive, or in Case C-534/11 *Arslan* [ECR TBC], discussed below in s IV.C.

[90] YA Kramo, 'The European Union's Response to Irregular Migration and the Problem of Criminalisation' (2014) 1 *New Journal of European Criminal Law* 26, 46.

[91] See, eg Advocate General Wathelet's opinion in *Arslan* (n 89), which stated that the examination of circumstances must be detailed because liberty is at stake (paras 65, 77), and in *G and R* (n 71), where Wathelet reminded the parties that the right to liberty is 'one of the most fundamental human rights' (para 55). Moreover, the Advocates General sometimes go outside the EU legal order to consider how the case law of the ECtHR, or even soft law such as the Council of Europe's Twenty Guidelines on Forced Return (adopted 4 May 2005 by the Committee of Ministers of the Council of Europe), impact the validity of national law, especially in relation to the use of detention. See, eg the AG opinions in *Kadzoev* (n 69) para 52 and fn 17; *Mahdi* (n 73) para 45; and *Celaj* (n 21) paras 1–2. It is important to emphasise that the Advocates General do not ignore the language of effectiveness either. See, eg Advocate General Bot's Opinion in *Bero, Bouzalmate and Pham* (Joined Cases C-473/13 and C-514/13 *Bero and Bouzalmate* and Case C-474/13 *Pham*) and Advocate General Mazák's opinions in *Achughbabian* (n 18) para 28 and *El Dridi* (n 19) para 33.

[92] Philippe De Bruycker and Sergo Mananashvili, '*Audi alteram partem* in Immigration Detention Procedures, between the ECJ, the ECtHR and Member States: *G & R*' (2015) 52 *Common Market Law Review* 569.

[93] ibid 587.

to terminate detention in all cases of a breach, it is disappointing that the CJEU did not give proper weight to the fact that the decision in question related to extending the initial six-month period of detention. As convincingly argued by De Bruycker and Mananashvili, the Court's review power should increase as the length of detention increases.[94] The judgment in *G and R* is especially interesting given the Court's subsequent ruling in *Mahdi*, which did not refer to the balanced approach in concluding that the same procedural guarantees must be applied to decisions to extend the initial period of detention.

Moreover, scholars have contrasted the Court's decision to base its judgment on effectiveness against the specific discussion of the importance of fundamental rights in the interpretation of the Family Reunification Directive.[95] One cannot help but think that this difference in treatment is due to the fact that the Return Directive deals with irregular migration, whereas the Family Reunification Directive is aimed at reuniting third-country national family members with third-country nationals lawfully resident in the EU. Regardless of the motive behind the use of effectiveness, its use thus far has resulted in rights-protecting outcomes in the CJEU case law. The CJEU therefore acknowledges the application of fundamental rights principles in its judgments, but relies primarily on the principle of effectiveness to justify its decisions.

IV. IMPACT OF DETENTION TIME LIMITS ON JUDICIAL DECISION-MAKING

Detention time limits are drawn out separately in this section to consider the extent to which a maximum detention period in the law (Return Directive in the EU) or guidance from the courts regarding length of detention (*Zadvydas* in the USA) impacts judicial decision-making, and whether there is a noticeable difference between these jurisdictions and the UK, which has neither. The judgments from the three jurisdictions suggest that, while setting a maximum time limit may not be essential in safeguarding the liberty of immigration detainees, it may be a helpful tool, especially where it is obligatory without exception. For example, in the EU context, once the 18-month maximum period in the EU Returns Directive is reached, release must be ordered, even where removal is likely, where the detainee is a flight risk or a danger, or where the detainee is pursuing legal remedies against removal.[96] As such, the maximum serves as a clear cut-off which ensures that immigration detainees are not detained in connection with return proceedings beyond a certain period. However, this may not preclude the states from detaining such people under other powers.[97] The USSC, though

[94] ibid 585.

[95] ibid 578, discussing the Court's judgment in Case C-578/08 *Chakroun* [2010] ECR I-1839 under the Family Reunification Directive 2003/86/EC.

[96] *Kadzoev* (n 69) paras 60, 68–71.

[97] ibid, view of Advocate General Mazák, para 101 and text accompanying fn 38.

not setting a maximum period of detention, did establish a presumptively reasonable period of detention at six months. What has happened in practice in the NY federal district courts is that this has become a compulsory minimum, which, until reached, forecloses the possibility of habeas corpus, without reference to whether the individual in question poses a genuine flight risk or danger – two factors which were identified as important by the Supreme Court in *Zadvydas*. The UK comes in as a softer third option, where no guidance has been offered by the courts or otherwise as to what constitutes a reasonable duration of detention. Rather, the focus of the *Hardial Singh* principles is determining reasonableness in light of all circumstances, no matter when the individual makes an application for judicial review. In comparison to the USA, average detention lengths in the UK cases are shorter, suggesting that the UK approach is more sound.

The impact of the maximum period of detention in the Return Directive is less clear. According to a Communication from the EU Commission on EU Return Policy, legal time limits for detention increased in eight Member States with the entry into force of the 18-month maximum in the Directive.[98] However, maximum detention periods across the Member States have reduced overall, and in practice, the average length of detention in the Member States seems to be much lower than legally permitted.[99] Therefore, it would seem that a maximum period may still be preferable, at the very least by functioning as a tool by which judges can draw a clear line of legality when faced with conflicting evidence regarding issues such as risk and non-co-operation. Each of these is explored in more detail in the following sections.

A. United Kingdom

The UK is the only jurisdiction of the three to have no temporal guidance regarding the length of detention, other than that it must be reasonable in all the circumstances, including the length of detention to date.[100] This means that 'There is no red line, in terms of months or years, applicable to all cases, beyond which time for detention becomes unreasonable'.[101] The Administrative Court has not been persuaded otherwise. In fact, in two cases, the claimants attempted to argue that the maximum period of detention in the EU Return Directive should apply in the UK;

[98] Communication from the Commission to the Council and the European Parliament on EU Return Policy, COM(2014) 199 final (28 March14) 18.

[99] ibid 17.

[100] *Kumar* (n 29) 22: 'The period of detention to date, which is from approximately July 2002 to March 2003, is not so long, in my judgment, as to be at present unreasonable.'

[101] *R (Mahfoud) v SSHD* [2010] EWHC 2057 (Admin) 6.

they were, however, unsuccessful.[102] Moreover, as discussed further in section V.A below, when the ECtHR reviewed the lawfulness of the UK's detention framework, it agreed that a maximum period was unnecessary. The Court reminded the parties of its numerous judgments to the effect that what matters is not that there is a maximum time limit on detention, but rather that there are sufficient safeguards in place to prevent arbitrary detention.[103] Applying those principles to the case, the Court held that the existence of a time limit would be one of many factors for it to consider in assessing lawfulness, but alone would not satisfy Article 5(1)(f) ECHR and that therefore the lack of such a limit in the UK does not amount to a breach of the Article.[104] Approval at the regional level has not stopped numerous calls to put an end to indefinite detention. Bodies including parliamentary committees and non-profit organisations have argued convincingly that there should be a time limit, citing the fact that the UK is the only European state without one.[105] At the time of writing, however, the idea of imposing a maximum period has yet to be taken seriously by Parliament.

Rather than attempt to identify a presumptively reasonable period of detention, like the USSC in *Zadvydas*, Administrative Court judges have specifically remarked on the extent to which referring to previous lengths of detention is helpful in determining whether detention is lawful. In those cases, the judges remind the parties that each case is dependent upon the facts, and therefore comparison with other cases is not helpful.[106] This approach is sensible when one recalls that the UK does not have a maximum time limit for detention, and that therefore the test is one based on an evaluation of whether detention is reasonable in all the circumstances. It is interesting that, despite the absence of any time-based guidance, UK detainees are more successful than US detainees in securing a grant of relief. This would suggest that a time limit may not be necessary if the applicable legality test is being applied with full consideration. However, it does not eradicate the risk of indefinite detention, which is evident from the UK pool of cases, where detainees were held on average for 2.1 years.

B. United States

In the USA, the *Zadvydas* line of cases makes it clear that many detainees have misunderstood the holding in *Zadvydas* to mean that once the presumptively

[102] *R (Azaroal) v SSHD* [2013] EWHC 1248 (Admin) 41, stating that the court is 'wholly unpersuaded' by the argument, and *R (JM) v SSHD* [2014] EWHC 151 (Admin) 10, noting simply that the UK has opted out of the Return Directive.

[103] *JN v UK* [2016] ECHR 434, paras 83–86.

[104] ibid paras 94–96.

[105] See, eg Medical Justice, which emphasises the negative impact of indefinite detention on the mental and physical health of detainees: www.medicaljustice.org.uk/healthcare-in-detention/impact-of-detention-on-health/.

[106] *Lamrani* (n 31) 62; *R (Egal) v SSHD* [2009] EWHC 2939 (Admin) 59.

reasonable period of six months has been reached, detainees should automatically be released. The courts' resistance to this interpretation is exhibited in many cases where detainees are reminded that the fact alone that they have been detained for six months does not automatically mean they are entitled to release under *Zadvydas*: 'the mere passage of time, [is] insufficient to meet the petitioner's burden to demonstrate no significant likelihood of removal'.[107] What is perhaps more remarkable is that, on occasion, judges chastise detainees for seeking habeas relief immediately upon the expiry of the six months. In the *Haidara* case, for example, the judge expressly noted that the petitioner applied for habeas relief just 'days after the six months ha[d] run'.[108] Though it is certainly evident from these cases that time alone is insufficient to obtain release, this comment implies that the petitioner had acted inappropriately or foolishly in petitioning for relief so soon after six months had been reached, and that there was no possibility that detainees similarly situated might have a case for release at that point, let alone before the six months has accrued. This tone is quite common in judgments from the district courts, not just relating to the six-month period of reasonable detention. Moreover, although in several cases concerning post-removal order detention the court determines that the petitioner's claim under *Zadvydas* is premature, it is sometimes the case that the court goes on to consider whether the petitioner would succeed with a *Zadvydas* claim should one be made in the future, thus seemingly pre-empting such a claim once it becomes ripe.[109]

What this behaviour demonstrates is that the presumptively reasonable six-month period has in fact become a default minimum as applied by the NY district courts. This means that the courts are not considering whether release might be appropriate in an individual case at a point following the end of the 90-day removal period and the culmination of the six-month period. The reasons for this are unclear on the face of the judgments, but can perhaps be partially attributed to the general role played by federal district courts. The USSC attempted to resolve an indeterminacy in the law by creating a legality test for cases of prolonged detention under section 241(a) INA. This is part and parcel of the role played by a supreme court in not only reviewing lower court judgments for errors of law, but also interpreting the law. Federal district courts, by contrast, are primarily responsible for fact-finding and applying the law to

[107] See, eg *Fofana v Holder* (2013 WDNY) 947 F Supp 2d 329, 334; *Haley v Holder* 2013 WL 1945704 (WDNY) 7; *Alzubi v Tryon* 2015 WL 860792 (WDNY) 9.

[108] *Haidara v Mule* 2008 WL 2483281 (WDNY) 3: 'Furthermore, petitioner commenced this action days after the six months has run. Just because an alien has been in BICE custody for more than six months does not justify his release under *Zadvydas*.' See also *Roberts v Bureau of Immigration and Customs Enforcement* 2007 WL 781925 (WDNY) 2, remarking that the petitioner filed 'only weeks after the six-month period ha[d] expired'.

[109] See, eg *Gabriel v Immigration and Customs Enforcement* 2009 WL 1272291 (WDNY); *Blackman v US Dept of Homeland Security Bureau of ICE* 2007 WL 4404930 (WDNY); *Singh* (n 60).

the facts.[110] They are not interpreters of the law. I show in chapter seven that the NY district court judges do not necessarily uphold their duty to fact-find in detention cases, but at this point it is important to understand that it is not the task of the federal district courts to question the interpretation of the law as set forth by the USSC, even if the USSC did not make it absolutely clear whether the six-month period was intended to apply in every case. Thus, the district judges faithfully apply the Supreme Court's interpretation of the law until they are told otherwise.

Compounding this situation is the fact that some of the cases demonstrate a disagreement about whether the presumptively reasonable six-month period includes the initial mandatory 90-day removal period under section 241 INA or is in addition to it.[111] In 2010, the WDNY adopted a Second Circuit Court of Appeals decision which held that the six months is inclusive of the 90-day removal period.[112] The Supreme Court did not make this clear in the *Zadvydas* decision, but the American Bar Association indicates that it is six months from when the removal order becomes final, and therefore inclusive of the 90 days.[113] This more rights-protecting approach is seemingly uncharacteristic of judgments from that district. Despite this, these cases ultimately demonstrate that the presumptively reasonable period of six months is, in practice, an obligatory minimum detention period that cannot be easily rebutted. As such, detention remains prolonged far beyond the six-month period in many cases, rendering *Zadvydas* not much help to detainees, at least in the NY federal district courts.

C. European Union

By contrast, it is clear from the case law of the CJEU that the Advocates General and the judges are acutely aware of the fundamental rights basis for the maximum period of detention.[114] In any case discussing detention, including Category B cases on criminalisation, the opinions and judgments are replete with warnings that detention should be used sparingly, and that the maximum must be respected. For example, detention is a 'last resort',[115] or 'only by way of an exception'.[116] Advocate General Wathelet, in *G and R*, emphasised that

[110] R Anderson IV, 'Law, Fact, and Discretion in the Federal Courts: An Empirical Study', Pepperdine University School of Law Legal Studies Research Paper Series, Number 2011/12 (2011) 3.

[111] See, eg *Roberts* (n 109) (holding that it is cumulative); *D'Alessandro* (n 42) (holding that the six months includes the 90 days).

[112] *Leslie* (n 13) 2, citing *Wang v Ashcroft* (2nd Cir 2003) 320 F3d 130.

[113] American Bar Association, 'A Legal Guide for ICE Detainees: Petitioning for Release from Indefinite Detention' (2006) 8.

[114] EU Return Directive 2008/115/EC, Art 15(5), (6).

[115] *Kadzoev* (n 69), view of Advocate General Mazák, para 101.

[116] *Arslan* (n 89), view of Advocate General Wathelet, 60.

> a detention measure which, although it is not a criminal-law penalty, none the less entails total deprivation of liberty, is designed to be a measure of last resort, provided for only where enforcement of the return decision in the form of removal is liable to be jeopardised by the conduct of the person concerned.[117]

In addition, the criminalisation cases discussing the permissibility of criminal imprisonment as a result of legal stay deserve a mention. In refusing to permit imprisonment in this context, the Court has reminded the Member States that criminal imprisonment would undermine the effectiveness of the Return Directive and its common standards on the deprivation of liberty.[118] In so doing, the Court is ensuring that the maximum is enforced and that additional detention cannot be imposed through criminal sanctions.[119]

Chapter five discussed the effect of pursuing legal remedies against return in the EU context, but it is worth reemphasising here the holding in *Kadzoev* that the time spent pursuing judicial review of the return decision must be included when calculating whether 18 months has been reached. In so holding, the Court reiterated that the objective of including a maximum period in Article 15 is to ensure that detention does not exceed 18 months.[120] If such periods were not counted, there would be varied detention periods across the Member States, which would undermine the objective of the Directive, which is to harmonise the maximum time that people can remain in immigration detention under the framework of returns.[121] Similarly, time detained prior to the entry into force of the Directive must also be included because, even though there was no maximum period when Kadzoev was initially detained, the Directive applies immediately to the consequences of a situation which arose prior to its entry into force.[122]

The referring court also queried whether Kadzoev must be released at the expiry of the 18 months, even though he did not possess identity documents, had displayed aggressive behaviour and had no means of financial support or accommodation. In response, the Court held that the Return Directive cannot serve as a basis for detaining individuals on public order or safety grounds, and therefore detention under the Directive is in no way to be exceeded.[123] Ultimately, the maximum is there to limit deprivations of liberty and cannot be subverted by the Member States through exceptions and exclusions.[124] In writing about *Kadzoev*, Cornelisse emphasises that the case demonstrates that the Return Directive includes important safeguards with which the Member States must comply.[125]

[117] *G and R* (n 71), view of Advocate General Wathelet, para 54.
[118] *Md Sagor* (n 77) para 36.
[119] Of course, *Celaj* (n 21) and *Achughbabian* (n 18) are exceptions to this general rule.
[120] *Kadzoev* (n 69), paras 37, 62.
[121] ibid para 54.
[122] ibid para 38.
[123] ibid paras 68–71. See also Mitsilegas (n 82) 99.
[124] *Kadzoev* (n 69) para 56.
[125] G Cornelisse, 'Case Note Case C-357/09 PPU, Proceedings Concerning Said Shamilovich Kadzoev (Huchbarov) Judgment of the Court (Grand Chamber) of 30 November 2009' (2011) 48 *Common Market Law Review* 3.

She suggests that this is an under-acknowledged aspect of the Directive.[126] Indeed, while certain judgments of the Court under the Return Directive have been the subject of scholarly writing, less attention has been paid to the power of the Return Directive in relation to safeguarding rights.[127]

By contrast, note the Court's separation of the Return Directive framework from the CEAS in *Kadzoev* and *Arslan*, and its impact on the duration of detention. As discussed, in *Kadzoev*, the Court made it clear that the maximum is absolute. However, unlike in the context of judicial review, even if a third-country national has made a legitimate application for asylum, it is possible for the maximum to be extended if the Member State makes a separate decision to detain him or her under asylum law.[128] Such detention is not to be counted for purposes of the Return Directive, though any time spent in detention prior to the entry into force of the Return Directive should be counted, if such detention was ordered in connection with a national removal procedure.[129]

In *Arslan*, the Court continued the idea of separate regimes, making it clear that the framework of the Return Directive does not apply once someone has made a genuine application for asylum. In so concluding, the Court explicitly noted that:

> the mere fact that an asylum seeker, at the time of making his application, is the subject of a return decision and is being detained on the basis of Article 15 of [the Return Directive] does not allow it to be presumed, without an assessment on a case-by-case basis of all the relevant circumstances, that he has made that application solely to delay or jeopardise the enforcement of the return decision and that it is objectively necessary and proportionate to maintain detention.[130]

Though it may be logical to consider the CEAS separately from the Return Directive, if, as the Court stated in *Kadzoev*, the aim of including time spent pursuing judicial review in the calculation of the maximum period is to avoid varied detention periods across Member States, it seems strange that the Court would not also see fit to include time spent in legitimate pursuit of asylum. To not count that time would present similar risks of variations in detention periods across the Member States. Ultimately, however, the maximum time period seems to be an effective tool to which judges can turn to ensure that, no matter what, release must be ordered after 18 months. In that way, a maximum should be considered a plus in terms of safeguarding liberty and arriving at rights-protecting judgments.

[126] ibid.

[127] But see Mitsilegas (n 82) discussing the way in which the Directive limits Member State sovereignty over immigration.

[128] *Kadzoev* (n 69) paras 40–48.

[129] ibid paras 34–39.

[130] *Arslan* (n 89) para 62.

V. QUALITY OF LAW

Chapters two and three traced the development and content of the main immigration laws under consideration in this book. That discussion demonstrated that, in the UK and USA, detention is not heavily regulated at the statutory level beyond providing the grounds for detention in certain circumstances. It does not address situations where detention has become prolonged. Judges in the UK and USA are consequently left without any statutory guidance on how to make determinations of legality when detention has become prolonged. The EU Return Directive offers the opposite scenario, with its detailed provisions supplying a test of legality not just for immigration officials, but also for the CJEU and national judiciaries. This section uses a different approach to the foregoing sections to illustrate the impact that the quality of law has on decision-making, and to emphasise the similarities between the UK and USA in particular.

The rule of law requires that the state act in accordance with the law.[131] Referred to as 'legality', this requires not only that its action must conform to the law, but that the law itself possess certain qualities. The ECtHR has expressed these as: (i) sufficiently accessible; (ii) sufficiently precise; (iii) foreseeable in application (so that individuals may regulate their conduct accordingly); and (iv) non-arbitrary (ie that there are adequate procedural safeguards in the law).[132] For the ECtHR, the fourth characteristic varies according to which limb of Article 5 ECHR is at issue. For example, in a judgment on stop and search powers in the UK under anti-terror legislation, the ECtHR held that the applicable statute's lack of a necessity requirement, and hence a proportionality analysis, meant that the statute conferred an arbitrary power.[133] This should be contrasted with the more lenient approach of the ECtHR towards immigration detention, where necessity is not required.

A. United Kingdom and United States

Looking only at the statutory law in the UK and USA, there are clear problems with accessibility, foreseeability and precision. As discussed in chapters two through four, the law governing detention in those jurisdictions is virtually non-existent, apart from a list of the grounds upon which detention can be based.

[131] See, eg T Bingham, *The Rule of Law* (Penguin Books, 2010) 37–47; J Jowell, 'The Rule of Law and its Underlying Values' in J Jowell and D Oliver (eds) *The Changing Constitution*, 7th edn (Oxford University Press, 2011) 17–20.

[132] See, eg *Gillan and Quinton v UK* [2010] ECHR 28, para 77; *JN* (n 103) para 77; Bingham (ibid) 60–65; Venice Commission, 'The Rule of Law Checklist', adopted by the Venice Commission at its 106th Plenary Session, Venice, 11–12 March 2016, II.C and cited case law.

[133] *Gillan* (ibid) paras 80, 87.

It is devoid of any detail regarding the implementation of detention on those grounds, applicable review procedures (judicial or administrative) and standards of review. More pertinent to the topic examined in this book, the law certainly does not address situations of prolonged detention. Though the US Government adopted regulations following the USSC judgment in *Zadvydas* aimed at helping ICE officials determine the likelihood of removal, immigration regulations (though binding on the relevant agency) are not subject to normal legislative processes and can be amended or deleted easily, which poses problems for foreseeability and non-arbitrariness.

In addition, the non-statutory guidance in the UK is patchy at best and does not cover all phases of detention.[134] UKVI guidance is predominantly concerned with the initial decision to detain, conditions of detention and administrative periodic review. It does not address situations of prolonged detention where removal is unlikely, and it is not aimed at judicial actors. Like the US immigration regulations, UKVI guidance is not subject to normal parliamentary scrutiny processes and therefore vulnerable to change. Ultimately, the focus of the law in both jurisdictions is on the narrow and preliminary issue of whether there is a lawful power to detain. The extent to which this situation can be considered accessible, precise and foreseeable is questionable.

The presence of procedural safeguards within the law is a way of ensuring that the law is not arbitrary. Though there are limited grounds upon which detention can be based, there are no additional safeguards in the laws in the UK and USA. The US INA and the UK Immigration Act each make provision for the availability of release on bond or bail in certain circumstances, but neither refers explicitly to judicial review powers. Mention of judicial review of detention is only made in Chapter 60 of the UKVI EIG and, as explained in chapter four, the availability of habeas corpus for immigration detainees in the USA was at one time unclear. Perhaps most importantly, neither the UK nor the USA has a statutory maximum period of detention.

These factors may likely have contributed to the decisions of the Administrative Court in *Hardial Singh* and the Supreme Court in *Zadvydas* to give the law more flesh by developing their own tests to determine whether ongoing detention is lawful. These tests effectively supplement the limited statutory law and guidance, and require additional conditions to be fulfilled in order for detention to be considered lawful. However, these judicially created standards raise rule of law issues of their own.

First, while the statutory law and guidance are both publicly available in the UK and USA, because they are not sufficiently precise or foreseeable, case law

[134] Moreover, addressing the more granular issues of detention in non-statutory guidance, which is not subject to parliamentary scrutiny and is frequently updated, presents significant problems for the rule of law requirement of stability and consistency of the law. See Venice Commission (n 133) II.B.4.

has come to form a substantial part of the law in this field. However, whether judgments are sufficiently accessible for detainees to understand their legal position, especially where detainees do not have legal representation, is unclear. This is a particular problem in the USA, where most of the detainees in my pool of cases were unrepresented. The likelihood that unrepresented detainees can access case law, or are even aware that they need to do so, seems low.

In addition, reliance on case law triggers difficulties with the requirement that the law be foreseeable in its application because, though there are applicable judicial tests of legality, they are heavily fact-dependent, and involve a subjective evaluation of factors. This means that outcomes vary in similar situations and in sometimes seemingly arbitrary ways, especially when courts have to assess risk or state efforts to pursue removal or deportation. This makes it extremely difficult for detainees to regulate their conduct accordingly. Indeed, I question whether it is possible at all for detainees to regulate their conduct under these tests. For example, the state can clearly decide whether or not it is going to act diligently in pursing removal. By contrast, detainees have little sovereignty over their conduct other than choosing whether or not to co-operate. They can do little to erase their past conduct (criminal or otherwise), or even judge how much their past is going to factor into the courts' analysis or what weight factors like criminal history or family ties will have.

The ECtHR judgment in *JN*[135] specifically addressed the question of whether the UK system for regulating detention satisfied the requirement of legality. In concluding yes, the Court largely based its conclusion on the existence of the *Hardial Singh* principles.[136] In the Court's discussion of the legality requirement, there was no consideration of the quality of the 1971 Act or of the EIG provisions on detention.[137] This suggests that, absent the *Hardial Singh* principles, the UK legal framework may not be rule of law compliant. However, given the discussion immediately above, even the *Hardial Singh* principles present rule of law problems. It is therefore, to my mind, difficult to see how the ECtHR could validly conclude that the UK legal framework satisfies the principle of legality, and therefore Article 5 ECHR, even though, as the ECtHR said, detainees can challenge their detention through judicial review at any time.[138] *JN* was used to dismiss a similar claim in *Draga v UK*.[139] These judgments firmly maintain a course that is at odds with the EU approach to managing detention, and,

[135] *JN* (n 103).
[136] ibid para 89.
[137] ibid paras 74–99. The judgment also did not refer to provisions in the Immigration Act 2016, which received Royal Assent just four days prior to the judgment in *JN*, and includes the additional safeguard against arbitrariness in the form of a requirement that the Secretary of State refer detainees for a bail hearing before the Immigration and Asylum Chamber of the First-tier Tribunal if they are detained pending examination for entry or pending removal, and have been detained for four months (c 19, Sch 10, s 11).
[138] ibid para 98.
[139] *Draga v UK* ECtHR App No 33341/13; Communicated Case [2015] ECHR 73, para 37.

as Simpson points out, ignores the advice and criticism by UN and European human rights bodies of the UK's lack of a maximum period as a vital safeguard against arbitrariness.[140]

In addition to legal certainty, a 'thick' conception of the rule of law requires that the law must respect fundamental human rights.[141] This is clearly not the case with the statutory law on detention in the UK or USA, primarily because of their lack of a statutory maximum period of detention, but also because of their lack of procedural safeguards. Whether the same can be said for the judicial tests in each jurisdiction is less clear. When the *Hardial Singh* principles were created by the Administrative Court, the discussion was based on reasonableness, not human rights. However, several judgments in the pool of Administrative Court cases demonstrate that judges are thinking about human rights when they apply the test – and, indeed, when they consider their role in the process of applying the test.[142] In the USA, the Supreme Court's judgment in *Zadvydas* was clearly based on constitutional principles and the right to liberty, but these values seem to have been lost in translation in the lower courts, which predominantly assess detention mechanistically without any meaningful reference to the role that the right to liberty should play in cases of prolonged detention.

B. European Union

On the opposite side lies the Return Directive, for which a number of observations can be made. First, though criticisms have been levied at the Directive,[143] one cannot deny that it is precise and accessible in a way that the laws in the UK and USA are not. The Directive goes beyond a mere listing of the grounds for detention to include specific conditions that must be fulfilled before a decision to detain can be made, and standards to apply in determining whether prolonged detention is lawful. Most importantly, the Directive includes a vital safeguard against arbitrariness in the form of a maximum period of detention. Perhaps the EU's long tradition of respect for fundamental rights means that it is keenly aware of the need to ensure that any legislation which it adopts conforms to the requirement of lawfulness, as prescribed by the ECHR and the ECtHR. Indeed, the CJEU judgment in *Al Chodor* on detention under the CEAS underscores the weight that the ECtHR's description of lawfulness is given by the CJEU in its assessment and interpretation of EU law.[144] In a similar vein, the EU's high

[140] F Simpson, 'Article 5 ECHR does not require time limits for detention pending deportation', UK Human Rights Blog (24 May 2016).

[141] Bingham (n 132) 66.

[142] See earlier discussion in s III.A.

[143] See ch 3, s II.C above.

[144] *Al Chodor*. See also ch 5, s V.C above.

regard for respect of fundamental rights is made explicit several times in the preamble of the Directive,[145] which sets the tone for its interpretation in a way that is not present in the law or guidance in the UK and USA. However, it must be said that, despite these positive qualities, like the judicially made tests in the UK and the USA, the Directive requires Member States to engage in a subjective evaluation of due diligence and likelihood of removal. This presents problems of foreseeability for detainees challenging their detention in the same way that arises under the UK and US judicially made tests.

The point of this discussion is to re-emphasise the vague nature of the law in the UK and USA, contrast it to the EU Return Directive and argue that the quality of the law is a factor in case outcomes. The cases demonstrate that, where the law is of insufficient quality and judges are forced to fill the legislative holes, the result can a poorer quality of decision-making. This is exemplified most obviously by the US judgments, which were made in a context where detainees are at a procedural disadvantage and where judicially created devices, such as the attribution principle, operate in favour of the state.

VI. CONCLUSION

The aim of this chapter has been to illustrate the types of tools that the judges in the pool cases have used to assist in their decision-making on immigration detention. Reference to precedent, fundamental rights principles and temporal limits on detention can be used in ways to create either rights-protecting or rights-limiting outcomes. For example, judges can either choose to fully engage with and understand decision-making in prior case law to ensure that they arrive at a decision which is fully justified by the facts, as is the case in the Administrative Court and the CJEU, or they can simply copy and paste the language from previous cases without much evaluation of the relevant factual circumstances, which is evidenced in the NY federal district courts. Whichever approach is taken, it is important to caution that thorough engagement with precedent alone will not automatically result in rights-protecting outcomes, especially where the precedential rules are themselves not rights-protecting. This is somewhat exemplified in the US cookie-cutter judgments, which nearly exactly adhere to precedent that is not well-reasoned. What is more important is for the judge to engage fully with precedent and understand the previous courts' reasoning so that precedent can be applied consistently, even where fact patterns differ.

When it comes to fundamental rights principles, it is difficult to argue that they can be manipulated to arrive at anything other than rights-protecting outcomes in the context of deprivations of liberty. However, they can be ignored

[145] EU Return Directive 2008/115/EC, paras 2, 17, 24.

as a useful decision-making mechanism, which is often the case in the US judgments, or they can be tempered by reference to other competing norms, such as policy objectives, as in the case of the judgments on the EU Return Directive.

The presence or absence of a maximum can impact decision-making on detention either positively or negatively, depending on the role that fundamental rights play in the decision-making process. In the UK, the lack of a maximum period of detention did not prevent the Administrative Court judges from arriving at rights-protecting outcomes because of the high value placed on the fundamental right to liberty. This approach can be most starkly contrasted with the USA, which also has no maximum period, but operates according to a presumptively reasonable period of detention, which has been clung to by judges in such a way that it has become a default minimum period that must be reached before a challenge can be mounted. Because the Administrative Court did not set a presumptively reasonable period in *Hardial Singh*, like the Supreme Court did in *Zadvydas*, the UK does not suffer the problematic 'default minimum' phenomenon that is evident in the US cases.

Finally, this chapter argues that the quality of the laws at play in the UK and USA is poor when assessed against rule of law standards and that, as a result, case outcomes are generally poor, especially in the latter jurisdiction. By contrast, the detail in the EU Return Directive gives judges the specific tools and tests they need to review detention with certainty and arrive at rights-protecting outcomes. In contrast, the lack of detail in the UK and US statutory law made it necessary for judges to step in and develop standards for legality that have been applied with mixed results.

In addition to the tools discussed in this chapter, institutional factors play a role in the judicial review of immigration detention. The following chapter considers two main factors present in the case studies and their impact on case outcomes: the role of judges and the place of deference to the state.

7

The Business of Judging

I. INTRODUCTION

THIS CHAPTER TAKES its name from a collection of essays by Lord Bingham reflecting on 20 years of his life as a judge.[1] It picks up some of the themes explored in Bingham's book by examining whether the role of judges and deference impact the way that judges consider the facts and analyse the law during judicial review. Broadly, this chapter concludes two things. First, judges who view themselves as playing a key role in the safeguarding of liberty undertake judicial review in a more careful and meaningful manner. Secondly, though deference has traditionally played a role in judicial review of state action, and continues to play a role today, there is no evidence that it has been improperly applied in any of the three jurisdictions under examination.

II. JUDGES AS FACT-FINDERS, REVIEWERS OR LAW-MAKERS

Various scholars have discussed the different roles that judges might play.[2] Which role judges will perform depends on a number of factors, such as the environment in which they operate, the level of discretion that they enjoy, the specific characteristics of the legal and social systems in which they operate and their education.[3]

When hearing habeas corpus applications, US federal district judges must determine the facts in accordance with the law. This reflects the primary role of district courts as trial courts. In contrast, the role of the Administrative Court in judicial review is normally limited to a determination of whether the state has acted reasonably. Similarly, the task of the CJEU in the preliminary

[1] T Bingham, *The Rule of Law* (Penguin Books, 2010).

[2] See, eg C Guarnieri and P Pederzoli, *The Power of Judges* (Oxford University Press, 2002); CK Rowland and RA Carp, *Politics & Judgment in Federal District Courts* (University Press of Kansas 1996); Bingham (ibid).

[3] Guarnieri and Pederzoli (ibid) 11; B Markesinis, 'Judicial Style and Judicial Reasoning in England and Germany' (2000) 59 *Cambridge Law Journal* 294. See also S Keslowitz, '*The Simpsons*, *24*, and the Law: How Homer Simpson and Jack Bauer Influence Congressional Lawmaking and Judicial Reasoning' (2008) 29 *Cardozo Law Review* 2787, arguing that pop culture influences the development of statutory and common law.

reference procedure is not to determine facts, but rather to interpret the law. However, these courts' official functions may not necessarily correspond to the behaviour of the courts in individual cases of detention review. Instead, the way in which judges view their own roles may differ in a way that reflects the level of importance they attach to these sorts of hearings and, ultimately, the right to liberty. This impacts the way they reason their judgments and arrive at conclusions. This section considers the role played by the judges as demonstrated by the pool judgments, and reflects upon the extent to which such roles explain case outcomes.

The cases highlight three interesting differences between the three jurisdictions. Administrative Court judges in the UK have given themselves a review role that exceeds the reasonableness standard that applies to regular cases where the Court is reviewing government action. They do so on the basis that the right to liberty is of a fundamentally important nature that should be given sufficient protection. This means that the Administrative Court engages in a full review, including establishing facts. The US judges, though they appear technically to be performing the same role, in fact only make findings in relation to whether removal is likely. Unlike the Administrative Court judges, US federal district judges do not reflect upon their role in any of the judgments. This might indicate a feeling that it is inappropriate to take an active stance in safeguarding the liberty of non-citizens, but the cases do not firmly point one way or the other in this regard. Finally, even though the CJEU must ensure that the Member States are taking the Charter of Fundamental Rights into account when they implement EU law, as a court which provides preliminary rulings to Member States, its primary task is arguably to interpret EU law and ensure that the law is being applied properly and consistently. This objective may explain the reliance by the Court on the principle of effectiveness as it has evolved in the criminal, and now immigration, law context.

A. United Kingdom

About one-third of Administrative Court judges in the pool were quite explicit about the role they should play in determining the legality of detention, underscoring their role as the primary decision maker. This exceeds the role they play in the context of typical judicial review proceedings;[4] that is, the role of the Court is not merely to determine 'whether the Home Secretary's judgment was unreasonable; rather it is for the court to decide whether the period of detention is lawful'.[5] The Court is the 'primary decision maker'[6] because

[4] H Woolf et al, *De Smith's Judicial Review*, 7th edn (Sweet & Maxwell, 2013) 4-048.
[5] *R (Daq) v SSHD* [2009] EWHC 1655 (Admin) 8.
[6] *R (A (Iraq)) v SSHD* [2010] EWHC 625 (Admin) 8.

'the liberty of the individual is being curtailed'.[7] Though the Court typically acknowledges that the Secretary of State may be better placed to determine incidental questions of fact, ultimately, it is for the Court to determine the reasonableness of detention.[8] Authority for this contention can be found in the opinion of Toulson LJ in a leading Court of Appeal case on immigration detention, *R (A)*,[9] and in *R (I)*, where Keene LJ stated that:

> It is to my mind a remarkable proposition that the courts should have only a limited role where the liberty of the individual is being curtailed by administrative detention. Classically the courts of this country have intervened by means of habeas corpus and other remedies to ensure that the detention of a person is lawful, and where such detention is only lawful when it endures for a reasonable period, it must be for the court itself to determine whether such a reasonable period has been exceeded.[10]

Speaking with a former High Court judge about the character of judicial review in the context of immigration detention,[11] he made the point that judicial review is flexible enough to incorporate a fact-finding role for the Court. He also noted that because Article 5 ECHR is engaged, it is for the Court, and not the Executive, to determine whether there has been a human rights violation. This is a significant principle.

Even in judgments which do not explicitly acknowledge this role, it is clear that the Administrative Court judges are aware that their task is to make a *de novo* determination of the facts. What makes the UK–USA comparison so interesting is that in the UK, judges not only designate themselves as the primary decision maker, but they often do so because of a recognition of the severity of detention and its impact on liberty.[12] Moreover, part of their self-ascribed role sometimes includes an element of stewardship, where the Administrative Court reserves decision until specific circumstances take place (such as a bail hearing within a certain number of days) or facts are clarified.[13]

B. United States

In the habeas cases examined in this book, US district judges weigh facts and make a determination of whether detention on those facts is lawful according

[7] *R (SM) v SSHD* [2011] EWHC 338 (Admin) 60. See also *MA & TT v SSHD* [2010] EWHC 2350 (Admin) 10.

[8] *R (Badah) v SSHD* [2014] EWHC 364 (Admin) 20; *R (Saleh) v SSHD* [2009] EWHC 2395 (Admin) 4.

[9] *R (A) v SSHD* [2007] EWCA Civ 804, 62.

[10] *R (I) v SSHD* [2002] EWCA Civ 888, 71, cited by the Administrative Court in *R (Lumba) v SSHD* [2008] EWHC 2090 (Admin) 59.

[11] Anonymous Interview, August 2017.

[12] *SM* (n 7) 60. See also *MA & TT* (n 7) 10.

[13] See, eg *R (Lubana) v SSHD* [2003] EWHC 410 (Admin); *R (Kumar) v SSHD* [2003] EWHC 846 (Admin); *R (M) v SSHD* [2009] EWHC 629 (Admin).

to the law. Indeed, one of the most important aspects of the federal judicial role is that of fact-finder. This is underscored by the mandate in 28 USC 2243 that judges 'summarily hear and determine the facts'.[14] District judges have become experts at striking a balance between accuracy of facts and efficiency,[15] especially considering their increasing case load. Partially because of this, Walker argues that federal district judges are the most efficient fact-finders.[16] Although what they are technically doing in habeas corpus is reviewing the state's decision to detain, they are forced under the applicable test to weigh facts to determine probability. Bingham claims that the resolution of factual issues is more difficult than making determinations on points of law because, ultimately, no precedent is wholly on point, which means that judges have to rely on their own judgment.[17] The difficulty increases where one considers that a misreading of the facts will necessarily result in a flawed decision.[18] A judge must therefore give a 'considered judgment as to the truth' in a given situation by weighing probabilities.[19] This is inherently a subjective exercise, which can, in certain circumstances, result in the judge consulting his or her own preferences.[20] This is cause for concern especially because in the context of immigration, which is always rife with politics, judicial preferences may be quite strong.

Though it is evident that they are intended to and behave as fact-finders, the district judges in my pool do not discuss their role in relation to assessing detention in the way the Administrative Court judges do. One can only speculate as to what this means, if anything. For example, it could mean that the role of judges in these cases is so fundamentally understood as to not bear repeating. Or, it could represent an unwillingness to explicitly designate themselves (for political reasons) as the arbiter of facts in the context of immigration matters. Perhaps this contention is a stretch. In assessing the Fifth, Ninth and Tenth Circuits post-*Zadvydas*, Silva proposes that courts should have *de novo* review of detention.[21] This implies that, unlike the Administrative Court, the federal district courts do not have *de novo* review of detention decisions. The federal case law reflects this by demonstrating that, though the courts may have *de novo* review over determining whether removal in the foreseeable future is likely, when it comes to assessing risk, the courts really only consider

[14] ch 4, s III.B above.

[15] JB Weinstein, 'The Roles of a Federal District Court Judge' (2011) 76 *Brook Law Review* 439, 441.

[16] VR Walker, 'The Most Efficient Finder of Fact: The Federal District Judge' (2015) 69 *University of Miami Law Review* 385.

[17] Bingham (n 1) 3.

[18] G Care, *Migrants and the Courts: A Century of Trial and Error?* (Ashgate, 2013) 109.

[19] Bingham (n 1) 4.

[20] O Raban, *Modern Legal Theory & Judicial Impartiality* (The Glass House Press, 2003) 111.

[21] T Silva, 'Toward a Constitutionalized Theory of Immigration Detention' (2013) 32 *Yale Law and Policy Review* 227.

whether the state made a reasonable assessment. Silva notes that, in fact, there is a split between the federal circuits as to which standard should apply to judicial review of detention generally, but that none apply *de novo* review to risk.[22] I would argue, based on the pool of cases in this book, that the NY district courts take a dual approach to review: they apply *de novo* review to the issue of whether removal in the foreseeable future is likely, but they apply a reasonableness standard to state determinations of risk.

C. European Union

The EU context is different and not so readily compared to those of the UK and USA. As discussed earlier, cases about the Return Directive come before the CJEU as requests for preliminary references. This means that the CJEU will provide an analysis of whether the national law or action at issue is compatible with the Return Directive, which entails interpreting specific provisions in the Directive. The CJEU does not establish facts like the Administrative Court or the US district courts. However, the nature of the CJEU's interpretive role is sometimes discussed prior to the legal analysis. For example, in *Kadzoev*, the Advocate General stated that 'The Court … has no jurisdiction to assess the facts of the case or to rule on the lawfulness of Mr Kadzoev's detention' and that the 'Court must rather confine itself to giving a ruling on the questions of interpretation of Community law referred to it which will be of use in the main proceedings'.[23] It is therefore the task of the national court

> to define the legal and factual context of a question referred for a preliminary ruling and to determine, in the light of the facts and the relevant provisions of national law, the subject-matter of the questions referred for a preliminary ruling and, ultimately, to apply the rules of Community law, as interpreted by the Court, to the particular case.[24]

Likewise, the Court in *G and R* stated that it

> need not adjudicate on the circumstances in which, under European law, there is an infringement of the obligation to ensure the right to be heard, but need only indicate to the referring court the consequences, under European Union law, of such an infringement.[25]

The Member States do not always get the questions right. In *Zaizoune*, the Court began its ruling by observing that the role of the CJEU is to give the referring court a useful answer.

[22] ibid 262.
[23] Case C-357/09 PPU *Kadzoev* [2009] ECR I-11189, view of Advocate General Mazák, para 25.
[24] ibid para 24.
[25] Case C-383/13 PPU *G and R* [ECR TBC] para 28. See also Case C-146/14 PPU *Mahdi* [ECR TBC], view of Advocate General Szpunar, paras 40–41.

> To that end, the Court may have to reformulate the questions referred to it [because] the Court has a duty to interpret all provisions of EU law which national courts need in order to decide the actions pending before them, even if those provisions are not expressly indicated in the questions referred to the Court of Justice by those courts.[26]

The Spanish tribunal had asked whether, in consideration of the principles of sincere co-operation and effectiveness of directives, Articles 4(2), 4(3) and 6(1) of the Directive prevent national law from substituting a financial penalty for return. The CJEU felt that the question referred should also take into account the impact of Article 8(1), which requires Member States to issue a return decision to any illegally staying third-country national, and adjusted the question accordingly.[27]

III. THE ROLE OF DEFERENCE

The role of judges, especially in the context of immigration law, cannot be considered without mentioning the role of deference. As explained in chapter five, the UK and USA in particular have both had a chequered history when it comes to the extent to which courts can intervene in immigration issues. While it seems that the impact of the prerogative has waned in the UK, it is unclear whether the same can be said of plenary power in the USA. In the EU context, the issue is one of deference to the Member States rather than any EU-level Executive, and for that reason, the CJEU does not make an easy comparison. Thus, this discussion will focus on the UK and the USA.

It is clear that, though they may have begun otherwise, immigration issues are justiciable in the UK and US courts. Therefore, the issue facing judges is not whether they can judicially review detention, but rather, to what extent (if at all) they should defer to the Executive. Deference can be given for a number of reasons. For example, it is clear that the judiciary will typically defer to the state when it comes to foreign affairs. This includes issues such as the interpretation of treaties or customary international law,[28] or diplomatic relations.[29] The latter becomes relevant when examining arguments for and against removal within the foreseeable future. Deference may also be given out of a desire on the part of the judiciary to maintain the respect of the other branches of government, because the topic before the court is politically

[26] Case C-38/14 *Zaizoune* [ECR TBC], para 25.

[27] ibid para 28.

[28] J Ku and J Yoo, '*Hamdan v Rumsfeld*: The Functional Case for Foreign Affairs Deference to the Executive Branch' (2006) 23 *Constitutional Commentary* 179.

[29] AB Cox, 'Deference, Delegation, and Immigration Law' (2007) 74 *University of Chicago Law Review* 1671.

salient or because of political pressure on the bench.[30] For example, Kavanagh suggests that when the Human Rights Act 1998 first entered into force in the UK, judges took a more cautious (and therefore more deferential) approach to interpreting the Act to allay concerns about negative public reactions to their judgments.[31] Immigration has been, and remains, politically contentious. It evokes strong feelings not only in policy and lawmakers, but in average individuals, and thus can be linked to the discussion above regarding personal preferences. It is difficult to conclude that judges would be excepted, especially where there is evidence that public interest informs the judiciary in the context of immigration and personal liberty.[32] Though courts may be reluctant to act in a rights-protecting manner when it comes to the rights of non-citizens, especially in the context of illegal migration, they 'must be prepared to protect the rights of individuals against public opinion'.[33]

Perhaps most relevant to this book is the idea that it is rational for judges to give proper weight to the judgments of those with expertise in a given area.[34] Government departments and agencies are created to deal with specific subject matter and, as a result, develop specialised expertise.[35] In that vein, Aman and Mayton suggest that the agencies' repeated exposure to the same issues enables them to perfect and improve upon their approach to certain issues.[36] As will be discussed below, deference to agencies and government departments can come in the form of deference to their interpretations of the law or their determinations of fact.

The fact that a certain decision maker or subject area requires deference does not mean that the courts are faced with an all-or-nothing proposition.

[30] A Kavanagh, *Constitutional Review under the UK Human Rights Act* (Oxford University Press, 2009) 169, 199, 345; G Beck, *The Legal Reasoning of the Court of Justice of the EU* (Hart Publishing, 2012) 390–91. Some also argue that judicial reasoning may be affected by a judge's ties to the region in which he or she operates and its predominate political orientation, the particular judicial ideology of the Federal Circuit in which they operate, and even the extent to which their immediate geographical location has been urbanised (suggesting that the more urban an area is, the more likely it is that judges will issue liberal decisions and be subject to influence by civil society organisations that tend to operate more in urbanised areas). See Rowland and Carp (n 2) 59, 68–72. Fischman and Law warn that there is no consensus regarding the meaning and use of the term 'judicial ideology' in the context of judicial motivation, and therefore that any claims that judicial ideology is a main driver of judicial decision-making might be based on a misunderstanding of the term, or improper methodologies due to the inability of someone's 'ideology' to be directly observed. See JB Fischman and DS Law, 'What is Judicial Ideology, and How Should We Measure It?' (2009) 29 *Washington University Journal of Law and Policy* 133, 137–42.

[31] Kavanagh (ibid) 197.

[32] JAG Griffith, *The Politics of the Judiciary*, 5th edn (Fontana Press, 1997) 334. Griffith speaks only about the senior judiciary in this regard.

[33] S Mosk, 'The Common Law and the Judicial Decision-Making Process' (1988) 11 *Harvard Journal of Law and Public Policy* 35, 41.

[34] Kavanagh (n 30) 179.

[35] AC Aman Jr and WT Mayton, *Adminitrative Law*, 3rd edn (West Academic Publishing, 2014) 353; Woolf et al (n 4) 1-032.

[36] Aman and Mayton (ibid) 353.

Rather, they can engage in what Elliot refers to as 'targeted deference' – the notion that deference can be applied, as appropriate, to specific issues during the judicial review process, rather than applying it wholesale to the case.[37] This is exemplified in the *Belmarsh* case, where the Administrative Court deferred to the state on the question of whether there was a public emergency, but not on the issue of whether detention without trial was necessary.[38]

Of the three jurisdictions examined, the NY federal district courts seem the most willing to defer to the state on issues of risk determination and likelihood of removal, though the text of the judgments does not explicitly include an engagement with the extent to which deference is appropriate. The conclusion is inferred from the short attention given by the courts to assessing these issues. The Administrative Court, by contrast, does occasionally acknowledge that the state is best equipped to assess certain issues, including the time necessary to obtain travel documents or to conclude return negotiations. However, there is no evidence in the pool of cases that the Administrative Court has improperly applied deference. Finally, though it has been suggested that politics plays a role in the CJEU's decision-making process, nothing in the judgments indicates that the CJEU has improperly deferred to Member States' interests.

The following subsections give an overview of how deference has traditionally been manifested in each jurisdiction and then evaluate the extent to which the three courts can be viewed as deferring to the state.

A. United Kingdom

In the UK, it is rare that something will be completely immune from judicial review. Rather, the question is the extent to which the court should limit its scrutiny and defer to the state. Elliot highlights two options. The first is to undertake a rational basis review, which is limited to asking only whether the decision maker acted unreasonably. This is an inherently deferential approach to judicial review, and is often based on an assessment that the subject at issue is largely non-justiciable, such as where the court would be required to

[37] M Elliott and JNE Varuhas, *Administrative Law Text and Materials*, 5th edn (Oxford University Press, 2017) 285–86. See also Kavanagh (n 30) 169; R Dennis, 'National Security and Fundamental Rights: the Redundancy or Illegitimacy of Judicial Deference' (2009) 2 *University College London Human Rights Review* 70; TRS Allan, 'Human Rights and Judicial Review: A Critique of "Due Deference"' (2006) 65 *Cambridge Law Journal* 671, 694 (arguing that deference should not be elevated to the status of 'an independent doctrinal requirement'). Similarly, Benesch suggests that, although judges must sometimes defer to the Executive's discretion, the judiciary can still question the way in which such discretion is exercised. This is less of an issue for judges in the UK and USA, who are performing the role of primary decision maker in most aspects of the judgments. The exception would be those district court judgments (discussed in ch 5, s V.B) concluding that the Executive acted reasonably in concluding that a risk was present. See S Benesch, 'Due Process and Decision-Making in U.S. Immigration Adjudication' (2007) 59 *Administrative Law Review* 557.

[38] *A v SSHD* [2004] UKHL 56. See also Elliott and Varuhas (ibid) 287.

make judgments of a political nature. This approach is characterised by the opinion of Lord Sumption in *R (Carlile) v Secretary of State for the Home Department*.[39] Lord Sumption felt that rational basis review was appropriate in cases involving 'predictive and other judgmental assessments, especially those of a political nature'.[40] Alternatively, the court might engage in a proportionality review which considers the nature of the relevant restriction and whether it can be justified by the proposed objective and methodology. This is especially important when a fundamental right has been restricted as a result of state action. Because proportionality review involves several steps, the court can choose whether or not to exercise deference at specific stages in its analysis. Elliot argues that this approach is preferable because it gives the court the flexibility it needs to assess whether a particular restriction was justified by the circumstances, in light of any relevant expertise to which the court should defer.[41]

Though these approaches to judicial review might inform the Administrative Court's process while reviewing immigration detention, it is important to re-emphasise here that judicial review in the immigration detention context is atypical. Rather than considering whether the state has acted reasonably or in excess of its powers, as it might normally do, the Administrative Court takes on the role of primary decision maker. This means that the Court itself is interrogating and weighing the evidence supplied by the state and by the detained individual. It is during this balancing process that the Court sometimes defers to the state, particularly with regard to its expertise in foreign affairs.

The previous section of this chapter underscored the role that the Administrative Court gives to itself in the context of judicial review of detention: it is the primary decision maker. This implies that the Court engages in *de novo* review of the facts and the application of the law to those facts. However, the cases show that the Court understands that it is appropriate to acknowledge, and sometimes defer to, the expertise of the UK's immigration authorities. This is illustrated by deference to the Secretary of State on determinations regarding the average time to obtain travel documents or matters dependent upon the UK's relations with foreign nations. The Administrative Court also seems to allow the Secretary of State some latitude to pursue enhanced strategies to effect deportation in light of external events that the Court believes might move matters on.[42] This deference is given because the Court realises that the Secretary of State has certain knowledge and experience that the Court does not have. It is simply the case, for example, that the Secretary of State is able to say with educated certainty that it will take a certain number of months to

[39] *R (Carlile) v Secretary of State for the Home Department* [2014] UKSC 60.
[40] ibid 32.
[41] Elliott and Varuhas (n 37) 287.
[42] *R (Giwa) v SSHD* [2013] EWHC 3189 (Admin) 82; *R (Abunasir) v SSHD* [2015] EWHC 2145 (Admin) 122, 136.

successfully conclude return negotiations with other countries. Indeed, this is borne out in the judgments. One judgment in particular states that 'matters such as the assessment of the progress of negotiations with foreign governments or commercial carriers as to the facts stated, and opinions and predictions of senior officials', are generally accepted as true absent 'clear evidence to the contrary'.[43]

Apart from these examples, deference plays no part in the UK pool of cases. In fact, many cases reinforce the fact that the primary purpose of the Administrative Court is to hold the state to account. This is especially demonstrated in relation to the Court's assessment of whether the Secretary of State has acted with due diligence in pursuit of removal. For example, the Court has criticised the Secretary of State when she has supported detention based on a 'mere hope' that negotiations with the target country will yield a positive result.[44] In other cases, the Court has commented that the claimant has remained detained while the Secretary of State engaged in 'fruitless negotiations'.[45]

In discussing the role of the Administrative Court with a retired Administrative Court judge, I asked whether judges felt any pressure to defer to the state in immigration matters. Without hesitation, the judge indicated to me that the word 'deference' is considered a 'bad word' among the judiciary, and that it is out of fashion.[46] In a similar vein, during arguments I observed at the Administrative Court, upon hearing the facts as presented by the claimant, the judge urged claimant's counsel to abandon a weaker argument that he felt would not achieve success, so as not to dilute the strength of the more palpable argument.[47] This judge, at least, certainly did not consider that his relationship to the state was subordinate in any way. This is supportive of the findings from the UK cases.

B. United States

The exercise of deference to the Executive by US judges was once characterised by an ad hoc approach.[48] However, since the 1940s, various doctrines of deference applicable to agency decision-making have been developed. In 1944, the

[43] *R (A) v SSHD* [2006] EWHC 3331 (Admin) 35.

[44] *R (Babbage) v SSHD* [2016] EWHC 148 (Admin) 94; *M* (n 13) 21–23; *R (Adewale) v SSHD* [2009] EWHC 1289 (Admin) 27.

[45] *M* (n 13) 7; *I* (n 10) 20.

[46] There is support for and against this point in the literature. Support can be found in Kavanagh (n 30) 178. However, Mark Elliot writes that, although the term 'deference' is 'deprecated by some judges, it is commonplace': Elliott and Varuhas (n 37) 284.

[47] *G v SSHD* [2016] EWHC 3232 (Admin). Hearing dates 15–16 November 2016. The substantial argument was that the conditions of house arrest violated the ECHR, whereas the weaker argument was focused on claiming that the individual was being falsely imprisoned, which the Court ultimately rejected (see para 12).

[48] Cox (n 29).

USSC held in *Skidmore v Swift & Co* that agency interpretative rules should receive deference as long as they are persuasive in terms of their rationalisation.[49] Though they are not binding on the court, because of the expertise developed by agencies over time, agency interpretative rules are entitled to a certain level of respect.[50] One year later, in *Bowles v Seminole Rock & Sand Co*, the USSC held that courts should defer to agency interpretations of their own regulations unless the interpretation is 'plainly erroneous or inconsistent with the regulation'.[51] Fast-forward to 1984, when in *Chevron*[52] the USSC attempted to halt the otherwise ad hoc approach to deference by holding that to agency interpretations of statutes should be given deference if the statutory language is unambiguous as to its meaning.[53] This can be quite challenging.[54] Finally, and perhaps most relevant to this discussion, a number of other doctrines require courts to defer to agency findings of fact as long as they are supported by substantial evidence.[55]

Like the Administrative Court, habeas corpus review of detention involves atypical review procedures in that the court does not limit itself to review of the law, as in judicial review proceedings, but also determines the facts. The habeas corpus statute itself mandates this.[56] This means that the federal district courts are not confined to determining whether the immigration authorities acted unreasonably; rather, their review is *de novo*. However, the fact of *de novo* review does not preclude the application of deference. It is therefore important to consider why the cases under review seem to indicate little judicial evaluation of the facts.

Compared to the cases heard by the Administrative Court, the NY federal district courts seem more willing to accept the view of the state in arguing that continued detention is appropriate. For example, Das suggests that federal courts have assumed that *Chevron* deference should be applied to detention cases, especially cases of mandatory detention, despite a modern trend moving away from deferring to the Executive in the superior courts.[57] It may therefore be the case that federal district courts are deferring to the Executive's decision-making regarding detention and related aspects of removal because they are accustomed to being directed to give effect to the intent of the Executive.

[49] *Skidmore v Swift & Co* (1944) 323 US 134.

[50] ibid 139.

[51] *Bowles v Seminole Rock & Sand Co* (1945) 325 US 410, 414. This type of deference is now known as *Auer* deference, as it was reaffirmed in 1997. See *Auer v Robbins* (1997) 519 US 452.

[52] *Chevron v Natural Resources Defense Council* (1984) 467 US 837.

[53] Cox (n 29).

[54] See ch 6, s III.B above, and related references.

[55] See, eg *Allentown Mack Sales & Service, Inc v National Labor Relations Board* (1998) 522 US 359.

[56] 28 USC 2243. Discussed in ch 4, s III.B above.

[57] A Das, 'Unshackling Habeas Review: Chevron Deference and Statutory Interpretation in Immigration Detention' (2015) 90 *New York University Law Review* 143, 158–59.

The situation is different when it comes to reviewing agency findings of fact, especially when it comes to determining if removal is likely in the foreseeable future. As chapter five illustrated, in many cases, especially the cookie-cutter judgments, a statement by the government that successful repatriations to a given country have occurred in the past, and will likely continue to do so in the future, seems to convince the court that the state is correct without any independent consideration of whether that is indeed the case. Perhaps the courts unconsciously feel caught out by the discrepancy between the mandate in the habeas statute to determine questions of fact anew and the administrative rule that deference should be given to agency findings of fact that are supported by substantial evidence. Indeed, on the latter point, the Administrative Procedure Act, which applies to judicial review of agency actions outside of the habeas context, reserves *de novo* review for extraordinary cases.[58] The courts may therefore feel uneasy about second-guessing agency determinations of fact. However, one might argue, as Bernick has, that fact deference is unconstitutional where core private rights, such as the right to liberty, are at stake.[59] This is perhaps one of the reasons why the habeas corpus statute requires *de novo* review.

Alternatively, Chen suggests that decisions by immigration officials are entitled to deference more than other agency decisions because immigration officials 'exercise especially sensitive political functions'.[60] In support of this, Chen points to jurisprudence confirming that immigration powers should be subject to a narrow judicial review because of their political character.[61] This viewpoint hearkens back to the role that plenary power played in early judicial discourse on the limited role of the courts in reviewing the exercise of immigration powers. Perhaps more realistic might be the notion that the federal district courts are engaging in deference based on the expertise of the immigration authorities, in particular, when it comes to estimating the progress of return proceedings. As return depends largely on the conduct of diplomatic and foreign affairs, the courts may presume agency estimations to be reasonable.

The concern is that, unlike the Administrative Court, which sometimes explicitly acknowledges that the state's expertise deserves some deference, the NY federal district courts are not transparent about how they arrive at their conclusions. Consequently, what we are faced with is a review that is not quite *de novo* because of the courts' general willingness to take ICE/INS at its word, but also not obviously deferential because they do not refer to particular expertise or consider whether the agency findings are supported by substantial evidence. At the very least, the cases suggest that courts are not engaging in

[58] Pub L 79–404, 60 Stat 237, enacted 11 June 1946, codified at 5 USC 706(2)(E)–(F).

[59] ED Bernick, 'Is Judicial Deference to Agency Fact-Finding Unlawful' (2018) 16 *Georgetown Journal of Law and Public Policy* 27, 38.

[60] EF Chen, 'Judicial Deference after United States v Mead: How Streamlining Measures at the Board of Immigration Appeals May Transform Traditional Notions of Deference in Immigration Law' (2006) 20 *Georgetown Immigration Law Journal* 657, 658, citing the USSC in *INS v Abudu* (1988) 485 US 94, 110.

[61] ibid, citing *Abudu* (ibid) 110; *Hampton v Mow Sun Wong* (1976) 426 US 88, 101–02.

de novo review as mandated by the habeas statute. This is a considerable problem given the gravity of the right at stake.

An additional factor may contribute to judicial behaviour in the USA that is not at play in the UK. Though it has been suggested that judges are best able to arrive at judgments without political pressure,[62] the political nature of US federal courts is undeniable. The fact that federal district court judges are appointed by the ruling political party potentially renders them susceptible to political pressure in a way that does not occur in the context of Administrative Court judges.[63] This pressure may manifest itself in undue deference to the state; however, it is not possible to state with certainty whether this is occurring in the USA detention cases considered here. In the mid-1990s, Posner suggested that there was a move from liberal to conservative judgments, not because of any pressure from the other branches of government, but because of an increase in the number of conservative judges appointed to the bench, and because of the pressures of an increased caseload.[64] This resulted in less activism among the federal courts. Looking at the 27 judges in the cases in the pool,[65] just over one-third (ten) were nominated by Republican presidents, with the remaining 17 coming from Democratic appointments.[66] However, the conservative/liberal split within the WDNY is 5:2; in the SDNY, it is 3:16; and in the EDNY, 2:2. Given the very low success rate of habeas cases across districts, it is unclear whether these statistics carry any meaning. However, the SDNY, the district with the highest proportion of liberal judges in the pool, saw the highest rate of relief granted, at nearly 40 per cent of the cases.

C. European Union

Because the EU is a supranational court, concerns about the improper exercise of deference are typically expressed in relation to the CJEU's treatment of Member State arguments and evidence, rather than specific EU agencies. Beck suggests that the CJEU will engage in expansive interpretation of a subject where it is viewed favourably politically,[67] which implies that the converse is true.

[62] J Waldron, 'Judges as Moral Reasoners' (2009) 7 *International Journal of Constitutional Law* 2, 3.

[63] P Cane, *Controlling Administrative Power: An Historical Comparison* (Cambridge University Press, 2016) 101. See also Kavanagh (n 30) 345, noting that because judges in the UK are not elected, they do not depend on popular support to get on the bench.

[64] RA Posner, *The Federal Courts* (Harvard University Press, 1996) 319.

[65] Excluding magistrate judges.

[66] Tolley suggests that the Republican Senate during the Clinton administration purposely frustrated appointments of democratic nominees in response to the previous rejection by Democrats of the nomination of Judge Robert Bork in 1987 by George HW Bush. See MC Tolley, 'Legal Controversies over Federal Judicial Selection in the United States' in K Malleson and PH Russell, *Appointing Judges in an Age of Judicial Power* (University of Toronto Press, 2006) 86–87. A similar phenomenon occurred in 2003 with the withdrawal of George W Bush's nomination of Miguel Estrada to the DC Circuit. See DS Law, 'Appointing Federal Judges: The President, the Senate, and the Prisoner's Dilemma' (2005) 26 *Cardozo Law Review* 479.

[67] Beck (n 30) 350, 390–91.

He specifically cites immigration law as one such area where the Court typically exercises restraint, and claims that the Court's ability to defer in these areas is typically bolstered by, for example, vague legislative provisions or the lack of any clear standards on point.[68] In any case, the standards on the Return Directive are quite clear – especially the maximum period of detention and the requirement to use detention only where necessary. There is little evidence in any of the judgments that the Court is deferring to the Member States, though reliance on the principle of effectiveness, rather than fundamental rights, to justify their conclusions may signify a desire to maintain a reputation of impartiality.[69] Bengoetxea suggests that preliminary references require the Court to engage in legal analysis by reference to norms beyond the text in order to arrive at a solution.[70] Beck points out that this may include general principles.[71] Effectiveness is an accepted general principle of EU law, which has been traditionally applied so as to give effect to safeguarding the rights of EU nationals.[72] Only recently has the CJEU begun to talk about effectiveness in the sense of the proper functioning of the law.[73] Therefore, while it is logical for the Court to continue to turn to general principles to assist in its legal reasoning, the evolution of this concept in recent cases is not so easily explained.

It has also been suggested that politics may play a role in the CJEU's decision-making process.[74] In particular, it is claimed that the CJEU has the ability to issue judgments contrary to Member States' interests, and to further an agenda of European integration.[75] This is particularly so in the context of preliminary references. However, such power is limited by two things: first, the possibility of overturning the Court's rulings with new EU legislation or Treaty revisions; and secondly, Member States' non-compliance with judgments against their interests.[76] Research suggests that the Court is mindful of these risks and that they have a large effect on case outcomes.[77]

Apart from wanting to avoid politically contentious issues, equally plausible is an awareness on the part of CJEU judges of their broader role as guardians of

[68] ibid 352.

[69] Kavanagh (n 30) 197.

[70] J Bengoetxea, *The Legal Reasoning of the European Court of Justice: Towards a European Jurisprudence* (Clarendon Press, 1993) 182.

[71] Beck (n 30) 168–71.

[72] See ch 2, s IV above.

[73] V Mitsilegas, 'The Changing Landscape of the Criminalisation of Migration in Europe' in M João et al (eds), *Social Control and Justice: Crimmigration in the Age of Fear* (Eleven International Publishing, 2013) 99–105.

[74] CJ Carrubba, M Gabel and C Hankla, 'Judicial Behaviour under Political Constraints: Evidence from the European Court of Justice' (2008) 102 *American Political Science Review* 435.

[75] ibid 437.

[76] ibid.

[77] ibid 449. See also G Garrett, RD Kelemen and H Schulz, 'The European Court of Justice, National Governments, and Legal Integration in the European Union' (1998) 52 *International Organization* 149, arguing that the Court anticipates Member State reactions and takes them into account in its decision-making.

the law and their responsibility to ensure that EU law functions properly. Perhaps it is only a coincidence that the application of effectiveness by the Court in most of the cases to date indirectly safeguards fundamental rights. It is impossible to anticipate whether the Court would employ effectiveness to such a degree in cases where the outcome would counsel strongly against safeguarding fundamental rights, though effectiveness has not always functioned in this manner. I refer specifically here to the outcomes in *G and R* and *Arslan*.

IV. CONCLUSION

This chapter on institutional impacts on detention case law follows the discussion in chapter six on how judges make use of the law and legal principles at their disposal to arrive at decisions on the legality of detention so that the reader can see that judicial review outcomes are informed not just by the way the judges apply the law, but also by the institutional architecture at play in each jurisdiction. Though these two chapters have covered a significant amount of material, it is important to understand that myriad additional factors may impact judicial review of detention that were not obvious from the text of the judgments, and that it is likely that different factors might present themselves in detention cases from other federal districts.

This chapter reveals a trend in the case law that has been emerging since chapter five, and that is that, though these three jurisdictions employ essentially similar standards to test the legality of detention, they each take a different approach that is rooted in their history, constitutional structure, legal framework and legal architecture. This chapter demonstrates that the judges in each jurisdiction view their tasks differently. The Administrative Court judges consider themselves as the guardians of liberty. They therefore perform the role of primary decision maker, engaging with the facts anew and only deferring where reasonable in light of state expertise. The NY federal district courts, by contrast, do not engage in any existential reflection on their role and do not seem to understand the importance of the part they play in safeguarding liberty. As a result, they are more willing to take factual determinations by the immigration authorities at face value without any exploration of whether it is warranted. Finally, the CJEU, though rooted in a strong tradition of fundamental rights protection, demonstrates that its primary mission is to ensure that the law is interpreted and applied correctly so that it can properly function. As such, deference does not play any role in its Return Directive decisions.

The final chapter in this book draws together the review, in chapters two to four, of the law and policy on liberty and immigration detention with the practical realities of judicial review of immigration detention, examined in chapters five to seven, to suggest that case outcomes are impacted by a series of key factors. After reviewing those factors, a number of recommendations for improvement are offered.

8

Conclusion

I. INTRODUCTION

The aim of this book has been to explore the utility of judicial review as a means of safeguarding the liberty of immigration detainees. It has done so by reference to the law and policy in the UK, USA and EU, and, along the way, has explored the historic and legislative context of immigration detention in each jurisdiction. This discussion has identified many similar characteristics, including a common set of standards for reviewing the legality of detention. However, some important differences are at play that have led to varied outcomes in practice, despite these shared standards. This chapter now seeks to explore the reason for these differences and, ultimately, to provide an answer to the question of whether judicial review offers a meaningful safeguard for the right to liberty.

II. DETENTION: AN ORIGIN STORY

Detention in the UK shares an especially similar history to that in the USA. Initially employed as an exception during times of insecurity, detention in these two jurisdictions has evolved into a tool that is considered essential in enforcing immigration law and policy. Moreover, the rise of 'crimmigration' and the specific legislative link between criminal history and eligibility for automatic deportation has necessarily led to increased use of detention pending deportation, especially in the USA, where the mandatory deportation and detention provisions feature routinely in the 110 federal district court cases considered here. Despite the great reliance upon detention in both jurisdictions, the legislative history of modern immigration law demonstrates virtually no discussion of the appropriateness or necessity of using detention to enforce immigration law. I would suggest that this is because detention had become such an integral part of immigration enforcement that the question of whether it should continue to be used was not within the scope of most debate.

The view that detention is part and parcel of immigration enforcement has also influenced the way that detention provisions in the law have been drafted. US and UK legislation supplies the grounds for detention, but does not detail the parameters for its implementation, especially where it has become prolonged. This gap has been addressed partially in the UK through non-statutory guidance from the state, but no equivalent exists in the USA. Perhaps even more surprising is the complete lack of reference to fundamental rights or due process principles in the statutory provisions addressing detention, which is alarming, considering that the laws permit restrictions on the right to liberty, which is constitutionally guaranteed in both jurisdictions.

The legislative gap has primarily been addressed in the UK and USA through judicially created standards on the lawfulness of detention. Both the UK and USA use a reasonableness standard to determine whether continued detention is lawful, which includes an evaluation of several factual components, including the detainee's behaviour and the likelihood that removal will occur within a reasonable period. In addition to being quite subjective in nature, other factors come into play – especially in the USA – which put the detainee at an immediate disadvantage. These will be addressed in more detail in section II below. Moreover, though the right to liberty arguably underpins the application of these standards, an explicit requirement that detention comply with fundamental rights principles is not present. Thus, it may be difficult for the courts to resolve cases by reference to fundamental rights principles. As will be discussed below, this has led to unsatisfactory results in a context where fundamental rights ought to be the starting point of judicial review.

This brings us to the EU, whose history and context should be contrasted with the UK and USA. Unlike the modern legislative histories in the other two jurisdictions, when the Return Directive was being adopted by the Member States, much debate and discussion was focused on the detention provisions, and especially the appropriate maximum period. As a result, the Directive includes detailed provisions that: expressly limit the use of detention to situations where less coercive measures would not be sufficient; mandate due diligence on the part of the state; provide for, and discuss the nature of, judicial review of detention; and delimit a maximum period of detention. Though the Directive has been the subject of criticism, and the CJEU has had to further define various aspects of the Directive, the Directive is largely self-sufficient and comes equipped with a host of standards to which national judges can refer in support of their decisions. In addition, the Directive was drafted with reference to the right to liberty as contained in the EU Charter of Fundamental Rights and the ECHR. This is expressly acknowledged in paragraph 24 of the Directive's preamble. One criticism arising not out of the case law, but out of the text of the Directive itself, is the option under Article 2(2) for Member States to disapply the Directive in cases where third-country nationals are subject to return because they have committed a qualifying crime under domestic law. If, as in the USA, large numbers of non-citizens are detained and subject to deportation based on criminal wrongdoing, vast numbers of individuals may not benefit from the protections of the Directive or its case law. Indeed, the

EU Commission reported in 2014 that a majority of the Member States elected to apply the derogations provided for in Article 2(2) of the Directive.[1]

III. ACCOUNTING FOR OUTCOMES

One of the most interesting discoveries in this book is that each of the three jurisdictions assesses the legality of detention using similar parameters. Because the UK and US legislative standards are so basic, and certainly do not contemplate situations where detention has become prolonged, the courts have stepped in to fill in the legislative gaps. Despite being developed years apart and on different continents, these standards share characteristics and are built upon the basic tenet that detention must be reasonable in all the circumstances. Thus, in the UK, the *Hardial Singh* principles require removal to take place within a reasonable period,[2] and in the USA, the Supreme Court judgment in *Zadvydas v Davis* permits detention if removal in the reasonably foreseeable future is likely.[3] These essentially mirror the standard set forth in the EU Return Directive, which requires a reasonable prospect of removal.[4]

More narrowly, though the calculation of what is reasonable differs between jurisdictions, some elements are common. In the UK and USA, courts must consider whether the detainee poses a risk of flight or danger to the community, and the length of detention to date. The UK goes beyond this to include consideration of the effect of detention on the detainee and his or her family, and the conditions of detention.[5] The EU Return Directive permits Member States to consider factors such as whether the person poses a risk of absconding, or is avoiding or interfering with the return process.

Moreover, the state must work actively to secure removal. In the UK and EU, this is expressed as 'diligence', whereas in the USA, diligence is implied by evidence in the judgments of the courts considering the quality of state efforts to remove. Detention may be considered unreasonable if the state is making little or no effort to remove the individual in question, for example, by failing to regularly communicate with the relevant foreign embassy or consulate to obtain identity documents.

[1] Communication from the Commission to the Council and the European Parliament on EU Return Policy, COM(2014) 199 final (28 March 2014) 22.

[2] *R (Hardial Singh) v Governor of Durham Prison* [1983] EWHC 1 (QB).

[3] *Zadvydas v Davis* (2001) 533 US 678.

[4] EU Return Directive 2008/115/EC, Art 15(4).

[5] See, eg *R (Asekun) v SSHD* [2009] EWHC 1707 (Admin); *R (Mjemer) v SSHD* [2011] EWHC 1514 (Admin); *R (Rashid) v SSHD* [2011] EWHC 3352 (Admin); *R (JM) v SSHD* [2014] EWHC 151 (Admin), where the individual had been 'detained in a strict prison regime, locked alone in a cell for over 20 hours a day with limited use of a pay phone' but release was not ordered because of a significant risk of reoffending (91).

Assessing reasonableness also includes an evaluation of the length of detention to date. The UK has no maximum period of detention, nor is any indicative period of reasonableness contemplated by the Administrative Court. The USA is essentially the same, except the US Supreme Court set a presumptively reasonable period for post-removal order detention of six months in *Zadvydas*. Finally, the Return Directive explicitly limits detention to six months, extendable by 12 months only where the detainee is not co-operating, or where there are delays in obtaining the requisite documents from the target country – either of which must be causally linked to a delay in effecting return. The Directive also stresses that detention must be as short as possible and necessary in each individual case. Necessity is not required in the UK or USA.

Despite the use of similar principles across each jurisdiction, the detainees in the cases examined had varied levels of success with their applications. Whether a detainee has a successful outcome means two different things in the context of these cases. In the UK and US cases, 'successful' indicates that the court has ordered release, a bond or bail hearing, has issued a declaration of unlawfulness, or has given the state a deadline for removal or deportation. In the CJEU cases, 'successful' denotes a rights-protecting interpretation of the Return Directive that directly or indirectly implies that the domestic courts should make a finding that detention is unlawful.

Of the 63 Administrative Court decisions, 31 (49.2 per cent) judicial review applications were successful. By contrast, only 15 of the 110 NY district court cases (13.6 per cent) resulted in a successful habeas corpus application. However, the percentages in the UK and USA should not be compared without reiterating the fact that the judicial review procedure in the UK includes a preliminary step of applying for permission to have the case heard fully.[6] This means that the cases which receive a full hearing have already been adjudged to have some merit.[7] This is not part of the USA habeas process, which means that the federal district judges do not benefit from an initial filtering of applications.

Because the CJEU judgments are given within the context of the preliminary reference procedure, it is impossible to calculate case outcomes at the national level in the same way as the UK and US judgments. Rather, the approach of the CJEU is evaluated in each case to determine whether, overall, it is rights-protecting or rights-limiting. Nine of the 14 cases from categories A and B (64 per cent) resulted in rights-protective interpretations of the Directive,

[6] See ch 4, s III.A above.

[7] Between 2009 and the end of 2018, 129,895 cases were lodged for permission, 88,447 actually reached permission stage and, of those, only 17,049 (19.3%) were granted permission. Of the total cases lodged for permission, 87,971 were immigration and asylum cases, including immigration detention. However, the UK Government does not keep separate statistics on case progression under that category, so it is not possible to ascertain how many of those types of cases were granted permission. See Ministry of Justice, 'Civil Justice Statistics Quarterly: October to December 2018' www.gov.uk/government/statistics/civil-justice-statistics-october-to-december-2018.

though in most cases this was the result of applying the principle of effectiveness rather than an explicit desire to safeguard fundamental rights.

Given that the standards applied in each jurisdiction share so many qualities, it is necessary to explore what accounts for differences in case outcomes. After reviewing a number of common themes, my research suggests that the root cause of the difference in outcomes is the role that fundamental rights play in each jurisdiction.

In the context of immigration, respect for human rights is key. As Crosby points out, fundamental rights are the only tools that non-citizens can use to protect themselves when they are subject to domestic immigration regimes that treat non-citizens differently than citizens.[8] Fundamental rights should play a prominent role in cases involving deprivations of liberty, and should form part of the fabric of the judicial review analysis. A strong fundamental rights framework can impact several aspects of judicial review, including the judges' own view of the role they play in this context, the way they assess facts and even how detention legislation is drafted. These are each discussed in turn below.

A. The Right to Liberty and the Role of the Judge

Beginning with the Administrative Court, two points are worth highlighting. First, the Administrative Court judicially reviews the lawfulness of continued immigration detention in a manner which differs from its conduct of judicial review in other contexts. 'Classic' judicial review generally sees the Court being tasked with assessing whether public bodies have exercised their (usually discretionary) powers lawfully. Thus, the primary role of the Court is to assess whether the law (including applicable procedures) has been followed in relation to the decision or action at issue, usually according to a standard of reasonableness. The Court is not meant to conduct a merits review of the decision itself. For example, where it is alleged that detention is unlawful due to breach of a public law duty, such as the requirement to follow published policy or to give reasons,[9] the court is limited to reviewing whether the decision maker acted within the limits of his or her discretionary power.[10] By contrast, the cases

[8] A Crosby, 'The Political Potential of the Return Directive' (2014) 3 *Laws* 117.

[9] For failure to conduct period reviews, see *Kambadzi (SK (Zimbabwe) v SSHD* [2011] UKSC 23; for failure to follow published policy, see *Lumba (WL) v SSHD* [2011] UKSC 12; for failure to provide reasons for detention, see *R (Faulkner) v SSHD* [2005] EWHC 2567 (Admin) 17 and *R (Mahajna (Salah)) v SSHD* [2011] EWHC 2481 (Admin). There is one exception to the rule that a public law error which is material to the decision to detain will render detention unlawful: Sch 3, s 2(1) of the 1971 Act requires the Secretary of State to detain certain individuals. In *R (Francis) v SSHD* [2014] EWCA Civ 718, the Court of Appeal found that the provision allows no discretion on the Secretary of State and that therefore it was not possible to find a breach of a public law duty.

[10] *R (LE (Jamaica)) v SSHD* [2012] EWCA Civ 597, 28(iii). However, in other cases, the Court of Appeal has held, contrariwise. See *R (Anam) v SSHD* [2010] EWCA Civ 1140, 77.

have borne out that, where the right to liberty is involved, the Court acts as the primary decision maker and fact-finder to make its own determination of whether detention is lawful. This approach is necessary, according to the Court, because of the severity of detention and its impact on liberty.[11] For example, the Court has stated on occasion that it is the 'primary decision maker'[12] because 'the liberty of the individual is being curtailed'.[13] In other cases, judges have explicitly stated that liberty is the starting point for their review, and that any restrictions on liberty must be closely scrutinised.[14]

Perhaps this is owing to the judgment of the late Lord Bingham in the well-known case of *Tweed*, in which he discussed the relationship between fundamental rights cases and factual determinations: 'human rights decisions ... tend to be very fact-specific and any judgment on the proportionality of a public authority's interference with a protected Convention right is likely to call for a careful and accurate evaluation of the facts'.[15] Indeed, it therefore seems that many Administrative Court judges recognise the importance of their role as fact-finder in safeguarding the right to liberty in the context of judicial review. Indeed, it is important to recall here the statement made by a former High Court judge underlining the fact that when human rights are involved, the court is the appropriate decision maker.[16]

The second point relates to the general role of the Administrative Court. The UK's participation as a signatory to the ECHR and its adoption of the Human Rights Act in 1998 means that the Administrative Court is well versed in assessing state action against the fundamental rights contained in the ECHR. The Administrative Court, whose task it is to review the legality of state action, is thus no stranger to passing judgment on the compatibility of state action with fundamental rights. This perhaps makes judges more willing to engage with fundamental rights in their judicial analysis.

The NY district courts present a different picture. Not only is there very little evidence that the right to liberty is a concern for judges at all,[17] but there is also no indication that the judges in these cases view themselves in the same way as the Administrative Court judges. Indeed, when the INA was being debated in Congress, great concern was expressed that judges engaged in judicial review

[11] *R (SM) v SSHD* [2011] EWHC 338 (Admin) 60. See also *MA & TT v SSHD* [2010] EWHC 2350 (Admin) 10.

[12] *R (A (Iraq)) v SSHD* [2010] EWHC 625 (Admin) 8.

[13] *SM* (n 11) 60. See also *MA & TT* (n 11) 10.

[14] ch 6, s III.A above.

[15] *Tweed v Parades Commission for Northern Ireland* [2006] UKHL 53, 3.

[16] ch 7, s II.A above.

[17] One of the main exceptions to this discussion is the judgment in *D'Alessandro v Mukasey* (WDNY 2009) 628 F Supp 2d 368. In that case, the Western District of NY court discussed in detail the importance of the right to liberty stemming from other judgments concerning confinement and procedural due process (80).

of immigration decisions should be examining the facts at all.[18] Though, in practice, the judges do seem to be performing the same role as the Administrative Court judges in terms of examining facts rather than just reviewing compliance with the law, they are certainly not explicit about doing so.

This could be because habeas review of detention used to be primarily concerned with whether a lawful decision to detain had been made by the Executive, but, since *Zadvydas* and the proliferation of indefinite detention post-removal order, the district courts have had to change their approach and examine the facts to determine whether it is reasonable to continue detention in those circumstances.

A lack of fundamental rights language and ownership of their role as decision makers may also result from the fact that immigration is increasingly perceived as a threat to national security in US policy. Thus, judges may struggle to view their role as something other than protecting the security of the nation. Indeed, Koulish has observed, and it is borne out in the cases considered in this book, that immigration law in the USA focuses on sovereignty rather than constitutional principles.[19] Labelle goes one step further to argue that one of the reasons detention is used so extensively in the USA is because the USA lacks a general theory of respect for human rights, despite its Constitution and Bill of Rights.[20] Thus, whereas Administrative Court judges view themselves as guardians of liberty, the NY federal district court judges seemingly approach their role from a national security/immigration control point of view.

Comparing this to the situation in the UK, where immigration is also increasingly viewed as a security threat in light of the refugee 'crisis' and seemingly uncontrolled migration from other EU Member States, but where the Administrative Court is still able to apply the *Hardial Singh* principles in a more rights-protecting, rights-emphasising manner, one cannot help but conclude that the UK's strong tradition of respect for fundamental rights has made a positive impact in this regard. Indeed, there seems to be a connection between the court's perceived role and the way it views the purpose of judicial review. For example, the Administrative Court views itself largely as a guardian of liberty, and its cases as being about liberty; in contrast, the US federal district courts seemingly view their role as protector of the nation, and their cases as being about immigration control rather than liberty. Whatever the reason, the district court judgments are virtually devoid of any indication that a desire to safeguard liberty motivates this approach.

[18] Joint Hearings before the Subcommittees of the Committees on the Judiciary, 82nd Congress, First Session on S 716, HR 2379 and HR 2816, bills to revise the laws relating to immigration, naturalization and nationality, 6–9, 12–16, 20–21 March and 9 April 1951: 6 March 1951, 24–25.

[19] R Koulish, *Immigration and American Democracy: Subverting the Rule of Law* (Routledge, 2010).

[20] D Labelle, 'Bringing Human Rights Home to the World of Detention' (2008) 40 *Columbia Human Rights Law Review* 79.

More broadly, despite its Constitution and Bill of Rights, the USA does not have a legal tradition rooted in human rights protection in a way similar to Europe. The US immigration detention machinery is primarily concerned with deportation, and the law and policy are directed at ensuring that deportation will be achieved. Thus, the use of immigration detention is practically a given – and automatic in many cases. Moreover, only recently has the US Supreme Court acknowledged the risk of indefinite post-removal order detention and a need to ensure that the due process rights of non-citizens in detention are safeguarded through the application of a reasonableness test. This will undoubtedly impact the extent to which fundamental rights are acknowledged in the judgments, or play a part in shaping the role of the courts in habeas review.

It is perhaps unfair to criticise the USA on this point without reiterating the relationship between the federal courts and the Executive. For many years, the federal courts have been instructed to defer to Congress on immigration matters and, more generally, to agency decision-making.[21] For these reasons, the federal courts may be reluctant to vigorously review the state's decision to detain, especially with regard to agency decisions regarding risk.

The CJEU's Return Directive case law presents a third judicial approach to fundamental rights. The EU's tradition of respect for fundamental rights was effectively launched by the CJEU, which developed a set of general principles that included respect for fundamental rights as defined by the ECHR long before the adoption of the EU Charter on Fundamental Rights. Once the Charter became legally binding in 2009, the CJEU became obligated to interpret it at least in line with the ECHR and the case law of the ECtHR where rights overlapped.

Despite this background, the CJEU's approach to fundamental rights in Return Directive cases has been twofold. In Category B cases, focused purely on the operation of the detention provisions in Article 15, the CJEU has, for the most part, directly confronted the issue of fundamental rights protection. For example, the Court clarified that any time spent in detention under the Directive, including time spent pursuing relief against removal, must be counted towards the 18-month maximum to ensure that the objective of the Directive – to limit deprivations of liberty – is given effect.[22] In another case involving the right to be heard prior to a decision to extend detention beyond the initial six-month period, the CJEU engaged in a lengthy discussion of the constitutional status of that right and its place within broader defence rights, rooted in general principles of EU law and the ECHR.[23]

[21] ch 7, s II.B above.

[22] Case C-357/09 PPU *Kadzoev* [2009] ECR I-11189, para 56.

[23] Case C-383/13 PPU *G and R* [ECR TBC], para 32; Case C-166/13 *Mukarubega* [ECR TBC], paras 42–52.

In Category A cases, on criminalisation (and in some Category B cases), the CJEU turned to the principle of effectiveness as its chief justificatory device. Effectiveness in the context of the Return Directive operates to ensure that national law does not impair the effective functioning of the Directive. In these judgments, the CJEU focuses not on fundamental rights principles, but on whether the national measure at issue, such as imprisonment as a consequence of unlawful presence, interferes with the aims of the Return Directive. Scholars have been critical of the Court's approach, especially in relation to the right to be heard, and the Court's failure in one case to discuss the ECHR and its detention provisions in Article 5(1)(f).[24]

The outcome of judgments based on effectiveness has been indirectly protective of the right to liberty in the sense that additional periods of detention outside of the Return Directive are not permissible. Therefore, though the principle of effectiveness is not outwardly concerned with fundamental rights, thus far, using effectiveness as an interpretive aid has resulted in rights-protecting outcomes. Its use also reveals that, despite its strong human rights tradition and its liberty-focused decision-making in the Article 15 cases, the CJEU seems to view itself primarily as a guardian of the law, rather than as a guardian of liberty or security, as in the UK and USA. Though using effectiveness has had an indirectly rights-protecting outcome in most cases, the CJEU should avoid employing this approach routinely, especially in cases where fundamental rights could expressly be used to respond to the questions referred by national courts. Employing fundamental rights language at the EU level is valuable because it signals to Member States the importance of those rights, especially in the context of immigration detention, and enables them to use fundamental rights language and jurisprudence in their own judgments.

Ultimately, the cases demonstrate that a strong fundamental rights context has the power to shape the manner in which judicial review is conducted and, more specifically, the way that judges view their role in relation to reviewing the legality of immigration detention.

B. Fact Assessment

The fundamental rights framework also seems to impact the way that judges weigh the facts by introducing an element of proportionality into judicial analysis. For example, in the UK, whether or not a detainee has a history of criminal activity or has absconded in the past is to be regarded as one consideration among many, none of which are to function as a trump card signalling

[24] P De Bruycker and S Mananashvili, '*Audi alteram partem* in Immigration Detention Procedures, between the ECJ, the ECtHR and Member States: *G & R*' (2015) 52 *Common Market Law Review* 569.

that continued detention is appropriate.[25] Administrative Court judges generally evaluate evidence of such conduct according to its degree and in light of when it occurred in time. Therefore, violent crimes will be weighted more heavily in favour of detention than crimes involving property, just as criminal activity from years ago will counsel towards release more than recent activity.[26] The NY district courts, by contrast, rely much more on the simple presence or absence of past criminal conduct or instance of absconding, rather than the circumstances or nature of either.[27] The courts seemingly rely on determinations of risk by the immigration authorities rather than engage in their own risk assessment. Turning to the EU, remarkably, the Return Directive does not include criminal history as a factor justifying detention, though it does permit detention based on flight risk where non-custodial alternatives are unsuitable.[28] Though this specific issue has yet to reach the CJEU, the decision in *Zh and O*, which concerned voluntary return under Article 7(4) of the Return Directive, makes clear that the fact that a third-country national is suspected, or has been convicted, of a criminal offence is not enough on its own to justify withholding return.[29] Thus, the CJEU appears to take an approach similar to that of the Administrative Court, where it is just one factor of many to be considered.

Another positive approach at the EU level is the Court's determination that any detainee non-co-operation must bear a causal relationship to delays in effecting removal. The fact of non-co-operation is not enough on its own to justify extending the initial six-month period of detention. Thus, like the Administrative Court, the CJEU recognises that factors such as criminal past or non-co-operation are to be construed proportionately and should not be considered black or white issues.

C. Legislative Drafting

Finally, a state's fundamental rights framework can also impact the way legislation is drafted or affect the development of judicially made standards. As has been discussed above, there is no reference in the statutes regulating detention in the UK or USA law to fundamental rights principles, or even a recognition that at some point detention may no longer be appropriate. There is also no mention of the right to judicial review of detention. The converse is true for the Return Directive, which acknowledges its fundamental rights footing in its preamble and considers in detail the circumstances under which detention may no longer be lawful. It also provides for judicial review in Article 15(2).

[25] ch 5, s V.A above.
[26] ibid.
[27] ch 5, s V.B above.
[28] ch 5, s V.C above.
[29] ibid.

The impact of fundamental rights on legislative drafting can be illustrated by two specific examples. First, with regard to the placement of the burden of proof in the UK and US cases,[30] the operation of the burden of proof is of profound importance to the case outcomes.[31] In the context of criminal law, if the state bears the burden of proving criminal liability, it means that the accused is presumed innocent. This presumption of innocence sets the tone for the ensuing hearing or trial, and requires the state to produce enough probative evidence to persuade the decision maker that the state has made its case for guilt. Thus, from the outset, the criminally accused is at a procedural advantage. This is not the case for immigration detainees.

Placement of the burden of proof in the pool of cases considered in this book is relevant only for the UK and USA. The EU Return Directive does not prescribe the operation of the burden, which is governed by domestic law. In the USA, the burden of proof rests with the detainee to demonstrate that there is no significant likelihood of removal in the reasonably foreseeable future.[32] Thus, immigration detainees in the US federal district courts begin at a procedural disadvantage from which, as the cases demonstrate, it is difficult to recover. It is further compounded by forcing the detainee to demonstrate that he or she is not dangerous, should the initial burden be sustained. By contrast, the Administrative Court has commented that placing the burden of proof on the detainee would strictly contradict Article 5 ECHR.[33] Indeed, the case law of the ECtHR on Article 5 and the burden of proof, though not explicitly differentiating between detention under subsection (1)(f) and other types of detention under Article 5, does seem to imply quite strongly that the state bears the burden in the context of detention generally.[34]

Why the US Supreme Court chose not to correct the burden issue in *Zadvydas* is not clear, especially given its review of how the burden operates in other contexts. These contexts include mental health detention, where the Supreme Court overturned a law that placed the burden of proving non-dangerousness on patients, and pre-trial detention, where the Court noted the state's burden to prove dangerousness by clear and convincing evidence.[35] Immigration detainees in the USA are therefore in a situation where they receive less procedural protection than other types of detainees, even though in all cases of detention the same right to liberty is at risk. Such a fundamental right should be given heightened protection.

[30] The Return Directive does not prescribe the operation of the burden, which is instead governed by domestic law.

[31] HG Watkins, 'The Ninth Circuit Versus the Board of Immigration Appeals: Conflicts Over Burden of Proof on Section 291 Deportation – Burden, Burden, Who's Got the Burden?' (1987) *Immigration and Nationality Law Review* 341.

[32] ch 5, s IV.A above.

[33] ch 5, s IV.B above.

[34] See, eg *Bykov v Russia* [2009] ECHR 441, 64 (and cited cases).

[35] *Zadvydas* (n 3) 690–91.

The second legislative impact relates to the decision to impose a maximum period of detention. A maximum time limit on detention provides judges with a failsafe means of ordering release which prevents indefinite immigration detention. No matter the state of return negotiations or detainee co-operation (for example), once 18 months is reached, individuals detained under the Directive must be released. Moreover, the 18 months includes time spent pursuing judicial remedies against removal. Though the length of the maximum has been criticised,[36] it still falls short of the average lengths of detention in UK and US cases in this book, at 2.1 and 2.4 years, respectively. Indeed, those averages gloss over some more lengthy instances of detention in both jurisdictions, which include lengths of four and five years[37] in the UK and two exceeding five years in the USA.[38] Though a reasonableness test is better than not having any judicial review standards at all, it still allows for the possibility of indefinite detention. Moreover, the NY federal district courts seem to be requiring at least six months in detention before detainees are even permitted to apply for review. An obligatory maximum would guard against these extraordinary deprivations of liberty that have occurred despite the operation of tests of reasonableness.

A word of caution: the existence of a statutory maximum alone is not evidence of a liberty-friendly legal framework. The maximum should be chosen by reference to important factors, such as the average length of detention and the time it reasonably takes to complete the immigration processes at issue. Consideration of these factors will help prevent the setting of an arbitrary time limit which may still result in prolonged detention. In addition, it is vital that a review process with binding legal standards is part of the framework. This will help ensure that any maximum set does not become a default minimum and that detention is only maintained as long as it is necessary.

IV. MOVING FORWARD

Ultimately, this book concludes that the place of fundamental rights in the legal system has a bearing on the effectiveness of judicial review, especially in jurisdictions like the UK and USA, where judicially made standards are employed to evaluate the legality of detention. A strong tradition of respect for fundamental rights will inform the nature of the judicial role. If the court does not view itself as playing a role in safeguarding liberty, its judgments are less likely to emphasise liberty or fundamental rights, and may have negative consequences on case outcomes in terms of safeguarding the right to liberty. This is supported by a

[36] ch 5, s V.B, above.

[37] *R (Raki) v SSHD* [2011] EWHC 2421 (Admin); *R (Mhlanga) v SSHD* [2012] EWHC 1587 (Admin).

[38] *Scarlett v US Department of Homeland Security Bureau of ICE* (2009 WDNY) 632 F Supp 2d 214 (five years, 228 days); *Sanusi v INS* 2003 WL 21696945 (EDNY) (five years, 287 days).

similar finding by Thwaites, who concluded that rights-protecting approaches to detention are typically set against a presumption of the right to liberty, which consequently limits the state's power to employ detention.[39]

Bearing this conclusion in mind, and the need to provide non-citizens with 'proper limits' on their detention,[40] this book closes with a number of recommendations for each jurisdiction to take into account in any future attempts to develop immigration detention law or improve the quality of judicial review of immigration detention. As a first step, each jurisdiction, especially the USA, should make more explicit the impact of detention on the fundamental right to liberty. This discussion should take place in the context of any legislative changes to the detention framework and should be imbued in the relevant legislation. In so doing, the courts may feel more free to speak in the language of fundamental rights, which may in turn lead to better case outcomes. Linked to this, it is important to provide judges with training on judicial review of immigration detention that underscores the right to liberty for all individuals and impresses upon them the important role they play in safeguarding it. This is particularly needed in the USA. A stronger fundamental rights architecture may also lead to less reliance by the state on detention as a tool of immigration enforcement, especially where the individual does not present a risk of absconding or is not especially dangerous.

What follows is a set of jurisdiction-specific recommendations. The UK should enact legislation that provides detailed standards regarding judicial review of immigration detention. This would entail going beyond just a codification of the *Hardial Singh* principles to include a maximum period of detention and clear guidance to assist courts in making determinations of risk of dangerousness or absconding. The USA should enact similar legislation, but with one further addition: a requirement that the state bear the burden of proving that detention is lawful. Finally, in the EU, the CJEU should, where possible, explicitly rely on fundamental rights to reach conclusions rather than the principle of effectiveness. This would send a clear message to national courts and tribunals that the protection of liberty is of the utmost concern within the EU framework. More specifically, the Return Directive should be amended to: repeal the exception in Article 2(2)(b) allowing Member States to exclude from the scope of the Directive third-country nationals subject to return because they have committed a qualifying crime under national law; reduce the maximum duration of detention, for example, by eliminating the possibility to extend detention beyond six months; and provide explicit guidance on what is meant by risk of absconding and lack of co-operation.

[39] R Thwaites, *The Liberty of Non-Citizens: Indefinite Detention in Commonwealth Countries* (Hart Publishing, 2014) 305–06.

[40] D Wilsher, 'The Administrative Detention of Non-Nationals Pursuant to Immigration Control: International and Constitutional Law Perspectives' (2004) 53 *International and Comparative Law Quarterly* 897.

Judicial review plays an important role in the legal architecture. It not only addresses wrongdoing and helps victims of such wrongdoing to obtain compensation, it also encourages good decision-making at the administrative level[41] and mitigates the 'mission-oriented' ethos of government agencies.[42] But judicial review is only as good as its constituent parts. Chief among them, as I argue in this book, is respect for fundamental rights. Such respect must be part of the fabric of the legal architecture of the state, woven into the law applicable to citizens and non-citizens alike. When it becomes commonplace to link liberty to detention, judicial review is likely to result in more positive case outcomes for detainees.

[41] SH Legomsky, 'Fear and Loathing in Congress and the Courts: Immigration and Judicial Review' (2000) 78 *Texas Law Review* 1615, 1631.

[42] AC Aman Jr and WT Mayton, *Adminitrative Law*, 3rd edn (West Academic Publishing, 2014) 352–53.

Bibliography

BOOKS

Aleinikoff, M, et al, *Immigration and Citizenship Process and Policy*, 7th edn (West, 2011).
Arnull, A, *The European Union and its Court of Justice*, 2nd edn (Oxford University Press, 2006).
Ashworth, A and Zedner, L, *Preventive Justice* (Oxford University Press, 2015).
Beck, G, *The Legal Reasoning of the Court of Justice of the EU* (Hart Publishing, 2012).
Bengoetxea, J, *The Legal Reasoning of the European Court of Justice: Towards a European Jurisprudence* (Clarendon Press, 1993).
Bingham, T, *The Business of Judging* (Oxford University Press, 2000).
Bingham, T, *The Rule of Law* (Penguin Books, 2010).
Bosworth, B, *Inside Immigration Detention* (Oxford University Press, 2014).
Cane, P, *Controlling Administrative Power: An Historical Comparison* (Cambridge University Press, 2016).
Care, G, *Migrants and the Courts: A Century of Trial and Error?* (Ashgate, 2013).
Clayton, G, *Textbook on Immigration and Asylum Law*, 7th edn (Oxford University Press, 2016).
Cornelisse, G, *Immigration Detention and Human Rights: Rethinking Territorial Sovereignty* (Martinus Nijhoff, 2010).
Denholm, G and Dunlop, R, *Detention Under the Immigration Acts: Law and Practice* (Oxford University Press, 2015).
Dow, M, *American Gulag: Inside USA Immigration Prisons* (University of California Press, 2004).
Farbey, J and Sharpe, RJ (with Atrill, S) *The Law of Habeas Corpus*, 3rd edn (Oxford University Press, 2011).
Galligan, DJ, *Due Process and Fair Procedures: A Study of Administrative Procedures* (Clarendon Press, 1996).
Golash-Boza, T, *Due Process Denied: Detentions and Deportations in the United States* (Routledge, 2012).
Gordon QC, R, *Judicial Review and Crown Office Practice* (Sweet & Maxwell, 1999).
Griffith, JAG, *The Politics of the Judiciary*, 5th edn (Fontana Press, 1997).
Guia, MJ, Koulish, R and Mitsilegas, V, *Immigration Detention, Risk and Human Rights* (Springer, 2016).
Guild, E, *Security and Migration in the 21st Century* (Polity Press, 2009).
Guarnieri, C and Pederzoli, P, *The Power of Judges* (Oxford University Press, 2002).
Halliday, PD, *Habeas Corpus* (Belknap Harvard, 2010).
Hanratty RD, J, *The Making of an Immigration Judge* (Quartet, 2016).
Kavanagh, A, *Constitutional Review under the UK Human Rights Act* (Oxford University Press, 2009).
Koulish, R, *Immigration and American Democracy: Subverting the Rule of Law* (Routledge, 2010).
Legomsky, SH and Rodríguez, CM, *Immigration and Refugee Law and Policy*, 5th edn (Foundation Press, 2009).
Legomsky, SH, *Immigration and the Judiciary: Law and Politics in Britain and America* (Clarendon Press, 1987).
Lyles, KL, *The Gatekeepers: Federal District Courts in the Political Process* (Praeger, 1997).
MacCormick, N, *Legal Reasoning and Legal Theory* (Oxford University Press, 1994).

Macdonald, IA and Toal, R, *Macdonald's Immigration Law and Practice*, 8th edn (LexisNexis Butterworths, 2012).

Malleson, K, *The Legal System*, 3rd edn (Oxford University Press, 2007).

May, TE, *The Constitutional History of England Since the Accession of George III*, vol III (Corsby and Nichols 1862) 50.

Mill, JS, *On Liberty, Utilitarianism and Other Essays* (Oxford University Press, 2015).

Mitsilegas, V, *The Criminalisation of Migration in Europe: Challenges for Human Rights and the Rule of Law* (Springer, 2015).

O'Neill, A, *EU Law for UK Lawyers* (Bloomsbury, 2011).

Posner, RA, *The Federal Courts* (Harvard University Press, 1996).

Raban, O, *Modern Legal Theory & Judicial Impartiality* (The Glass House Press, 2003).

Rasmussen, H, *On Law and Policy in the European Court of Justice: A Comparative Study in Judicial Policymaking* (Martinus Nijhoff, 1986).

Rowland, CK and Carp, RA, *Politics & Judgment in Federal District Courts* (University Press of Kansas, 1996).

Shetreet, S and Turenne, S, *Judges on Trial: The Independence and Accountability of the English Judiciary* (Cambridge University Press, 2013).

Sokol, RP, *Federal Habeas Corpus* (The Michie Company, 1969).

Surrency, EC, *History of the Federal Courts* (Oceana Publications, 2002).

Thwaites, R, *The Liberty of Non-Citizens: Indefinite Detention in Commonwealth Countries* (Hart Publishing, 2014).

Tridimas, T, *The General Principles of EU Law* (Oxford University Press, 2006).

Wilsher, D, *Immigration Detention: Law, History, Politics* (Cambridge University Press, 2012).

Woolf, H, et al, *De Smith's Judicial Review*, 7th edn (Sweet & Maxwell, 2013).

ARTICLES

Acosta, D, 'The Good, the Bad and the Ugly in EU Migration Law: Is the European Parliament Becoming Bad and Ugly? (The Adoption of Directive, 2008/115: The Returns Directive' (2009) 11 *European Journal of Migration & Law* 19.

Acosta Arcarazo, D, 'The Returns Directive: Possible Limits and Interpretation' (2011) in K Zwann (ed), *The Returns Directive: Central Themes, Problem Issues, and Implementation in Selected Member States* (Wolf Legal Publishers, 2011).

Acosta Arcarazo, D, 'Latin American Reactions to the Adoption of the Returns Directive' (CEPS, 2009).

Allan, TRS, 'Human Rights and Judicial Review: A Critique of "Due Deference"' (2006) 65 *Cambridge Law Journal* 671.

Aliverti, A, 'Exploring the Function of Criminal Law in the Policing of Foreigners: The Decision to Prosecute Immigration-Related Offences' (2012) 29 *Social & Legal Studies* 511.

Aliverti, A, 'Making People Criminal: The Role of the Criminal Law in Immigration and Enforcement' (2012) 16 *Theoretical Criminology* 417.

Anello, FR, 'Due Process and Temporal Limits on Mandatory Immigration Detention' (2013) 65 *Hastings Law Journal* 363.

Anonymous, 'Making Outcasts Out of Outlaws: The Unconstitutionality of Sex Offender Registration and Criminal Alien Detention' (2004) 117 *Harvard Law Review* 2731.

Appleman, LI, 'Justice in the Shadowlands: Pretrial Detention, Punishment & the Sixth Amendment' (2012) 69 *Washington & Lee Law Review* 1297.

Auerhahn, K, 'Selective Incapacitation and the Problem of Prediction' (1999) 27 *Criminology* 703.

Baldaccini, A, 'The EU Directive on Return: Principles and Protests' (2010) 28 *Refugee Survey Quarterly* 114.

Baldaccini, A, 'The Return and Removal of Irregular Migrants under EU Law: An Analysis of the Returns Directive (2009) 11 *European Journal of Migration & Law* 1.
Baker, DJ, 'Punishment Without A Crime: Is Preventive Detention Reconcilable with Justice?' (2009) 34 *Australian Journal of Legal Philosophy* 120.
Banias, BB, 'A "Substantial Argument" against Prolonged, Pre-removal Mandatory Detention' (2009) 11 *Rutgers Race & Law Review* 31.
Bast, J, 'Of General Principles and Trojan Horses – Procedural Due Process in Immigration Proceedings under EU Law' (2010) 11 *German Law Journal* 1006.
Benesch, S, 'Due Process and Decisionmaking in US, Immigration Adjudication' (2007) 59 *Administrative Law Review* 557.
Benson, LB, 'As Old as the Hills: Detention and Immigration' (2010) 5 Intercultural *Human Rights Law Review* 11.
Bhargava, S, 'Detaining Due Process: The Need for Procedural Reform in *'Joseph'* Hearings after *Demore v Kim*' (2006-2007) 31 *NYU Review of Law & Social Change* 51.
Bingham, T, 'Personal Freedom and the Dilemma of Democracies' (2003) 52 *International & Comparative Law Quarterly* 841.
Bleichmar, J, 'Deportation as Punishment: A Historical Analysis of the British Practice of Banishment and its Impact on Modern Constitutional Law' (1999) 14 *Georgetown Immigration Law Journal* 115.
Bloch, A and Schuster, L, 'At the Extremes of Exclusion: Deportation, Detention and Dispersal' (2005) 28 *Ethnic and Racial Studies* 491.
Bosworth, M and Guild, M, 'Governing through Migration Control' (2008) 48 *British Journal of Criminology* 703.
Bosworth, M and Kaufman, E, 'Foreigners in a Carceral Age: Immigration and Imprisonment in the United States' (2011) 22 *Stanford Law & Policy Review* 429.
Boyd, CL and Sievert, JM, 'Unaccountable Justice? The Decision Making of Magistrate Judges in the Federal District Courts' (2013) 34 *Justice Systems Journal* 249.
Bull, M, et al, 'Sickness in the System of Long-Term Immigration Detention' (2013) 2 *Journal of Refugee Studies* 47.
Caldeira, GA and Gibson, JL, 'The Legitimacy of the Court of Justice in the European Union: Models of Institutional Support' (1995) 89 *American Political Science Review* 356.
Caloz-Tschopp, M, 'On the Detention of Aliens: The Impact on Democratic Rights' (1997) 10 *Journal of Refugee Studies* 165.
Carrubba, CJ, et al, 'Judicial Behaviour under Political Constraints: Evidence from the European Court of Justice' (2008) 102 *American Political Science Review* 435.
Celaya, GA, 'USA Immigration Detention: Policy and Procedure from a Human Rights Perspective' (2010) 5 *Intercultural Human Rights Law Review* 177.
Chacón, JM, 'A Diversion of Attention? Immigration Courts and the Adjudication of Fourth and Fifth Amendment Rights' (2010) 59 *Duke Law Journal* 1563.
Chelgren, W, 'Preventive Detention Distorted: Why It Is Unconstitutional to Detain Immigrants without Procedural Protections' (2011) 44 *Loyola Los Angeles Law Review* 1477.
Choi, SJ, et al, 'What Do Federal District Judges Want? An Analysis of Publications, Citations and Reversals' (2011) 28 *Journal of Law, Economics & Organization* 518.
Cole, D, 'Jurisdiction and Liberty: Habeas Corpus and Due Process as Limits on Congress's Control of Federal Jurisdiction' (1998) 86 *Georgetown Law Journal* 2481.
Cole, D, 'In Aid of Removal: Due Process Limits on Immigration Detention' (2002) 51 *Emory Law Journal* 1003.
Cordelli, C, 'Judicial Appointments to the Court of Justice' (2013) 54 *Acta Juridica Hungarica* 24.
Cornelisse, G, 'The Constitutionalisation of Immigration Detention: Between EU Law and the European Convention on Human Rights', Global Detention Project Working Paper No 15 (October 2016).
Cornelisse, G, 'Case Note Case C 357/09 PPU, Proceedings Concerning Said Shamilovich Kadzoev (Huchbarov) Judgment of the Court (Grand Chamber) of 30 November 2009' (2011) 48 *Common Market Law Review* 3.

Cornelisse, G, 'Immigration Detention and the Territoriality of Universal Rights' in N De Genova and N Peutz (eds), *The Deportation Regime: Sovereignty, Space and the Freedom of Movement* (Duke University Press, 2010).

Costello, C, 'Human Rights and the Elusive Universal Subject: Immigration Detention Under International Human Rights and EU Law' (2012) 19 *Indiana Journal of Global Legal Studies* 257.

Craig, P, 'The ECJ and *Ultra Vires* Action: A Conceptual Analysis' (2011) 48 *Common Market Law Review* 395.

Crosby, A, 'The Political Potential of the Return Directive' (2014) 3 *Laws* 117.

Curtain, D, 'Directives: The Effectiveness of Judicial Protection of Individual Rights' (1990) 27 *Common Market Law Review* 709.

Das, A, 'Immigration Detention: Information Gaps and Barriers to Reform' (2013) 80 *University of Chicago Law Review* 137.

De Bruycker, P and Mananashvili, S, '*Audi alteram partem* in immigration detention procedures, between the ECJ, the ECtHR and Member States: *G & R*' (2015) 52 *Common Market Law Review* 569.

Deeks, AS, 'The Observer Effect: National Security Litigation, Executive Policy Changes and Judicial Deference' (2013) 82 *Fordham Law Review* 827.

Demleitner, NV, 'Immigration Threats and Rewards: Effective Law Enforcement Tools in the "War" on Terrorism?' (2002) 51 *Emory Law Journal* 1059.

Dennis, R, 'National Security and Fundamental Rights: The Redundancy or Illegitimacy of Judicial Deference' (2009) 2 *UCL Human Rights Review* 70.

Dumbrovský, T, et al, 'Judicial Appointments: The Article 255 TFEU Advisory Panel and Selection Procedures in the Member States' (2014) 51 *Common Market Law Review* 455.

Dyson, LJ, 'Some Thoughts on Judicial Deference' (2006) 11 *Judicial Review* 103.

Eagly IV and Shafer, S, 'A National Study of Access to Counsel in Immigration Court' (2015) 164 *University of Pennsylvania Law Review* 1.

Engle, E, 'The History of the General Principle of Proportionality: An Overview' (2012) 10 *Dartmouth Law Journal* 1.

Evans, JM, 'Immigration Act, 1971' (1972) 35 *Modern Law Review* 508.

Family, JE, 'Beyond Decisional Independence: Uncovering Contributors to the Immigration Adjudication Crisis' (2010) 59 *University of Kansas Law Review* 541.

Fialho, CM, 'Rethinking Pre-removal Immigration Detention in the United States: Lessons from Europe and Proposals for Reform' (2012) 31 *Refugee Survey Quarterly* 69.

Fennelly, N, 'Legal Interpretation at the European Court of Justice' (1996) 20 *Fordham International Law Journal* 656.

Firmacion, M, 'Protecting Immigrants from Prolonged Pre-removal Detention: When "It Depends" Is No Longer Reasonable' (2014) 42 *Hastings Constitutional Law Quarterly* 601.

Fischman, JB and Law, DS, 'What Is Judicial Ideology and How Should We Measure It?' (2009) 29 *Washington University Journal of Law & Policy* 133.

Fix, MP, 'Does Deference Depend on Distinction? Issue Salience and Judicial Decision-Making in Administrative Law Cases' (2014) 35 *Justice System Journal* 122.

Flynn, MB, 'From Bare Life to Bureaucratic Capitalism: Analyzing the Growth of the Immigration Detention Industry as a Complex Organization' (2016) 8 *Contemporary Readings in Law and Social Justice* 70.

Flynn, MB, 'There and Back Again: On the Diffusion of Immigration Detention' (2014) 2 *Journal on Migration and Human Security* 165.

Flynn, MB, 'Immigration Detention and Proportionality' (2011) Global Detention Project Working Paper No 4.

Friedman, B and Stumpf, J, 'Advancing Civil Rights through Immigration Law: One Step Forward, Two Steps Back?' (2002) 6 *NYU Journal of Legislation & Policy* 131.

Friendly, HJ, 'Some Kind of Hearing' (1975) 123 *University of Pennsylvania Law Review* 1267.

Garrett, G, et al, 'The European Court of Justice, National Governments and Legal Integration in the European Union' (1998) 52 *International Organization* 149.

Gibney, MJ, 'Deportation, Crime and the Changing Character of Membership in the United Kingdom' in KF Aas and M Bosworth (eds), *The Borders of Punishment: Migration, Citizenship and Social Exclusion* (Oxford University Press, 2013).

Gibney, MJ, 'Asylum and the Expansion of Deportation in the United Kingdom' (2008) 43 *Government & Opposition* 146.

Goldman, S, 'Federal Judicial Recruitment' in JB Gates and CA Johnson (eds), *The American Courts, A Critical Assessment* (Congressional Quarterly Press, 1991).

Grimmel, A, '"This is not Life as it is Lived Here": The Court of Justice of the EU and the Myth of Judicial Activism in the Foundational Period of Integration through Law' (2014) 7 *European Journal of Legal Studies* 56.

Groenendijk, K, 'Book Review: *The Human Rights of Migrants and Refugees in European Law*, by Cathryn Costello (Oxford: Oxford University Press, 2015)' (2017) 54 *Common Market Law Review* 943.

Gryll, S, 'Immigration Detention Reform: No Band-Aid Desired' (2011) 60 *Emory Law Journal* 1211.

Harman, M, 'Indefinite Detention of Excludable Aliens: An International Crisis on American Soil' (2000) 7 *Southwestern Journal of Law & Trade in the Americas* 193.

Heeren, G, 'Illegal Aid: Legal Assistance to Immigrants in the United States' (2011) 33 *Cardozo Law Review* 619.

Hepple, BA, 'Aliens and Administrative Justice: The Dutschke Case' (1971) 34 *Modern Law Review* 501.

Herlin-Karnell, E, 'Effectiveness and Constitutional Limits in European Crim Law' (2014) 5 *New Journal of European Criminal Law* 267.

Herlin-Karnell, E, 'An Exercise in Effectiveness?' (2007) 18 *European Business Law Review* 1181.

Hernández, DM, 'Pursuant to Deportation: Latinos and Immigrant Detention' in JA Dowling and JX Inda (eds), *Governing Immigration Through Crime: A Reader* (Stanford University Press, 2013).

Holper, M, 'The Beast of Burden in Immigration Bond Hearings' (2016) 67 *Case Western Reserve Law Review* 75.

Hopkins, WJ, 'Piercing the Veil: Executive Detention and Judicial Deference' (2005) 8 *Yearbook of New Zealand Jurisprudence* 239.

Jowell, J, 'The Rule of Law and its Underlying Values' in J Jowell and D Oliver (eds), *The Changing Constitution*, 7th edn (Oxford University Press, 2011).

Kalhan, A, 'Rethinking Immigration Detention' (2010) 110 *Columbia Law Review Sidebar* 42.

Kanstroom, D, 'Criminalizing the Undocumented: Ironic Boundaries of the Post-September 11th "Pale of Law"' (2004) 29 *North Carolina Journal of International Law & Commercial Regulation* 639.

Kenney, S, 'The Members of the Court of Justice of the European Communities' (1998) 5 *Columbia Journal of European Law* 101.

Keslowitz, S, '*The Simpsons*, *24* and the Law: How Homer Simpson and Jack Bauer Influence Congressional Lawmaking and Judicial Reasoning' (2008) 29 *Cardozo Law Review* 2787.

Kessler, B, 'In Jail, No Notice, No Hearing … No Problem? A Closer Look at Immigration Detention and the Due Process Standards of the International Covenant on Civil and Political Rights' (2009) 24 *American University International Law Review* 571.

Keyes, E, 'Expansion and Restriction: Competing Pressures on the United Kingdom Asylum Policy' (2003) 18 *Georgetown Immigration Law Journal* 395.

Kimball, KJ, 'A Right to be Heard: Non-citizens' Due Process Right to In-Person Hearings to Justify their Detentions prior to Removal' (2009) 5 *Stanford Journal of Civil Rights & Civil Liberties* 159.

Kline, A and Wittes, B, 'Preventive Detention in American Theory and Practice' (2011) *Harvard National Security Journal* 85.

Koh, JL, 'Waiving Due Process (Goodbye): Stipulated Orders of Removal and The Crisis in Immigration Adjudication' (2012) 91 *North Carolina Law Review* 475.

Koulish, R, 'Immigration Detention in the Risk Classification Assessment Era' (2016) 16 *Connecticut Public Interest Law Journal* 1.
Kramo, YA, 'The European Union's Response to Irregular Migration and the Problem of Criminalisation' (2014) 1 *New Journal of European Criminal Law* 26.
Kumm, M, 'Democracy Is Not Enough: Rights, Proportionality and the Point of Judicial Review' (2009) NYU School of Law Public Law & Legal Theory Research Paper Series, Working Paper No 09–10.
Labelle, D, 'Bringing Human Rights Home to the World of Detention' (2008) 40 *Columbia Human Rights Law Review* 79.
Lasch, CN, 'Enforcing the Limits of the Executive's Authority to Issue Immigration Detainers' (2008) 35 *William Mitchell Law Review* 164.
Law, DS, 'A Theory of Judicial Power and Judicial Review' (2009) 97 *Georgetown Law Journal* 723.
Law, DS, 'Appointing Federal Judges: The President, the Senate and the Prisoner's Dilemma' (2005) 26 *Cardozo Law Review* 479.
Legomsky, SH, 'Transporting *Padilla* to Deportation Proceedings: A Due Process Right to Effective Assistance of Counsel' (2011) 31 *St Louis University Public Law Review* 43.
Legomsky, SH, 'Restructuring Immigration Adjudication' (2010) 31 *Immigration & Nationality Law Review* 503.
Legomsky, SH, 'The New Path of Immigration Law: Asymmetric Incorporation of Criminal Justice Norms' (2007) 28 *Immigration & Nationality Law Review* 679.
Legomsky, SH, 'Fear and loathing in Congress and the Courts: Immigration and Judicial Review' (2000) 78 *Texas Law Review* 1615.
Legomsky, SH, 'The Detention of Aliens: Theories, Rules and Discretion' (1999) 30(3) *University of Miami Inter-American Law Review* 531.
Legomsky, SH, 'The Alien Criminal Defendant' (1977) 15 *San Diego Law Review* 105.
Lennox, M, 'Refugees, Racism and Reparations: A Critique of the United States' Haitian Immigration Policy' (1993) 45 *Stanford Law Review* 687.
Lenz, CO, 'The Role and Mechanism of the Preliminary Ruling Procedure' (1994) 18 *Fordham International Law Journal* 388.
Lobban, M, 'Habeas Corpus, Imperial Rendition and the Rule of Law' (2015) 68 *Current Legal Problems* 27.
Majcher, I, '"Crimmigration" in the European Union through the Lens of Immigration Detention' (2013) Global Detention Project Working Paper No 6.
Mancano, L, 'The Right to Liberty in European Union Law and Mutual Recognition in Criminal Matters' (2016) 18 *Cambridge Yearbook of Legal Studies* 215.
Markesinis, B, 'Judicial Style and Judicial Reasoning in England and Germany' (2000) 59 *Cambridge Law Journal* 294.
Marong, C, 'Protecting the Public? Challenging the Indefinite Preventive Detention of Non-Citizens' (2014) 3 *UCL Journal of Law & Jurisprudence* 115.
Martin, DA, 'Graduated Application of Constitutional Protections for Aliens: The Real Meaning of *Zadvydas v Davis*' [2001] *Supreme Court Review* 47.
Martin, DA, 'Making Asylum Policy: The 1994 Reforms' (1995) 70 *Washington Law Review* 725.
Mayr, S, 'Putting a Leash on the Court of Justice – Preconceptions in National Methodology v *Effet Utile* as a Meta-Rule' (2012) 5 *European Journal of Legal Studies* 3.
McGinty Borg, M, 'Freedom from the Deprivation of Liberty: The Supreme Court Imposes Limitations on Indefinite Detention of Criminal Aliens – *Zadvydas v Davis* (2003) *William Mitchell Law Review* 951.
Mead, JW, 'Stare Decisis in the Inferior Courts of the United States' (2012) 12 *Nevada Law Journal* 787.
Medina, MI, 'The Criminalization of Immigration Law: Employer Sanctions and Marriage Fraud' (1997) 18 *Immigration & Nationality Law Review* 643.
Melander, M, 'Effectiveness in EU Criminal Law and Its Effects on the General Part of Criminal Law' (2015) 5 *New Journal of European Criminal Law* 274.

Miller, TA, 'Blurring the Boundaries between Immigration and Crime Control after September 11th' (2005) 25 *Boston College Third World Law Journal* 81.

Miller, TA, 'Citizenship & Severity: Recent Immigration Reforms and the New Penology' (2003) 17 *Georgetown Immigration Law Journal* 611.

Mitsilegas, V, 'The Changing Landscape of the Criminalisation of Migration in Europe' in M João et al (eds), *Social Control and Justice: Crimmigration in the Age of Fear* (Eleven International Publishing, 2013).

Morawetz, N, 'Detention Decisions and Access to Habeas Corpus for Immigrants Facing Deportation' (2005) 25 *Boston College Third World Law Journal* 13.

Morriss, AP, et al, 'Signaling and Precedent in Federal District Court Opinions' (2005) 13 *Supreme Court Economic Review* 63.

Mosk, S, 'The Common Law and the Judicial Decision-Making Process' (1988) 11 *Harvard Journal of Law & Public Policy* 35.

Motomura, H, 'The Curious Evolution of Immigration Law: Procedural Surrogates for Substantive Constitutional Rights' (1992) 92 *Columbia Law Review* 7.

Murdoch, JL, *Article 5 of the European Convention on Human Rights* (Council of Europe, 2002).

Nason, S, 'The Administrative Court, the Upper Tribunal and Permission to Seek Judicial Review' (2012) 21 *Nottingham Law Journal* 1.

Nason, S, 'Regionalisation of the Administrative Court' (2009) 14 *Judicial Review* 1.

Neenan, C, 'Is a Declaration of Incompatibility an Effective Remedy?' (2000) 5 *Judicial Review* 247.

Neuman, GL, 'Habeas Corpus, Executive Detention and the Removal of Aliens' (1998) 19 *Immigration & Nationality Law Review* 307.

Noferi, M, 'Cascading Constitutional Deprivation: The Right to Appointed Counsel for Mandatorily Detained Immigrants Pending Removal Proceedings' (2012) 18 *Michigan Journal of Race and Law* 63.

Noferi, M and Koulish, R, 'The Immigration Detention Risk Assessment' (2014) 29 *Georgetown Immigration Law Journal* 45.

Olivares, M, 'Intersectionality at the Intersection of Profiteering & Immigration Detention' (2016) 94 *Nebraska Law Review* 963.

Olson, SM, 'Studying Federal District Courts through Published Cases: A Research Note' (1992) 15 *Justice Systems Journal* 782.

O'Nions, H, 'No Right to Liberty: The Detention of Asylum Seekers for Administrative Convenience' (2008) 10 *European Journal of Migration and Law* 149.

Peitzke, M, 'The Fate of "Unremovable" Aliens before and after September 11, 2001: The Supreme Court's Presumptive Six-Month Limit to Post-Removal-Period Detention' (2002) 30 *Pepperdine Law Review* 769.

Pershan, LS, 'Selective Incapacitation and the Justifications for Imprisonment' (1984) 12 *NYU Review Law & Social Change* 385.

Prakash, S and Smith, SD, 'How to Remove a Federal Judge' (2006) 116 *Yale Law Journal* 72.

Raffaelli, R, 'Case Note: The *Achughbabian* Case, Impact of the Return Directive on National Criminal Legislation' [2012] *Diritto Penale Contemporaneo* 176.

Raffaelli, R, 'The Returns Directive in Light of the *El Dridi* Judgment' (2011) 3 *Perspectives on Federalism* 32.

Sadl, U, 'The Role of *Effet Utile* in Preserving the Continuity and Authority of European Union Law: Evidence from the Citation Web of the Pre-accession Case Law of the Court of Justice of the EU' (2015) 8 *European Journal of Legal Studies* 18.

Samuels, A, 'The United Kingdom Immigration Act, 1971' (1972) 11 *University of Western Australia Law Review* 54.

Sartori, ME, 'The Cuban Migration Dilemma: An Examination of the United States' Policy of Temporary Protection in Offshore Safe Havens' (2003) 15 *Georgetown Immigration Law Journal* 319.

Savino, M, 'Irregular Migration at the Crossroads, between Administrative Removal and Criminal Deterrence: The *Celaj* Case' (2016) 53 *Common Market Law Review* 1419.

Sayed, FW, 'Challenging Detention: Why Immigrant Detainees Receive Less Process Than "Enemy Combatants" and Why They Deserve More' (2011) 111 *Columbia Law Review* 1833.

Schuck, PH, 'The Transformation of Immigration Law' (1984) 84 *Columbia Law Review* 1.

Schwarzer, WW, 'Case Management in the Federal Courts' (1996) 15 *Civil Justice Quarterly* 141.

Scott, K, 'The Impact of Common Law on Judicial Decision Making' (2007) 3 *International Journal of Punishment and Sentencing* 184.

Silva, T, 'Toward a Constitutionalized Theory of Immigration Detention' (2013) 32 *Yale Law & Policy Review* 227.

Silverman, SJ, '"Regrettable but Necessary?" A Historical and Theoretical Study of the Rise of the UK, Immigration Detention Estate and Its Opposition' (2012) 40 *Politics & Policy* 1131.

Singer, JM and Young, WG, 'Measuring Bench Presence: Federal District Judges in the Courtroom, 2008–2012' (2013) 118 *Penn State Law Review* 243.

Singh, R, 'The Declaration of Incompatibility' (2002) 7 *Judicial Review* 237.

Skouris, V, '*Effet Utile* versus Legal Certainty: The Case-Law of the Court of Justice on the Direct Effect of Directives' (2006) 17 *European Business Law Review* 241.

Stefanelli, JN, 'Disclosure in Immigration Bail Proceedings: Ensuring Equality of Arms' (2016) 30 *Journal of Immigration, Asylum & Nationality Law* 301.

Stefanelli JN, 'Taking Back Control? Parliamentary Sovereignty and UK Membership in the EU' (2016) 10 *Journal of Parliamentary & Political Law* 521.

Stefanelli, J, 'Book Review: The Liberty of Non-citizens: Indefinite Detention in Commonwealth Countries by Rayner Thwaites (Oxford: Hart Publishing Publishing, 2014)' (2015) 78 *Modern Law Review* 176.

Stevens, D, 'The Law's Approach to Detention of Asylum Seekers: Help or Hindrance?' (2010) University of Warwick School of Law Legal Studies Research Paper No 2010–21.

Stumpf, JP, 'Civil Detention and Other Oxymorons' (2014) 40 *Queens Law Journal* 55.

Stumpf, JP, 'The Process is the Punishment in Crimmigration Law' in KF Aas and M Bosworth (eds), *The Borders of Punishment: Migration, Citizenship and Social Exclusion* (Oxford University Press, 2013).

Stumpf, JP, 'Doing Time: Crimmigration Law and the Perils of Haste' (2011) 58 *UCLA Law Review* 1705.

Stumpf, JP, 'Fitting Punishment' (2009) 66 *Washington & Lee Law Review* 1683.

Stumpf, JP, 'States of Confusion: The Rise of State and Local Power over Immigration' (2008) 86 *North Carolina Law Review* 1557.

Stumpf, JP, 'Penalizing Immigrants' (2006) 18 *Federal Sentencing Reporter* 264.

Stumpf, JP, 'The Crimmigration Crisis: Immigrants, Crime and Sovereign Power' (2006) 56(2) *American University Law Review* 368.

Sivaprasad Wadhia, S, 'Under Arrest: Immigrants' Rights and the Rule of Law' (2008) 38 *University of Memphis Law Review* 853.

Taylor, MH, '*Demore v Kim:* Judicial Deference to Congressional Folly' in DA Martin and PH Schuck (eds), *Immigration Stories* (Foundation Press, 2005).

Thomas, R, 'Administrative Justice, Better Decisions and Organisational Learning' (2015) 1 *Public Law* 111.

Tolley, MC, 'Legal Controversies over Federal Judicial Selection in the United States' in K Malleson and PH Russell (eds), *Appointing Judges in an Age of Judicial Power* (University of Toronto Press, 2006).

Torrey, PL, 'Rethinking Immigration's Mandatory Detention Regime: Politics, Profit and the Meaning of "Custody"' (2015) 48 *University of Michigan Journal of Law Reform* 879.

Tridimas, T, 'Knocking on Heaven's Door: Fragmentation, Efficiency and Defiance in the Preliminary Reference Procedure' (2003) 40 *Common Market Law Review* 9.

Van Marle, K, Queen Mary University of London, Half-Day Workshop on 'Diversity and Legal Reasoning', 23 November 2016.

Waldron, J, 'Judges as Moral Reasoners' (2009) 7 *International Journal of Constitutional Law* 2.

Walker, VR, 'The Most Efficient Finder of Fact: The Federal District Judge' (2015) 69 *University of Miami Law Review* 385.

Watkins, HG, 'The Ninth Circuit versus the Board of Immigration Appeals: Conflicts over Burden of Proof on Section 291 Deportation – Burden, Burden, Who's Got the Burden?' [1987] *Immigration & Nationality Law Review* 341.

Waxman, MC, 'Guantánamo, Habeas Corpus and Standards of Proof: Viewing the Law through Multiple Lenses' (2009) 42 *Case Western Journal of International Law* 245.

Weinstein, JB, 'The Roles of a Federal District Court Judge' (2011) 76 *Brook Law Review* 439.

Wilsher, D, 'The Administrative Detention of Non-nationals Pursuant to Immigration Control: International and Constitutional Law Perspectives' (2004) 53 *International & Comparative Law Quarterly* 897.

ONLINE MATERIALS

Bail for Immigration Detainee's 'Submission to the APPG on Refugees and APPG on Migration's Parliamentary Inquiry into the Use of Immigration Detention in the UK' (September 2014) http://www.biduk.org/sites/default/files/media/docs/BID submission to detention inquiry_Access to legal advice in IRCs Sept 2014 (2).pdf.

Centre for Migration Law, 'Overview of CJEU Case Law' http://www.ru.nl/law/cmr/documentation/cmr-series/.

Cuauhtémoc García Hernández, C, 'In 1 Week, Private Prisons Announce New Contracts for 3000 Immigration Detention Beds', *Crimmigrationcom* (20 December 2016) http://crimmigration.com/2016/12/20/in-1-week-private-prisons-announce-new-contracts-for-3000-immigration-detention-beds/.

'Clarke Insists "I Will Not Quit"', *BBC News* (London, 25 April 2006) http://news.bbc.co.uk/1/hi/uk_politics/4944164.stm.

Doughty, S and Slack, J, 'Record Number of Jobless EU Migrants in Britain: Hammer Blow for PM as 270,000 EU Nationals Came Here Last Year', *Daily Mail* (London, 26 May 2016) http://www.dailymail.co.uk/news/immigration/index.html.

Drury, I, 'Criminal Notifications for EU Migrants Leap by 40% in Five Years: Now There Are 700 Every Week in the UK but Less Than 20,000 Foreign Criminals Have Been Deported', *Daily Mail* (London, 17 February 2016) http://www.dailymail.co.uk/news/article-3450323/Criminal-convictions-EU-migrants-leap-40-five-years-700-guilty-week-UK-20-000-foreign-criminals-deported.html.

Evans, K and Koulish, R, 'Under Trump, ICE No Longer Recommends Release for Immigrants in Detention', *Crimmigration* (26 July 2018) http://crimmigration.com/2018/07/26/under-trump-ice-no-longer-recommends-release-for-immigrants-in-detention/.

Federal Court Management Statistics, Table C-3: US District Courts – Civil Cases Commenced, by Nature of Suit and District, During the 12-Month Period Ending December 31, 2018 https://www.uscourts.gov/statistics/table/c-3/statistical-tables-federal-judiciary/2018/12/31.

Federal Court Management Statistics, Table D-3: US District Courts – Criminal Defendants Commenced (Excluding Transfers), by Offense and District, During the 12-Month Period Ending December 31, 2018 https://www.uscourts.gov/statistics/table/d-3/statistical-tables-federal-judiciary/2018/12/31.

Hennessy, P, 'Theresa May: I'll Bring in New Law to End Human Rights Farce', *The Telegraph* (London, 16 February 2013) http://www.telegraph.co.uk/news/uknews/immigration/9875052/Theresa-May-Ill-bring-in-new-law-to-end-human-rights-farce.html.

'How the Deportation Story Emerged' *BBC News* (London, 9 October 2006) http://news.bbc.co.uk/1/hi/uk_politics/4945922.stm.

'Malta: New Migration Strategy Ends Automatic Detention of Irregular Entrants', *Asylum in Europe* (8 January 2016) http://www.asylumineurope.org/news/08-01-2016/malta-new-migration-strategy-ends-automatic-detention-irregular-entrants.

Ministry of Justice, 'Civil Justice Statistics Quarterly: October to December, 2018' https://www.gov.uk/government/statistics/civil-justice-statistics-october-to-december-2018.

Ministry of Justice, 'Types of Cases' https://www.justice.gov.uk/courts/rcj-rolls-building/administrative-court/types-of-cases.

Nason, N, 'Home Office Belatedly Issues Guidance on Operation Nexus', *freemovementorguk* (24 April 2017) https://www.freemovement.org.uk/home-office-belatedly-issues-guidance-operation-nexus/.

Peers, S, 'The CJEU's Ruling in *Celaj*: Criminal Penalties, Entry Bans and the Returns Directive', *EU Law Analysis* (6 October 2016) http://eulawanalysis.blogspot.co.uk/2015/10/the-cjeus-ruling-in-celaj-criminal.html.

Poli, T, 'Immigration Detention and the Rule of Law: the ECJ's First Ruling on Detaining Asylum-Seekers in the Dublin System', *EU Law Analysis* (5 May 2017) http://eulawanalysis.blogspot.co.uk/2017/05/immigration-detention-and-rule-of-law.html.

Trump, DJ, 'State of the Union Address' (5 February 2019) https://www.whitehouse.gov/briefings-statements/remarks-president-trump-state-union-address-2/.

Rivas, J, 'ICE Quietly Updates Rule to Make It Easier to Detain Even More Migrants', *fusionnet* (24 March 2017) http://fusion.net/ice-quietly-updates-rule-to-make-it-easier-to-detain-ev-1793859312.

Shepherd, K, 'Government Quietly Increases ICE Detention to 48,000 Beds during the Shutdown', American Immigration Council, *Immigration Impact* (31 January 2019) http://immigrationimpact.com/2019/01/31/increases-ice-detention-beds-shutdown/.

Silverman, SJ and Griffiths, M, 'Immigration Detention in the UK', *Migration Observatory* (3 July 2018) https://migrationobservatory.ox.ac.uk/resources/briefings/immigration-detention-in-the-uk/.

'Theresa May Criticises Judges for "Ignoring" Deportation Law', *BBC News* (London, 17 February 2013) http://www.bbc.co.uk/news/uk-21489072.

'Theresa May Gets Cross-Party Backing in Article 8 Row', *BBC News* (London, 19 June 2012) http://www.bbc.co.uk/news/uk-politics-18511727.

Tidwell Cullen, T, 'ICE Released Its Most Comprehensive Immigration Detention Data Yet, It;s Alarming' (13 March 2018) https://immigrantjustice.org/staff/blog/ice-released-its-most-comprehensive-immigration-detention-data-yet.

Tiven, RB, 'The Airport Lawyers Who Stood Up to Trump Are Under Attack', *The Nation* (19 May 2017) https://www.thenation.com/article/the-airport-lawyers-who-stood-up-to-trump-are-under-attack/.

United Nations Office of the High Commissioner for Human Rights, 'UN Experts Express Concern about Proposed EU Return Directive' (2008) http://www.ohchr.org/en/NewsEvents/Pages/DisplayNews.aspx?NewsID=8440&LangID=E#sthash.vuMAfFKS.dpuf.

Other Documents

COUNCIL OF EUROPE

'Twenty Guidelines on forced return', adopted 4 May 2005 by the Committee of Ministers of the Council of Europe

Venice Commission, 'The Rule of Law Checklist', adopted by the Venice Commission at its 106th Plenary Session, Venice, 11–12 March 2016

EUROPEAN UNION

Court of Justice of the European Union, 'Annual Report 2018: Judicial Activity' (2019)

Court of Justice of the European Union (Skouris, V), 'Report on the Use of the Urgent Preliminary Ruling Procedure by the Court of Justice' (31 January 2012)

Court of Justice of the European Union, 'Information Note on References from National Courts for a Preliminary Ruling' [2009] OJ C297/1

European Commission, 'Communication on a Community Immigration Policy', COM(2000) 757 final, 22 November 2000

European Commission, 'Communication from the Commission to the Council and the European Parliament on a Community Return Policy on Illegal Residents', COM(2002) 564 final, 14 October 2002

European Commission, 'Green Paper on a Community Return Policy on Illegal Immigrants', COM(2002) 175 final, 14 March 2002

European Commission, 'Proposal for a Directive of the European Parliament and of the Council on Common Standards and procedures in Member States for Returning Illegally Staying Third-Country Nationals', COM(2005) 391 final, 1 September 2005

European Commission, Communication from the Commission to the European Parliament, the Council, the European Economic and Social Committee and the Committee of Regions, 'An Open and Secure Europe: Making It Happen', COM(2014) 154 final, 11 March 2014

European Commission, 'Communication from the Commission to the Council and the European Parliament on EU Return Policy', COM(2014) 199 final, 28 March 2014

European Commission, 'Communication from the Commission to the Parliament and the Council on a More Effective Return Policy in the European Union – A Renewed Action Plan', COM(2017) 200 final, 2 March 2017

European Commission, 'Communication from the Commission to the European Parliament, the Council, the European Economic and Social Committee, the Committee of the Regions and the Court of Justice of the European Communities Adaptation of the provisions of Title IV of the Treaty Establishing the European Community Relating to the Jurisdiction of the Court of Justice With a View to Ensuring More Effective Judicial Protection', COM(2006) 346 final, 28 June 2006

European Council, Presidency Conclusions, Brussels European Council, 4 and 5 November 2004, 14292/1/04 REV 1

European Parliament, 'Resolution Adopting the Declaration of Fundamental Rights and Freedoms' [1989] OJ C120/51

European Union Agency for Fundamental Rights, 'Detention of Third-Country Nationals in Return Procedures' (2010)
Third Activity Report of the Panel Provided for by Article 255 of the Treaty on the Functioning of the EU (13/12/2013) SN 1118/2014

UNITED KINGDOM

Administrative Justice & Tribunals Council, 'Right First Time' (2011)
All Party Parliamentary Group on Refugees & the All Party Parliamentary Group on Migration, 'The Report of the Inquiry into the Use of Immigration Detention in the United Kingdom: A Joint Inquiry by the All Party Parliamentary Group on Refugees & the All Party Parliamentary Group on Migration' (March 2015)
Hansard, HC Vol 819, cols 712–29 (17 June 1971)
Hansard, HC Vol 326, cols 37–129 (22 February 1999)
Hansard, HC Vol 698 (29 July 2002)
Hansard, HL Vol 639, cols 412–82 (10 October 2002)
Hansard, HL Vol 692, (13 June 2007), UK Borders Bill Second Reading
Hansard, HL Vol 637, cols 1048–84 (15 July 2002)
Hansard, HL Vol 606 cols 724–800 (2 November 1999)
Hansard, HL Vol 605, cols 1193–284 (20 October 1999)
Hansard, HL Vol 636, cols 1087–81 (24 June 2002)
Hansard, HL Vol 323, cols 1009–86 (3 August 1971)
Hansard, HL Vol 323, cols 1105–44 (3 August 1971)
Home Office, 'Rights Brought Home: The Human Rights Bill', Cm 3782 (October 1997)
Home Office, Detention Services Order 03/2016, 'Consideration of Detainee Placement in the Detention Estate' (April 2016)
House of Commons Home Affairs Committee Inquiry into Detention (announced 18 March 2018)
House of Lords and House of Commons Joint Committee on Human Rights, 'Immigration Detention', Sixteenth Report of Session 2017–19, HC 1484, HL Paper 278 (7 February 2019)
—— 'Human Rights Judgments', Seventh Report of Session 2014–15, HC 1088, HL Paper 13 (11 March 2015)
—— 'Legislative Scrutiny: Sixth Progress Report', Thirteenth Report of Session 2006–07, HC 538, HL Paper 105 (21 May 2007)
Judge Clements, President of the First-tier Tribunal (Immigration and Asylum Chamber), Presidential Guidance Note No 1 of 2018, 'Guidance on Immigration Bail for Judges of the First-tier Tribunal (Immigration and Asylum Chamber) (15 January 2018)
Ministry of Justice and Legal Aid Agency, Legal aid statistics: October to December 2015', Table 6.1 (31 March 2015)
Ministry of Justice, 'Response to Its Consultation on Proposals to Expedite Appeals by Immigration Detainees' (April 2017)
Review Body on Senior Salaries, 'Thirty-Eighth Annual Report on Senior Salaries 2016' Rep No 85, Cm 9248 (April 2016)
Secretary of State for the Home Department, 'Fairer, Faster and Firmer – A Modern Approach to Immigration and Asylum' (1998) Cm 4018
Shaw, S, 'Review into the Welfare in Detention of Vulnerable Persons' (January 2016) Cm 9186
Shaw, S, 'Assessment of Government Progress in Implementing the Report on the Welfare in Detention of Vulnerable Persons: A Follow-Up Report to the Home Office' (July 2018) Cm 9661
UK National Preventive Mechanism, Seventh Annual Report (January 2017)
UK Visas and Immigration, 'Enforcement Instructions and Guidance' Chapter 55
UK Visas and Immigration, 'Enforcement Instructions and Guidance' Chapter 60
UK Home Office, 'Operation Nexus – High Harm', version 1.0 (15 March 2017)

UNITED NATIONS

UN Human Rights Council, 'Report of the Special Rapporteur on the Human Rights of Migrants, François Crépeau: Regional Study: Management of the External Borders of the European Union and Its Impact on the Human Rights of Migrants', A/HRC/23/46 (2013)

UNITED STATES

Congressional Record, 104th Congress, 1st Session, Vol 141, No 88, S7497
Congressional Subcommittees of the Committees on the Judiciary, 82nd Congress, First Session on S 716, HR 2379 and HR 2816, bills to revise the laws relating to immigration, naturalization and nationality, 6–9, 12–16, 20–21 March and 9 April 1951, 09/04/1951
Department of Homeland Security, 'Immigration Enforcement Actions 2013' (September 2014)
Department of Homeland Security (DHS), 'Immigration Enforcement Actions 2013' (September 2014)
Department of Homeland Security, 'ICE Enforcement and Removal Operations Report 2014' (19 December 2014)
Department of Homeland Security Memorandum, 'Implementing the President's Border Security and Immigration Enforcement Improvements Policies' (20 February 2017)
Executive Office of Immigration Review Benchbook, 'Bond/Custody' (2008)
Immigration and Customs Enforcement (ICE), 'Parole of Arriving Aliens Found to Have a Credible Fear of Persecution or Torture' (2009), Directive No 11002.1, effective 4 January 2010
ICE, 2011 Performance-Based National Detention Standards
Senate Bill 36, the 'Keep Our Communities Safe Act of 2017', 115th Congress (2017–2018)
Senate Report, Vol 141, No 88, 104th Congress, 1st Session, S7479
Senate Report, Vol 141, No 88, 104th Congress, 1st Session, S7480
Senate Report, Vol 142, No 127, 104th Congress, 2nd Session, S10573
Senate Report 81-1515 (20 April 1950), Serial Set No 11373, 915
US Department of Justice, 'Report and Recommendations Concerning the Use of Restrictive Housing' (January 2016)

Index

www.ingramcontent.com/pod-product-compliance
Ingram Content Group UK Ltd.
Pitfield, Milton Keynes, MK11 3LW, UK
UKHW021908150926
475560UK00003B/244